THE NINE LIVES OF JOHN ASLIN

A Non-Fiction Novel

JILL CREECH BAUER

ISBN 9798663230520

Cover design by: Jill Creech Bauer
Library of Congress Control Number: 2018675309
Printed in the United States of America

DEDICATION

Dedicated to my parents, Jim & Sally Creech,
who planted the seeds of my passion for social justice.

CONTENTS

Nothing was your own except the few
cubic centimetres inside your skull.

— George Orwell, 1984

INTRODUCTION

While working as an attorney in Flint, Michigan in 2009, I was contacted by John Eric Aslin, an inmate in the Michigan Correctional System. He sought my assistance in applying to have his prison sentence commuted by then Governor Jennifer Granholm. I have remained in contact with John since that time. The events of his life are both remarkable and devastating. What you are about to read is based on real events.

To adequately tell John's story, I had to include the story of his father and his father's siblings. I did as much research as I could on the previous generation of the Aslin family, but little information exists because the entire generation has no offspring to whom they could pass along their stories. The lack of personal sources required me to fill in some of details of their lives with my imaginings, but these details are based upon the following: research of Ojibwe culture and traditions; John Eric's knowledge of his family and cultural history; media coverage of John's uncle, Fred Aslin, who filed a law suit against the State of Michigan; investigations of John Harvey Kellogg, the Michigan Eugenics movement and the Home for the Feeble-Minded, an actual place that was located in Lapeer, Michigan. Many of the story elements that happen at the Home in my book originate from stories that I uncovered in my research. I simply placed Fred Aslin and his siblings in the midst of the anecdotes that I discovered.

John was not raised in his culture and only came to know it as an adult. I have done my best to research Ojibwe traditions and present culturally accurate depictions of the Aslin family, but I am sure that I have made errors. My desire was to illustrate the entirety of what they lost when they were essentially kidnapped by the State of Michigan, so I ask for grace; if I fell short, I had good intentions. I would like to note that I sometimes use the word "Indian" in this text because that is how John and his family members refer to themselves—I am aware that some might view that word as problematic, but I felt it important to retain John's voice when I tell his story.

That being said, the vast majority of the story you are about to read blossomed from the seeds of my discussions with John Eric himself; other details came from the record of his criminal case. The depiction of the trial and related events is taken verbatim from court transcripts, so it is as accurate as the record allows. I have changed some of the names, but I have remained otherwise true to the record.

The stories from John's childhood are based on John's memories, with my creative additions to bring the outlines he has provided to life. I chose to relay John and Fred's experiences, for the most part, as a non-fiction novel, so I invite you to settle in for one of the most compelling life stories you might ever read. The movie, *White Boy Rick*, claims that Rick Wershe held the record as the longest-serving non-violent offender in Michigan after serving 30 years. Though John Aslin was sentenced for felony murder, his crime was non-violent; he has been imprisoned for 36 years so I believe that John is the longest non-violent offender in the Michigan system.

One more thing. John's spirit animal is a member of the cat family. The more I learned about his life journey—all of the things that he has survived—it became clear to me that John's ancestors chose a cat for him because he would need nine lives to survive his time on this earth. I use the "nine lives" concept metaphorically as a symbol of all of the challenges that John has survived, literally, emotionally and spiritually. He could have been destroyed by such a life, yet he has not been.

PROLOGUE

KINROSS CORRECTIONAL FACILITY
MICHIGAN'S UPPER PENINSULA
2009

If he squinted as he exited the sweat lodge, focusing on the trees on the horizon, John Aslin could almost forget the tall humming fence, the guns that might be pointed at his heart, and instead hear the call of his ancestors on the wind.

John had spent more time inside the dank concrete walls of the myriad penal institutions scattered across Michigan than outside, moving from prison to prison over the past 25 years and eventually ending up not far from where his pa, John Albert Aslin, was born in 1932. Pa started out about 25 miles away, in St. Ignace, a small coastal town that faced lower Michigan and overlooked the spot where Lake Huron and Lake Michigan kissed, a place now marked by the Mighty Mackinaw Bridge. John Eric wished he could walk those years back to that small town, before tragedy hit, a mile for each year, and undo all of the pain.

But John would have to be able to go back much further than 25 years to really fix things. He would have to fix himself out of existence—if his father had not been abducted by the state almost 75 years before, he would have never met John's mother and John Eric would not be here. In fact, according to the State of Michigan, John Eric shouldn't exist.

Would that have been better—to never exist? There was so much sorrow packed into his bloodline that some days he thought maybe it would have been better to have been erased by a twist of events; then other days he had hope that he still might be able to take all that had happened, all that he had learned, and live a meaningful life beyond prison walls. Make a difference. He had something more than such a small, sad existence to offer the universe.

John saw beauty in the smallest things. He noticed intricacies in the wings of a fly, the blue-black sheen in the pair of ravens that regularly visited his windowsill and the varied shades contained in a patch of grass. At his core, his was a gentle soul. He could take beauty in and push it back out into exquisite works of art. He yearned for more of a life than the one that he had been dealt. Was he really going to rot away inside the walls of his cell until he ceased to exist?

Some days the walls squeezed the breath out of him, leaving him panicked and panting on his bunk, each shallow breath an inhale of the rot that permeated his surroundings. Twenty-five years—over half of his life—had done nothing to erode his concrete cell, but he lost a tiny piece of hope each time the sun set. Hope used to fill him up almost halfway, but now his dreams had shrunken down to a walnut—a hard, protective shell with a soft inside that could only be harvested with a bit of effort.

He was responsible for a death. He had not stabbed, struck, shot, poisoned or even intentionally touched Ella Stephens, but he brought her to her end, nonetheless. He had lived with this knowledge for more than 9,000 waking ups and 9,000 going to beds and 9,000 spaces between. It broke his heart and chipped away at his spirit bit by bit. But responsibility didn't mean intention and he had served enough time—he had learned his lesson more than 9,000 times. Science told him that his life expectancy might only allow him 25,000 days on this earth, and he had already spent over a third of them in a cage.

He never claimed to be innocent. He was a thief—that was certain—but he wasn't a killer. It took more than the combination of a proclivity to take things that didn't belong to him and terrible, terrible luck to make him that. Things had reached a point where justice required that he be set free. Would justice ever prevail?

LIFE FIVE: WHERE JOHN ERIC LOSES A LIFE BY TAKING A LIFE

THE CRIME
FLINT, MICHIGAN
MAY 21, 1984

The black jacket had zippers and silver accents. John unconsciously lifted his arm near his nose regularly just to smell it. Every time he thought he saw a speck on a sleeve, he startled and inspected it to make sure the leather stayed pristine. The red converse shoes were still clean as was the red bandana he'd rolled up and tied around his head. His long, waving hair flowed below it. Life was pretty shitty, but at least he looked cool.

John walked on the edge of a two-lane road, trying to look like he had somewhere to go. Roy, an old friend from the neighborhood, rolled up beside him in his slick Trans Am. Roy had bought it used, but it was amazing what a bit of Bondo and some paint could do. It was now cherry-red with a yellow racing stripe down the hood.

"Hey, dumbass, you want a ride?" Roy was grinning when John turned.

John got into the car. "Damn, Roy. Did you spill a bottle of Drakkar Noire in here?"

"Got a hot date. Chick I met at the mall."

"Did she get a good look at you or just your car?"

Roy reached out and playfully smacked John on the back of the head, telling him to shut up.

"Poor thing. She doesn't know what a boring night she has ahead of her. Maybe you should do the right thing and introduce her to me."

Roy laughed. "Where you want me to drop you?"

"I was headed to the market. Can I grab some of this change?" The console of the Trans Am was full to the top with coins.

"Sure."

John grabbed a large handful. Roy glanced down but did not react. John's friends knew he was struggling after getting out of lock up. Roy had a good job at GM, living the life that John might have had if he had stopped his criminal activities, if he had buckled down to finish his GED and gotten a legitimate job.

Roy pulled into the nearby market parking lot and reached for his wallet. "Hey Johnny, here's the five bucks I borrowed from you a while ago."

John was confused for a split second, then realized that Roy was being kind, trying to help him out without embarrassing him. He razzed them through the awkward moment. "Thanks, man. I never thought a deadbeat like you was going to pay that back. Where's the interest?"

~~~

Generally speaking, Ella Stephens lived alone. She had experienced a few health issues over the past year. Her grandson, Glenn, lived with her to take care of her while she was recuperating, but she didn't want to be a burden on anyone and encouraged him to go live his life once she didn't need him.

His company had been nice, especially in the evenings. It was pleasant to have someone listen to her comments on the news or someone to try to beat to the answer of a gameshow question. Having a break from cooking and dishwashing was a bonus, though it was hard for her to sit back and let someone else take care of her. Usually she was the one taking care of others.

Glenn wasn't staying with her the evening of May 21, 1984. That night she was alone. The temperature was in the mid-60s. There was a light rain falling when Ella checked to make sure that her house was locked up; then she headed to bed.

The dishes had been washed and Ella had neatened up the kitchen, but her home was lived in. She had jars and knickknacks covering surfaces all over the house. Small piles of cash were tucked here and there, poking out from under lamps and other objects, in open view. Dozens of small jars filled with coins and bills served as at-home "savings plans" for things that she wanted to buy or needed to pay for, but most of her money was in her purse.

She took her handbag into the bedroom each night, tucking it under a pillow. It held the remaining cash from her pension check and social security allotment. Once her purse was hidden, she changed into a blue nightgown and made sure the flashlight she kept on her nightstand was in place. Then she pulled the string that led from the overhead light to her headboard, closed her eyes and fell asleep.

~~~

John had a plan for the five-dollar bill he'd gotten from Roy. It opened up a window in his evening. A pint of Jack Daniels would soften the edges, push the anxiety down to a comfortable level.

He slapped the bill down on the counter. Once he got to the parking lot, he twisted off the cap and took a swig. Then another and another. Soon he began to feel warm and tingly; lately he had to drink more and more just to reach a point of equilibrium.

Bobby, a neighborhood kid who sometimes mowed the lawn for John's mother, Norma, called to John, who was always nice to him even though he was just thirteen years old and still in junior high. It probably helped John's attitude that Bobby admired him.

"That's a cool leather jacket," the kid said. He reached out to touch the sleeve and John proudly held it out. "It's the nicest thing I own." John started to walk away and looked back over his shoulder. "I need to go see a girl named Sue. And I gotta get some money that someone owes me. You can come along if you want."

John flagged down a ride from an acquaintance. He and Bobby were dropped off in the parking lot of the Northgate Bar soon after. When John dropped the empty whiskey bottle as he headed to the back of the parking lot, it shattered. Bobby heard him say, "Wait here. I'll be right back."

Ella was startled by a loud crash coming from the kitchen. She sat up and fumbled for her flashlight and purse, holding them both tightly as she shuffled down the hall. "Who's there?"

A second later, she was standing in the kitchen doorway. She flipped the light on. She was stooped, stumbling a bit in surprise and then righting herself as she indignantly asked, "What are you doing in my house?"

The brightness caused John to freeze for a moment. John was not a tall man, so the elderly woman and he were almost eye-to-eye. He was uncomfortable meeting her piercing gaze. When he looked down, he saw the purse that she clutched tightly to her chest. "This is a robbery. Give me your money!"

Ella turned toward the front room. "I'm calling the police. Get out of my home!"

John should have left, but when she turned toward the phone in the front room, he rushed past her to make sure the phone was inoperable. On his way, he accidentally brushed against her. She fell back, landing in a sitting position on the couch.

The phone was sturdy and old-fashioned, with a thick coiled cord that wired the hand piece directly into the phone itself; it proved more difficult to pull apart than he expected. When it finally gave way, the side table that the cord had been wrapped around fell over and a lamp crashed to the floor, breaking into several pieces.

John was out of breath when he turned to see the old woman standing at the kitchen table, pulling a bank enveloped from her purse. She removed the cash inside and extended it over the table to him. "Take it. Take it. It's all I have."

She handed him a pile of small bills. He pushed them into the pocket of his jeans. Then she yelled an order. "You get out of here. Now!"

John ran faster than he had ever run in his life, terrified by his first encounter with one of his theft victims. Facing an actual person made everything real. He had never before thought about the emotional impact of his actions on the people he stole from. As scared as he felt in that moment after staring the woman down, he knew that she, and all of the others, felt worse.

As he turned the corner of the house, he tripped on some chicken wire and fell, hitting his head on the bumper of the woman's car. The impact stunned him; he almost passed out, but he got up and did something he knew how to do very well—run away.

~ ~ ~

Bobby was bored until he noticed the sports car. He ambled over to check it out, running his hand along the shiny black paint and trying to peek inside the tinted windows. He was testing the door handle when a young couple pulled in, parked nearby and went into the bar. Bobby followed them, hoping to get a peek inside to see what the bar looked like.

A man came out. "Hey kid, what are you doing hanging out here?"

"I'm waiting for my friend. He went up the road to get money from someone."

The man opened the sports car door, looked inside, then shut it gently. Bobby heard the door locks click into place. Bobby, nervous that he was in trouble, made small talk. "He'll be right back. Is this your car? It's neat."

The man was about to answer but was distracted by a noise coming from the other side of the fence.

~~~

Stanley Hissong was already the night manager of the Northgate Bar at only twenty years old. When some customers came in and told him that a kid might be messing with his Camero, he went out to investigate.

The kid seemed harmless.

Stanley locked up his car and decided to check the parking lot for mischief. He heard moaning noises from the other side of the wooden fence on the edge of the parking lot, but he couldn't see through it. At first, he thought it was children playing or crying, or even cats, but as he peeked around it, he saw a wavering light. An old woman came into focus.

He heard her call, 'Help!" He shouted to a regular who was getting out of his car, "There might be trouble over here. Come help me."

~~~

Bobby saw John run along some bushes, then cut through the parking lot and pause. Bobby hurried to join him.

John was out of breath. "Come on, let's get the hell out of here."

Bobby followed John, climbing the fence that John had hopped. He saw John's jacket fall to the ground and stopped to pick it up. "Hey you dropped this."

John looked back but did not reach for the jacket. Bobby grabbed the red bandana off the ground too and stuffed it in the jacket pocket, then sprinted to catch up with John. They ran a few more blocks and arrived at Sue's house—a friend who owed John money.

John tried to get inside but the door was locked. He tried a couple of windows, then the back door, but the lights were off and no one was home.

"Let's go." John jogged to the street and waved down a car.

The driver was a black man in his thirties. Shock washed over his face when John opened the car door. "Hey, man, can we get a ride? I'll give you $5. I gotta get out of here—some people are chasing me."

John was already in the passenger seat before the man replied. When John held out the cash, the man, relieved that he wasn't being robbed, put the car into drive. "Where you going?"

Bobby settled in the back seat and handed John the jacket. John gave the man the name of the trailer park where he had been sleeping on a couch since his release from prison and chatted him up as they headed off.

~~~

The woman was elderly, not very tall. She was barefoot, wearing a nightgown with a floral print. She was shaking and crying when Stanley reached her. "Somebody broke into my house and knocked me down. I don't want to go back in there."

Stanley tried to comfort her. "Well, they're not there now. Let me get you to your neighbor's house. I'll get you inside where you'll be safe."

The woman started calling her neighbor's name and stumbling toward his porch. She repeated. "I've been robbed," over and over again, clearly in shock. Stanley stooped over and held her arm as they walked.

~~~

Robert Edwards had lived across from Ella Stephens for forty years. He thought that kids were pranking when he heard someone calling for help, but he finally looked out the window and saw Ella stumbling around her front yard. The flashlight that she held bounced erratically.

As he got closer, he heard her say that there had been a break in. When he saw that a man from the bar was helping her, he ran into her house and out to the backyard to make sure that the robber was gone.

After assuring that her home was secure, Robert rushed over to support her from the other side. He held Ella Stephens while the other man went up and knocked on the neighbor's door.

It took the homeowner a while to answer. The neighbor invited Mrs. Stephens in but directed her toward the side door because there was a chain across the porch that would be difficult for her to step over.

The neighbor came out to help guide her to the house and the bar manager went back to the Northgate to call the police. Robert got in his car and drove around, looking for the bastard who had robbed a little old lady but soon returned to her house empty-handed.

~~~

Her rescuers were ushering Ella into the house next door when she said, "Oh, I feel faint," and collapsed. The men carried her inside by her arms and legs and laid her on the kitchen floor.

The paramedics arrived but didn't have enough personnel on the scene. They had Robert help with chest compressions for a few minutes until a professional could replace him.

They worked on Mrs. Stephens for twenty minutes, but she never regained consciousness. Ella Stephens was pronounced dead when she arrived at the hospital.

~~~

"Johnny, you got any smokes?"

"Don't you even think about smoking in my car." The driver looked sternly at Bobby in his rearview mirror.

John continued to make small talk, asking the man where he lived and worked, then, based on the answers, if he knew so-and-so.

"Johnny, you never said if you had any smokes." John handed him a couple of bucks so he would stop asking.

"Here, you can buy your own."

"I'm not old enough."

"I'm sure you can figure it out."

They let Bobby out near his house a few minutes later.

~~~

As John was dropped off at the trailer park, Ella's body was placed inside an ambulance headed to the coroner's office.

John was still drunk. He walked to the back of the park. He knew a lot of people and had several places he could go kill time before he went to bed. He needed to get rid of his jacket. The old lady, who was alive and well when he left her, might be able to identify him.

His friend, Tim, had been admiring the leather. Maybe Tim would buy it at a significant discount.

~~~

John was charged with adrenaline and Jack Daniels; nervous energy sparked off him, but as the alcohol receded, a feeling of dread emerged. He had crossed a line within his own set of boundaries by robbing a senior citizen.

John called up the street when he spotted his friend. "Hey, Tim."

Tim sat outside, finishing off the beer he was drinking. He crushed the can in his fist and tossed it to the ground. Tim's brother, also named John, walked outside just as John Eric was getting there.

John Aslin was ramped up, talking fast, pacing and waving his arms around. He wasn't making much sense and was constantly on the verge of tears.

"I just need money. You want it?" John took the jacket off and held it out to Tim. They worked out a price.

John stayed for an hour, his energy draining until he got quiet, playing the scene where he knocked the woman over repeatedly in his head.

Even though he had stopped smoking pot, John knew he was going to have trouble sleeping. It had been an extraordinary night, in the worst way possible.

He went to Glenn Stephens' trailer to buy some weed. Glenn was listening to the police scanner. "My grandma's house got broken into."

John's heart stopped beating for a moment; he turned white. "That's awful."

John heard enough details squawking out of the radio speaker to know that he was the cause of the commotion before Glenn reached over and turned it off. John's guilt made it hard to remain standing. He handed Glenn some cash and left with one joint.

~ ~ ~

John was staying with his friend, Sheila, and her grandmother, Marybell, who told him to call her grandma. He was still tipsy when he tiptoed into the trailer, but his liquid courage had seeped out.

He saw Marybell standing at the sink, washing dishes. He found a towel and stood beside her, drying the dishes as she handed them to him, then stacking them on the counter.

John was somber, the reality of his decisions and actions sinking in. He had robbed an elderly woman, even knocked her over, and now he realized that she belonged to someone he knew.

He should have turned and left as soon as she woke up, but Uncle Jack had clouded his judgment, created false bravado and dismantled his common sense to a point that he had done something he was truly ashamed of.

He felt utterly dejected, his shoulders weighed down by his remorse. He swiped at rogue tears as he dried the plates and bowls that Marybell handed him.

The old woman's voice played over and over in his head, her fierce insistence that he leave her alone as she looked up at him with determination. She was braver than he.

He would have to figure out a way to make things right. "Grandma, you go to church, right?"

"Yes, Johnny, I go to mass every week."

"Does God forgive sins?"

"Sure he does, as long as you repent."

"What does that mean?"

"You have to admit that you did something wrong, then ask God to forgive you."

"What if the thing you did is shameful—unforgiveable?" John's eyes were now brimming over with tears, steady streams running down his cheeks.

"Look Johnny, I don't know what's going on but whatever you've done, I'm sure God had heard much worse. You're God's child and he loves you."

John doubted God would have much interest in taking the burden of stealing from an old woman off his shoulders. He had never been face-to-face with someone he stole from, except for shoplifting, and he felt like he had crossed into a whole new level of badness by invading the sanctity of an old lady's home and insisting on taking her money.

"How do I do it?"

Marybell turned off the water, dried her hands and walked into the living room, gesturing for John to follow. She opened a drawer and removed a long necklace with a cross hanging from it and a small prayer book.

She sat on the couch and patted the space next to her for John to sit. "Praying is talking to God in your mind or out loud. It's best to find a quiet time to do it, fold your hands and bow your head, but you can pray while you're doing just about anything. I pray when I'm in the car driving and walking to get the mail."

She held up the necklace and displayed the cross on her palm. "This is a rosary. You don't need it to pray to God, but I use it when the thing I am praying about is important."

Marybell taught John how to use the rosary. She would have more time to teach him about God and learn what it was that had so upset him the next day; it was late and she needed sleep.

When she turned back to say goodnight, John was hunched over the prayer book, reading intently.

~~~

John ran the beads of the rosary through his fingers. "God, I feel so ashamed of what I done. I've been bad for a long time and I want to be better. I never knew how much I probably hurt the people I stole from. I'm gonna do better. I'm gonna stop drinking and I'm gonna go straight, finish school, get a job, be a man to my boy. Please forgive me and help me change."

After he finished his prayer, John went into the bathroom. The young man who looked back at him in the mirror was a mess. His beard was unkempt, his hair scraggly. His blue irises were surrounded by snakes of red veins.

He splashed water on his face, a baptism of his desire to change. He would clean himself up. He would look for a job the next day. He combed out his long hair and cut it off, giving himself a neater look—the kind of haircut that would not get him immediately rejected by a potential employer. He shaved his beard and mustache and trimmed his sideburns.

He dug through his bag, found a nice shirt and hung it up. He would iron it in the morning. There was still a lot of cleaning up to do on the inside, but his new look and his resolve to find a job were steps in the right direction.

~~~

Marybell was smoking and drinking coffee in the kitchen when John woke up. "Johnny, can you turn on the TV? I want to hear the news before I go to work."

John turned on the console and changed the channel to ABC-12 just in time to hear the newscaster breathlessly announce, "A 76-year-old was literally scared to death last night in Mt. Morris. Police say that Ella Stephens collapsed after an intruder broke into her home and was later pronounced dead."

John fell back into a seated position on the couch, too stunned to speak.

Sheila came out from the back bedroom and sat beside him. "You okay, Johnny?"

"Yeah... Just hungover... The news just said a lady died in Mt. Morris last night. They said it was a homicide. Do you know what

14

that is?"

"I think its murder." Sheila went to take a shower. John laid down, facing the back of the couch, pretending to sleep away the morning, but wide awake.

~~~

"Why did you kill that old lady?"

Bobby was shocked the first time a classmate asked him that question but when it happened dozens more times, he panicked and left school. He should have never told his friend that he was near the Northgate Bar the other night.

He needed a cigarette. He went to the party store to try to buy or bum one off someone there. After he had been loitering for twenty minutes, John Aslin showed up. "Hey, Johnny, can I bum a smoke?"

~~~

John composed himself enough to walk up to the corner store so he could buy a newspaper. Bobby Keene was standing outside and asked him for a cigarette.

"I told you, I don't smoke... Just a minute." John went into the store. When he came out, he handed a pack of cigarettes to the kid. "Do me a favor? If anybody asks if you saw anything last night, don't mention me."

"Sure Johnny." Bobby shuffled off, words unspoken and questions unanswered.

John called Tim from a payphone. "If anyone asks, will you say I was at your house last night?"

"Why? What's going on?"

"Nothing but can you just do that for me?"

"Sure.

~~~

A few days later, when Bobby was in math class, the intercom interrupted his thoughts. "Please send Bobby Keene down to the office."

Two police officers were waiting in the hallway. Bobby's mouth went dry. He had never been in any kind of trouble. Smoking cigarettes was the only law he had ever broken.

A silent police officer grabbed his shoulder and steered him toward the cruiser. Each step was more terrifying than the last. The officer directed him to the back seat. Bobby rode silently for a few minutes as he gathered his courage. "Why did you come and get me?"

"You're a suspect in a homicide."

"What's a homicide?"

"Murder."

~ ~ ~

Bobby was dumped in a small room with three chairs and a table. He eventually lost track of time. He put his head down on his arms and drifted into sleep.

While he was in that room, the lead detective called his parents. "Mr. Keene, we need to keep your son in juvenile lock up to protect him from a murder suspect. We believe he's in danger... no, the facility is not set up for visitors... I don't know how long we'll need to keep him, but I'll be in touch."

Bobby was abruptly awakened when the detective flung the door open so that it crashed against the wall. Bobby forgot where he was for a moment.

The detective growled, "You look pretty young to be a murderer."

Bobby was too shocked to speak. He stared at the menacing man then looked down.

"You think you're tough?" No one would ever say Bobby was tough. He was a scrawny kid who always had a smile on his face. He was not equipped to deal with the situation he found himself in.

"No, Sir."

"I agree. Tough guys don't pick on little old ladies, you piece of shit."

Bobby was silent, then squeaked out, "I didn't hurt anyone."

"But you know who did."

"I don't know what you're taking about."

"I know that John Aslin told you all about robbing that old lady."

"I don't know what you want me to say—I don't know anything about it."

"You better figure it out. You're going to prison today, and you might spend the rest of your life there, so you better think really hard."

~ ~ ~

Bobby didn't really spend the next week in prison, but he didn't know that. For a well-behaved eighth grader, juvie felt like death row.

"Here kid. Put these on." The guard handed him a cheap light brown cotton sweatshirt with matching pants. The clothing dripped over his small frame, making him look like a melting ice-cream cone.

As he was escorted to his cell, the other kids ran to the bars of their individual enclosures. They screamed threats; animal noises echoed in the small space. A few reached for him.

The guard swatted at their arms and screamed, "Knock it off." This only managed to increase the frenzy to a terrifying roar.

While the guard was distracted by threatening to hit an outstretched arm with his baton, Bobby took a step away from the scuttle, unknowingly moving closer to the cells on the other side.

A long thin arm yanked Bobby's ankle out from under him. He lost his balance and fell hard on his elbow. Tears streamed down his cheeks, a fatal revelation of his weakness that made him a mark for the rest of the week.

They ate in their cells, which should have assured that he got to keep his food, but once the tray was delivered and the guard moved on, the threats started.

"Give me your milk or I'll take it out of you in the yard." That voice came from the right side and belonged to a huge kid with a full beard. Bobby passed his milk around the wall that divided them.

A demand for his sandwich came from the other side. That kid wasn't very big but Bobby had seen him fight in the yard and knew the kid could do some damage to him.

Most meals, Bobby was left with just his vegetables since they were logistically hard to give away. On top of being hungry, he was bruised and battered—elbowed, tripped and sucker punched, but never on the face. The kids knew that they could have their fun with him as long as the marks didn't show.

~~~

Bobby was ready to talk when he was brought back to the precinct for questioning the next week, even though he still didn't really have much to say.

He scarfed down the cheeseburger and fries the detective gave him. He hadn't eaten a good meal in a week.

"Jesus, kid, slow down. If you barf, you're cleaning it up—not me."

Today the scary detective was all smiles, jokes and atta-boys, offering to go get another burger and keeping the Pepsi flowing.

"Time for the two of us to have a chat." The detective took a seat across from him and pushed the button to engage his pen, holding it expectantly over a pad of paper.

Bobby wiped across his mouth with the back of his hand. He sat up, took another swig of pop and burped softly.

"Tell me what happened the night you hung out with John Aslin."

Bobby told about riding along with John and waiting for him in the parking lot, then running to Sue's and hitching a ride with a stranger.

"John told you he killed Mrs. Stephens, right?"

"No, he didn't say anything."

"Bobby, are you suddenly having a hearing problem."

"Um, no, I mean, yes, John told me he killed Mrs. Stephens."

The detective spent the next hour telling Bobby what John said and did and then made Bobby repeat it back. Once he was satisfied with the story, he turned on the recording equipment and got Bobby's "official statement."

"Okay kid, if you testify to what you just told me in court, I'll put in a good word for you. Maybe your charges will be dropped. That means you wouldn't spend the rest of your life in prison."

~ ~ ~

John was cooking Hamburger Helper for breakfast when he noticed several police vehicles parked up the block. His first instinct was to run out the back door and never look back.

He peered out the window, watching them move toward Marybell's place. Then they crossed to the other side of the road. Four more cars pulled up at the other end of the street and eight officers jogged toward the trailer across from him.

John felt relief. Elmer Stone must have done something pretty bad for a dozen officers to take him in, but today was not John's day—not yet.

The police battered in the door across the street, dragged Elmer out and threw him on the ground, wrenching his arms behind him and cuffing them.

Then John heard the words that made his blood run cold. "John Eric Aslin, you're under arrest for the murder of Ella Stephens."

They didn't realize their mistake for several minutes. John could have taken off out the back door, run to the field a few rows down, crossed it and calmly hitchhiked his way out of town, but he was ready to take responsibility for what he had done.

It had been an accident.

Still, Mrs. Stephens' death was keeping him awake at night. He had run away his whole life.

This time he would stay put. He had vowed to change; taking responsibility for his terrible decisions was a necessary first step.

He calmly turned off the stove burner and walked toward the front door, intending to turn himself in to the policemen in the street, but they burst through the door as he pulled it open.

One of them cocked him in the head with the butt of his gun. John went down and his nightmare began.

The Prosecution

Within the Genesee County's prosecutor's office, John was known as the Teddy Bear Killer. His rap sheet showed thefts, but he had no history of violence or confrontation with his victims. The autopsy confirmed that he did not physically harm Mrs. Stephens or put his hands on her in any way.

He was 21 years old, but he looked younger, as well as terrified and remorseful. He was clearly no murderer but that didn't mean he couldn't become one, with the right spin.

John's crime created an opportunity for an ambitious prosecutor to expand the law and make a name for himself—perform a magic trick and show that he could send a poor, battered-by-life young thief to prison for the rest of his life.

So that's what happened—instead of an unarmed robber, John was painted as a cold-blooded killer. Michigan's felony murder law would provide the path for the Genesee County Prosecutor's office to elevate the terrible, yet unintended consequences of John's decisions and behavior to a life offense—a crime that he would spend the rest of his natural life paying for in prison if he was convicted.

Felony murder was generally used in situations where there was an unintended yet entirely foreseeable death during the commission of a felony, such as using a gun to commit a robbery and having it accidentally go off and kill someone. Felony murder was an odd choice for what happened to Ella Stephens but that's what the prosecutor was counting on to make his plan attention-grabbing and career altering.

In Michigan, felony prosecutions begin in District Court, a lower court that also handles misdemeanors and small civil cases. Evidence is presented to a judge, as opposed to a jury or a grand jury.

The prosecutor must provide proof of two things in order for a case to move forward to circuit court, where a trial or plea will take place. The prosecutor must show that it was more likely than not that a certain crime took place and that a particular defendant is the person who committed that crime.

The prosecutor's theory of why John's case deserved to be a felony murder—which sends the convicted to prison for life—rather than an unarmed robbery or even involuntary manslaughter (crimes that carry a maximum penalty of fifteen years) emerged at the Preliminary Exam when Ella Stephens' grandson, Glenn, took the witness stand.

Glenn told the court he had stayed with his grandmother after she had a heart attack during the prior year. Glenn dated Misty, who was Carrie's sister. John and Carrie had a baby together. Glenn claimed that one day when he was at Misty's parents' home, John Aslin called their house from jail and Glenn told John that he was staying with his grandmother because she had a heart attack.

Glenn, however, testified that John had never visited him at his grandmother's house. He said that no one beyond Ella's family knew that Ella cashed her pension checks and kept the money in her house. Glenn said he was suspicious of John on the night that Ella Stephens died because his grandmother kept jars of change all over her house and John had used coins to pay for the "cigarette" that John had bought from him.

Glenn misled the court about two things that were exposed quickly. The first thing Glenn lied about was exposed by Misty, who had been required to sit in the court hallway while he testified so that her testimony would not be impacted by Glenn's. Misty testified that John came over the night that Ella died to buy marijuana—not a cigarette.

The other mistruth was exposed during cross examination. Glenn was forced to admit that he never talked to John on the phone; he quickly covered his lie with a claim that he overheard someone else talking to John and somehow telling John the convenient detail that Ella Stephens had a heart condition.

John was puzzled by the made-up story—why the prosecution wanted to establish that he knew Mrs. Stephens or had knowledge of her heart condition—but he didn't put the pieces together about why that was important until later.

The court heard testimony from multiple witnesses and eventually "bound the case over to circuit court" for further proceedings.

As John was being collected by the deputies to return to jail, his attorney leaned over and turned on a lightbulb inside John's brain. "Looks like they're going to argue that you knew she was sick and somehow did this on purpose. That's how they'll sell it as murder."

The four months that John was in jail awaiting trial were a blur. It might seem like common sense that jail would be a place where he would be forced to dry out but there were plenty of substances available for an addict to feed his need inside his cage. He was able to chemically check out for much of the time.

And then the most important event of his life was suddenly upon him.

A couple facts penetrated the drug-induced haze. Visitors told John that his mother, Norma, was threatening to kill herself, so ashamed that any son of hers would be a murderer. This increased his need to somehow beat the case.

Norma had contemplated hiring an attorney for John, but everyone assured her—and John himself—that he was being overcharged and that the case would get sorted out to a more reasonable charge eventually. He had no choice but to face the prosecution's machine with a court-appointed attorney.

His mother's advisors underestimated the ambition of Genesee County Prosecutor Robert Weiss, who was in the midst of building a reputation for being tough on crime, advocating for harsher sentences and the building of more jails and prisons. In fact, he would be critical of the multi-million-dollar jail that the county would build in 1988, claiming it wasn't big enough.

The gall of Weiss' decision to prosecute the Teddy Bear Killer for murder gained him a lot of attention. If he succeeded, John Aslin would be sentenced the same as if he had walked into Ella Stephens' house intending to kill her, put a gun to her head and pulled the trigger—a first degree murderer with a life sentence and no chance for parole ever.

John would be worse off than if he had walked into her house with a gun, not intending to kill her and then decided to shoot her in the heat of the moment—that crime would have been second degree murder and he would have possibly been eligible for parole someday.

The plea offer never came. John's only option was to take the case to trial, hope that a jury would see the facts for what they were—an accident stemming from terrible judgment.

But a trial was exactly what the Genesee County Prosecutor wanted—it was more dramatic and would make bigger headlines.

As John sat in jail, he was bored out of his mind. He got his hands on a phonebook and decided to look up his last name. There was a single listing—Peter Aslin.

John's hands shook as he dialed the number. A friendly voice with an Upper Peninsula Indian accent answered. "Hello."

"Hey. Um, my name is John Aslin. I found your number in the phonebook. I was wondering if we're related."

"John? You Norma's boy?"

"Yes. Norma's my ma."

"My brother John is your pop then. And I'm your uncle. Hello nephew."

John was silent, any words stunned out of him. Was it that easy then? Just pick up a phonebook, push some buttons and have the mystery of half of your existence crack open?

"I've been following your case. Telling my brother about it. Saw your picture in the paper. You look just like him."

That gave John the first smile he had had in months. "Where is he?"

"He lives up north. I'll talk to him. Call back tomorrow. Maybe I'll have a number for you."

John couldn't sleep. He called early the next day. Peter picked up on the first ring. "I've got your pop's phone number. You got something to write with?"

John felt dreamy, almost happy. The thought of speaking to his father was surreal. There were little points of anxiety poking at the edges of his imaginings, but he decided that his father would not have allowed Uncle Peter to pass his phone number along if he planned to reject his son.

He dialed the number immediately. "Hello?"

The voice at the other end of the phone had the same Upper Peninsula Indian accent.

"Um, this is John Eric, your son."

"Son, I've been waiting for you to call for the longest time. I've kept my phone number in the book all these years, hoping you would look me up."

John was stunned. "I never would've thought you wanted that."

"I tried to see you over the years, but your ma would chase me off. If I showed up, she'd menace me with that old shotgun of hers—one time she even shot in the air over my head. She'd threaten to call the police, say that I was harassing her."

John could envision the exact scene that his father described. It rang true.

"So I just tried to keep track of you as best I could. There was an Indian family that lived near you. They would take pictures of you and send them to me until your ma put the brakes on that plan."

John remembered playing with those kids, how their dad always had his camera out—as interested in capturing John in his lens as he was in his own kids. Then Norma decided that John couldn't play with those "dirty Indians" anymore and banned their house to him. They were such fun playmates that he had gone back. When she found out, he suffered a beating.

"I want you to know that I never missed a child support payment all of these years and now that you're in the situation you're in, I'll support you as long as I'm breathing." (That statement held true. His father faithfully sent him $25 a month until he died.)

"I'm not trying to speak ill of your mother though. I want you to know what happened, but I won't speak of it again. I was a heavy drinker back then—so was she. We fought terrible and hurt each other so much that we couldn't go back. I haven't had a drink in twenty years. It ruined my life. I wish your ma could have gotten sober too—then maybe she would have let me back in enough to be your pa."

His father, John Albert Aslin, was a faithful letter writer. He talked to John Eric on the phone once a week.

This is how John Eric learned that he was Ojibwe and not just a smidge—more than enough to register with two tribes. He reexamined his life. Was he predisposed by blood to love the natural setting of the California redwoods and Northern Michigan woods, to almost commune with animals—a caged bear outside a store in Rose City that he would visit as a child that seemed to speak to him? His bond with his best friend and Siamese cat, Pretty One? Was his toxic addiction to alcohol a poison that was already inside him when he entered the world?

Getting to know his father brought a whole new set of stories to fill in the sketches of his childhood. The best story was about how his sister, Linda, became a hero when she was five years old.

The possibility of a future John Eric Aslin began on the Fourth of July in 1958 and was almost snuffed out in December of the same year.

Origin Story: John Albert Aslin and Norma White Meet Flint, Michigan July 4, 1958

John Albert Aslin had plans with his brother Ted to celebrate Ted's birthday in downtown Flint by watching the Fourth of July fireworks. These were boom years for General Motors Corporation—money for civic events flowed through the city. The light show was expected to be spectacular.

The Aslin men already had a few beers in them when they set up their cooler and blanket on the crowded banks of the Flint River. John Albert spotted a young woman with a little girl sitting nearby. There was no ring on her finger.

He mustered some liquid courage, slickly uncapped a bottle of beer and offered it to her.

"That's nice. Sure is hot tonight." She took a swig from the bottle, smiled appreciatively and wiped a speck of foam off her lips with the back of her hand.

"That your sister?" John nodded at the little girl.

The woman giggled. They chatted. John soon moved over to her blanket. Her name was Norma. Her daughter, Linda, ran around with other kids but rushed to her mother's lap when the first "boom" and explosion of light shattered the sky.

The trio laid back and watched the lit-up sky for almost forty minutes. When it was over, Norma folded up her blanket and packed up her picnic basket. John reached for it. "Let me carry your things."

When they got to the car, he made his move. "I'd like to see you again."

Norma pulled a small pad of paper from her purse and wrote down her phone number. "I'd like that."

LIFE TWO: WHERE JOHN ERIC'S FUTURE EXISTENCE IS PRESERVED BY HIS BRAVE SISTER AND AN ANGEL DOG

HOGBACK HILLS, DAVISON, MICHIGAN
DECEMBER 1958

Norma and John were not the types to pass up an invitation to a Christmas party that was sure to be fueled by booze, even if it took place out in the middle of nowhere in a blizzard. During the festivities, they had done their best to help empty the keg of beer and down the Christmas cocktails that their excellent hostess, Molly Newsome, kept replenishing.

After hours of intoxicated merriment, they headed home. Out of the two of them, Norma was in the best shape, so she got behind the wheel. John muttered in the passenger seat and Linda slept in the back in her holiday white fur cape. Norma had tucked the matching muff under Linda's head to pillow her slumber.

Norma tried to concentrate on the road, but every time she focused, she'd realize she was drifting toward the edges. She would startle and jerk the wheel back then be at risk of veering into the oncoming lane. Fortunately, the heavy snow that was coming down had discouraged most people from leaving their homes, but occasionally another car would pass by, horn blaring, an alarmed look on the face of the driver.

The roads were tricky because they wound their way along the edges of the thickly wooded and sparsely populated Hogback Hills. Norma got sleepy and allowed her eyes to droop for just a second. When she opened them, the car was headed into the opposite lane again. She reflexively whipped the wheel back to correct the car's path. When the vehicle, instead, veered toward the trees on the edge of her lane, she slammed on the brakes but that just put the car into a spin.

Suddenly the car was off the road, sliding backwards down an incline. Their descent was halted by a large bush. John pulled himself back into his seat from the passenger-side floor and began yelling at Norma. She could hear Linda whimpering in the backseat.

Norma clumsily opened the driver's side door and stumbled out into the snow. The car tilted dangerously toward the driver's side, but alcohol dulled Norma's thinking.

All Norma wanted was to get to Linda. Her dress pumps did not make things any easier and the back door of the car had been dented during the journey down. Norma yanked on the handle several times. Linda, whose little face had been pressed against the window, wailed as her mother battled to open the door.

Suddenly, the door flung open. Linda was projected from the car into Norma's arms and then through them, tumbling to the ground beyond where her mother stood. The car groaned and slowly tipped toward Norma. Her blunted reflexes made it impossible for her to move out of the way. The car fell in slow motion, pinning Norma to a tree.

Linda, mere inches from the bumper, narrowly avoided being crushed. Norma, barely able to breath, let go a piercing scream. "John!"

John lifted his head and reached toward the steering wheel. He was too inebriated to do anything but hold the car horn in and hope someone would hear them.

~~~

Five-year-old Linda shook her mother's shoulder. Norma's eyes fluttered then stayed closed.

Linda had worn her fancy clothes to the Christmas party. Her shiny black shoes with the silver buckle were not good for climbing up a snowy hill. Her hand muff was still somewhere in the car and her lovely white cape was getting less pretty by the moment as she slowly made her way, slipping and sliding, taking three steps up the muddy incline and then falling back two.

Her tights were ripped, and the wintry gusts blew up her dress, chilling her to the core. When she reached the road, snow blurred everything. It blocked any stars that might be out, blurred the moonlight and obscured everything around her. The only reason she knew she'd reached the road is because the land flattened out.

Linda took a moment to catch her breath. She was crying. Snot froze to her face and clogged her nose. She felt something nudge her from behind. She turned and was nose-to-nose with a giant black and white dog; it dipped its snout to nuzzle her, then licked her cheek. It walked away, then looked back, as if to say, "Come on!"

Linda caught up with the dog, grabbing some of its fur to steady herself. She was a big girl, five years old, but it was hard for her to walk so far. They turned off the road toward a house at the end of a long driveway. Christmas lights twinkled in the windows. The dog nudged her toward it and up to the front porch.

Linda pushed the doorbell. She turned back toward the dog, but it was gone. Santa Claus opened the door—at least that's who Linda thought he was. He had a thick white beard, a red sweater and a look of surprise. He hollered deeper into the house as Linda stumbled through the door, into the relative warm, swaying as she stood staring at Santa. She thought she might topple.

Mrs. Santa Claus appeared. When she saw Linda, covered in mud and snow, shaking so violently that she couldn't speak, she swooped down and wrapped the child in her warm bosom, hollering at her stunned husband to get some blankets and put the kettle on.

Mrs. Claus hurried Linda to a blazing fire and rubbed her arms vigorously to warm her up. Soon Linda was cocooned in several quilts. Her shivering subsided.

Mrs. Claus gave her a mug of hot chocolate. "I cooled it down so it won't burn your tongue. Can you take a sip for me, honey? It'll warm you up from the inside out."

Linda took several swallows. The warmth freed up her voice. "Mama crashed."

"What's that?"

"Mama. She's stuck."

"You're telling me about your mom?"

Linda nodded. Then sorrow crashed over her face. "The car fell on Mama down a hill."

Santa picked up the phone. He talked to someone about a car accident. Sometime later, Linda heard sirens. Later still, a police officer knocked on the door. The adults talked quietly, but Linda could hear them.

"That little girl saved their lives. The man was passed out—probably would've frozen to death. The woman is in bad shape. She was pinned under the car. They took her to the hospital."

Mrs. Claus had removed Linda's filthy clothes and dressed her in a nightgown that a granddaughter had long outgrown. She retrieved the child's clothes to show the officer. "This was all she was wearing. It's amazing that she made it all the way here."

The officer whistled in wonder. "It was almost a mile down the road, then they were pretty deep off the edge. No one would have seen them if she hadn't made it here. Can't believe she even found you—if she'd taken the other way on the road, she would've wound up nowhere."

Linda spoke up. "I followed your dog."

"We don't have a dog," said Mrs. Claus.

"It was big as me."

The adults smiled in a way that told Linda they thought she was telling a story.

When Norma woke up, she felt like she'd been beaten with a meat tenderizer. Her entire body oozed pain. She couldn't move. She was obviously in a hospital, but she couldn't remember why. "Hey!" She started yelling. "Hey!"

A nurse popped her head in the room, then disappeared. Norma could hear the woman's shoes tapping down the hallway as she called out, "205 is awake! Call the doctor!" She returned a few minutes later. "Dr. Lazar will be here shortly. We had to call him at home."

"What happened?"

"You were in a car accident. Your car went over a cliff."

Norma went white. "Where's my daughter?"

"She's with Mr. Aslin. They should be here soon. We called him too."

The doctor got there first. "You're lucky to be alive. You were half frozen when they pulled you up to the ambulance." He was speaking to her slowly, in a measured voice. "You've been unresponsive for five days. There may be permanent damage. The car pinned your middle to a tree. There was a lot of pressure on your chest, abdomen and spine. I'm not sure if you will regain your ability to walk. You probably won't be able to have more children. We'll have to see how it goes. In the meantime, you'll stay in here for a couple of weeks and heal up. Let us know if there's anything we can do to make you feel more comfortable. Miss White, do you have any questions for me?"

Norma shook her head slowly from side to side. A few tears leaked out. She quickly wiped them away. She was alone in her room, mulling over her predicament, when she heard Linda's chirpy voice floating down the hall. "Come on, John!" Norma heard the tap, tap, tap of her daughter's shoes and then she burst through the door. "Ma, you're awake!"

Linda ran to her, looking as though she would jump on the bed. John intercepted her just in time, lifting her and carefully setting her down near Norma's knees. Linda climbed toward her mother's face.

John hovered helplessly. "Lindy, be careful. Your ma's still sick. You could hurt her."

Linda slowed her pace but kept moving until her cheek was pressed to her mother's heart. "Did they tell you what she did?"

Norma shook her head.

"She saved us. Climbed up to the road and walked a mile in that storm to a house."

Linda's head popped up. "I followed the angel dog."

Norma laughed. "You did?"

Linda nodded soberly.

"You did real good, Lindy. The doctor said we need to let your ma sleep. We'll come back later."

The accident sealed Norma and John to each other. His guilt over being drunk and useless as she lay pinned and dying exacerbated the fact that their relationship had reached a point where it evolved around drinking.

John tended to Norma's needs when she came home in her wheelchair and he took care of Linda, but he was well on his way down an alcoholic path. The stress of her disablement eventually pushed Norma to almost keep pace with his consumption of booze as the aches and pains from that accident dulled her mood.

The fact that their drinking had brought them to their current predicament was lost on them. If they had been sober, would they have even headed out into that snowy night? If they had been sober, would they have been more careful? If they had been sober, would Norma have gotten pinned and trapped in the freezing cold? Would John have been able to get out of the car and help? These questions were never asked.

Though a blossoming drunk, John was a good caretaker. He held down a job, married Norma in a small ceremony and adopted Linda. He was a sweet step-father, bringing her treats and trinkets when he came home. They might have been happy, but alcohol punctuated each sentence in their story. Happy moments were eclipsed by angry, alcohol-soaked arguments.

Norma was tough as nails. Soon she was taking steps around the house while holding on to the furniture. Eventually she walked to the corner and back, leaning on John just a little.

John sat in the doctor's waiting room while Norma had a check up to make sure she was healing properly. Norma walked out with a smile on her face. She walked right by him, almost floating out to the parking lot. He hurried after her, afraid she would slip on the icy sidewalk. "What's gotten into you, Norma? You trying to fall?"

She gleamed as her helped her get seated in the car. Once he was settled behind the wheel, she turned to him, beaming. "We're going to have a baby." She expected excitement, but not of the angry variety.

"You been stepping out on me?"

Norma was confused. "What are you talking about?"

"I can't have kids. There's no way that baby is mine."

John stuck around until Norma healed, but things had changed. He left Norma emotionally long before he moved his things out. He was long gone before Amy was born in late August. He softened over time, came back, but the drinking and arguing continued. When he found out the second baby was coming, his sense of betrayal was too strong. He left and didn't look back for years. Something happened in his youth that made him believe Norma's children were not his and her pregnancies simply triggered that trauma.

We'll get to that later but it started when his grandfather had an accident.

The Happy then Tragic Childhoods
of John Eric's Father, Aunts and Uncles
St. Ignace, Michigan
1936

John Albert, who became the father of John Eric, was born in the woods of Northern Michigan, the seventh of nine children of Ojibwe parents. He was dearly loved. He especially loved his own father, Albert Aslin. Fred, John Albert's oldest brother, looked out for him. They were part of a happy family until their life changed in 1936 when Fred was ten and John Albert was four.

Albert Aslin talked softly to his oldest son, Fred, as they walked through the woods, bundles of blankets strapped to their backs.

Albert's pack held his wolf pelt. Fred carried a pelt from a raccoon that he had trapped earlier that spring.

The wolf was Albert's totem animal and spiritual guide. The fact that the wolf had chosen Albert highlighted the fact that Albert had a teaching spirit, spreading knowledge to his children and his tribe. He treated life like a never-ending journey; Albert was a pathfinder, always discovering a way through difficulties and challenges. These were the qualities that the wolf had recognized in him.

Fred had yet to journey on a Vision Quest, so he didn't know what his spirit animal would be, but he wore the raccoon pelt with pride during ceremonies. He would be honored if the raccoon appeared to him some day as his spiritual liaison.

Fred had a small axe and a colorful pouch tucked in his pack. The light mist that hovered above the ground added a sense of magic to the morning.

It was early. Fred repeated his father's instructions back to him to show that he had listened carefully and understood his responsibilities. "When Medewin gets there, I give him the pouch of tobacco and ask him to guide me today."

"That's close, but no words are needed. Giving him the tobacco is how you ask." Fred was solemn as he thought about his father's words. There were no silent understandings at the school that he and his siblings attended, where they learned to read, write and do their numbers.

Learning the rituals of his tribe made him feel mature. He was only ten years old, but the things his father was teaching him were steps along the road to manhood; they excited him, yet he kept a serious mask on his face.

His father continued in their native tongue. "The hut that we will build is like the womb that your mother carried you in. You go inside that womb, your spirit grows and, when you come out, you are reborn in some way. Maybe your spirit is renewed, maybe your body is healed or maybe both. Inside the lodge, you will breath the breath of life."

His father paused to allow the idea to sink in. "In this life, we have our physical self and our spiritual self. The purification ceremony makes it possible for these two parts to begin to become one. It's a joining ceremony—maybe even a marriage," his father laughed gently, "that takes place within yourself. Medewin will work with the spirits who live in the invisible realm to help you become aware of the healing process." The two continued on their journey, lost in thought.

Albert and Fred were the first to arrive at the meeting spot. Fred cut dozens of the small saplings they would need to build a new structure. Albert dismantled the weathered, dried-out wooden structure left over from a previous ceremony and snapped the branches easily with his strong arms. He piled them in the fire pit so that their power would be added to the spiritual event that would take place later that morning.

Fred dragged the fresh saplings to the small clearing where his father was working. Albert removed a large knife from his waistband and trimmed off smaller branches so that the long supple trunks could be bent to their purpose without the interference of twigs and leaves. He had built many sweat lodges in his forty years and quickly bowed the fresh wood into crisscrossed arches that he wove into a solid frame.

Fred followed his father's lead, holding things in place when Albert needed an extra hand. Once Albert was satisfied with the base, he motioned Fred toward the bundles. Fred unwrapped the pelts and blankets they had carried deep into the woods and brought a stack over to his father. He stood patiently as his father removed them from his arms, one-by-one, and placed them over the fresh wooden skeleton. Soon a sturdy dome stood in the glade, waiting to greet the men who would be arriving soon.

When Medewin arrived, Fred nodded respectfully as he handed the spiritual guide his pouch. This was the first time that Fred had prepared for a purification ceremony himself. The small bundle, which took him hours to assemble, held hundreds of tobacco ties that Fred had carefully constructed according to the directions the medicine man had given. Medewin was in communication with the spirit world and passed along the spirits' requests to each participant of the sweat lodge ceremony.

Fred gathered little pieces of cloth representing the six directions-- white for north, yellow for south, red for east, black for west, blue for the heavens and green for the earth mother—in the numbers that Medewin had told him, directing his prayers toward each as he tied them up.

Fred's medicine pouch held hundreds of small bundles that the spirits viewed as prayers. The tiny gifts would draw the spirits to Fred's assistance during the ceremony.

Medewin nodded back, placed the tobacco somewhere in the folds of his clothing and readied himself for the ceremony. He examined the new lodge, walked around the premises, and set up the altar. He placed a set of antlers from his pack atop a pile of stones that had been arranged to provide a surface for the implements of purification.

Medewin set up his pipes, the tobacco that Fred had given him and some small containers that held sacred herbs. He arranged grandfather rocks in the fire pit. They would be heated, then moved to the hut so that water could be poured on them and create sweat to fill the symbolic womb.

Soon, the other men arrived, each approaching Medewin and handing him a pouch of tobacco. Everyone helped prepare for the sweat. Some men laid out the food on a pelt. A few filled buckets from a nearby creek.

After Medewin lit the fire, the men circled it, praying silently. Medewin offered sacred herbs to the four directions of the winds, chanting his intercession to the spirits. Soon the fire was so hot that the air above it shimmered.

Fred, Albert and the other men entered the hut and crawled to the right around the perimeter until they evenly circled the center, but they kept the sacred spot to the left of the door free for Medewin.

Medewin used sticks to move the rocks into a pit in the center of the hut one at a time. He placed the north stone first, then south, east and west. Several other stones were placed in the center. He continued his prayers as he sprinkled sacred herbs—medicine—on the rocks and then moved some blankets to seal the entrance.

The small space was already heating up when he dipped into the cold buckets of water and threw ladles of it on the burning rocks—this was called "pouring sweat."

The forest was silent. Even the creatures respected the spiritual work of the men inside the hut and calmed their chatter. Fred was anxious as the room heated up. The men were draped in their sacred hides; Fred covered his head and shoulders with his own.

If he had prepared well, he would be able to endure the next couple of hours of intense heat and the spirits would bless him. He had to stay inside the hut until the process was finished. He could even go to sleep if he needed to, but it was important not to disrespect the spirits by leaving the lodge before the ceremony was complete.

Fred concentrated on managing the discomfort of the heat. Sweat poured into his eyes, burning them. He shut them tight, breathing slowly, as his father had taught him. He was able to stay alert for a while, but his thoughts eventually wandered. He got lost inside the hut and was gently awakened by his father, who motioned him to exit the sweat lodge.

Other men exited as well, contemplating the journey they had just taken. Several set out food while others arranged blankets to circle the feast. They ate and talked quietly once Medewin had taken his first bite.

When their stomachs were full, Albert and Fred bundled their belongings for the journey home. They walked silently until Fred was ready to talk about what had happened to him inside the hut.

"Pa, I saw something in there."

"Yeah? Was it a light?"

"You saw it too?"

"I did. I heard my father's voice speaking to me."

Fred nodded in agreement. "I heard Nimishoomis too."

Albert mussed his son's hair with affection. "That's real good, son. He was calling you to be a man. He'll be there when you're ready in a few years."

St. Ignace, Michigan
Summer 1936

The heatwave that hit the Midwest just after Independence Day in 1936 brought the most intense warmth Albert had ever known. Michigan was one of over a dozen states that experienced the highest temperatures ever tracked. St. Ignace hovered around 100 degrees for 5 days. The weather was relentless.

Though the furnace-like conditions continued through the summer and destroyed most of the crops suffering under its intensity, the worst of it was July 6th through July 10th. During that week, over 5000 people across the country lost their lives simply from overheating.

Draught had plagued the country for several years when the oven-like blasts of wind blew over the plains and settled in for that week of temperatures that reached over 100 in many places and set a record in North Dakota that still holds—121 degrees in the city of Steele.

The summer had been hotter than normal already and had followed the coldest winter ever recorded. Albert believed something had unbalanced the spirits. He felt that truth in his bones.

Albert performed a smudge—by creating sacred smoke from

tobacco, cedar, sage and sweetgrass— to cleanse his home so that the impurities that swirled around the ecosphere would not impact his precious family. His garden was sparse that summer and the animals he hunted for meat were harder to find. A smudge might turn the energy back to a more balanced state. He was out in the woods behind his home when he heard Fred calling for him.

"I'm here, son. What is it?

"Baby's coming."

Albert dropped the plant he was examining and rushed toward the house. He needed to start a sacred fire and keep it burning while Frances labored to bring their ninth child into the world. As the father, Albert was responsible for lighting the way so their child's spirit would succeed on its journey and would find them.

Albert had constructed a birth hut a few weeks earlier. He was grateful to have not delayed the project. His oldest girls, Doris and Alberta, were ushering Frances into the hut as he arrived. Layers of blankets and pillows had been arranged inside it so that Frances would be comfortable as she talked their baby into the world.

Normally, Albert would throw a few stones into the fire and use them to warm up the hut, but the weather had caused it to be too hot inside already. Frances and the girls disappeared inside the wigwam and Albert gathered wood.

The fourth Aslin girl was born many hours later. Doris caught her as she entered the world and turned to touch her feet to a small patch of dirt left uncovered near the opening of the hut. It was important to ground Eva in the physical world before she was passed over to her mother's arms so that her spirit would stay.

St. Ignace, Michigan
Late Summer 1936

The Aslin home was nestled slightly off the main road a short distance from town. There were Aslins in the community who had achieved a degree of success and several branches of the family lived closer to town in modest homes. School would begin the next day and there were six excited children and one disappointed boy sitting around the dinner table in the home of Albert and Frances.

The six students looked like stairsteps when they stood in a line— Doris (12), Alberta (11), Fred (10), Peter (8), Violet (7) and Theodore

(6). They would leave together in the morning while John, just four years old, would stay home with "the babies"—George, a toddler, and baby Eva. This fact was intolerable to John.

The older children chattered while John sulked and pleaded with his father to let him go with the "big kids" in the morning. "I'm not a baby," he growled.

"John Albert, I know you want to go to school, but I have to go out tomorrow and I need a little man here to help your ma. Can I count on you?"

John thought about it for a few seconds and then reluctantly nodded his head. He would have to wait until next fall to go to begin his education.

Violet, who loved the evening ritual of family readings, always reminded her mother when it was storytime. "Ma, can we hear some more of Dr. Doolittle?"

Doris chimed in, "I'll finish up the dishes."

Their mother, Frances was a mere thirty years old and had been pregnant for much of her adult life, but instead of being tired out, she was fun and energetic. "Sure. Go get the book."

Violet hurried to the bookshelf of borrowed books and other family treasures. Albert grabbed Baby Eva and sat in a chair, waiting for Frances to read.

Violet handed her mother the book with a look of anticipation and Alberta settled George on her lap on the floor. John lay on his back on the floor near his father and reached his hand out, resting it on Albert's foot, which he periodically patted softly. The other children arranged themselves near their mother, who sat close to the only light in the room.

Doris called from the kitchen, "Keep your voice up, Ma!"

Frances paused dramatically and took in a deep breath. "Everybody ready?"

Nine heads nodded—even Albert. Baby Eva was the only one who had not learned the nightly ritual.

"'Chapter Eight. The Leader of the Lions. John Doolittle now became dreadfully, awfully busy. He found hundreds and thousands of monkeys sick --gorillas, orangutans, chimpanzees, dog-faced baboons, marmosets, gray monkeys, red ones --all kinds. And many had died.'"

John interrupted. "Are there pictures, Ma?"

Fred answered, "Hush, John. Not now."

"I don't know what an orangutan looks like."

"I'll draw you one later." Fred spent many afternoons studying a set of encyclopedias at the Civic League Library in town and could draw a zoo's worth of animals. John was satisfied with that offer and quieted down as his mother resumed reading.

"'The first thing he did was to separate the sick ones from the well ones.'"

John interrupted again. "Why'd he do that, Ma?" "He thinks it will stop the strong ones from getting sick." John nodded. That answered made sense to him. "'Then he got Chee-Chee and his cousin to build him a little house of grass...'"

The next morning, six children exited their home like a line of ducklings. Doris carried a brown bag rolled at the top with six sandwiches inside. Fred and Alberta carried books and notebooks.

They were barely down the driveway when the younger children broke ranks and chased each other, yelling and laughing as they bolted down the road. The oldest three initially tried to corral the younger ones, but they soon gave up and ran to catch up.

Soon after, Albert walked out the front door carrying George; John was close on his heels. John stooped to pick up a feather and showed it to his father. They examined it together.

"What kind of bird do you think it came from?"

"It looks like a turkey feather."

Albert smiled. "That's right. Good boy. You're a smart one, alright." He tucked the feather behind John's ear.

Albert went to a small shack behind the house and took out some fishing nets, examined them, then set them against the side of the house. He took the children inside. John placed the feather carefully on the special bookshelf.

Frances was nursing Baby Eva. Albert leaned over and nuzzled the baby, kissed Frances on the cheek and tussled John's hair. "I'll be back once Henry and I have enough fish to take to market. John, watch your brother. Help your ma."

"I will, Pa."

"Tomorrow you can come with me to set some traps." John beamed and nodded at his father, then led George over to some toys; they played quietly as Albert left.

St. Ignace, Michigan
Late Fall 1936

John heard the wagon coming down the road. He went to the window so he could tell his mother who it was. He didn't recognize anyone but Henry. Several men hovered around something in the back and the driver urged the horses to hurry.

The wagon pulled into the yard a few moments later and a couple of men jumped to the ground to receive a large bundle that others lifted over the edge. Henry ran ahead toward the front door. He opened it without knocking. "Albert fell in the water. He's had a bad chill."

Albert was carried through the door, barely conscious. Frances motioned the men toward the bedroom, where Henry was already stoking up the fire. They laid Albert on the bed. Henry and Frances removed his wet clothes.

"He took in some water too." Emotion choked Henry's voice as he looked at his friend, pale and listless on the bed. Once Albert's clothing had been removed, Frances layered blankets over her husband.

Henry asked one of the anonymous men to get more wood from outside so that Frances could keep the fire going all night. John climbed on the bed and gently touched his father's face, whispering something in his ear that no one else in the room could hear. George hovered nervously at the door and Baby Eva cried in the other room.

"John, tend to the baby for me so I can get your pa set up. You can come back in a little while."

John was his father's little man. He had to help his ma when she needed him, so he climbed from the bed and took George into the other room to stop the baby from crying. After Albert was tucked in, the men and the wagon left.

Frances came out to the front room. "John, you can go see your pa now, but don't wake him up." John laid on his side, softly brushing his father's damp hair from his face and petting one of his hands. Sometimes he sang to him and sometimes he whispered more secret messages.

He stayed with his pa until the older kids got home. He heard them burst through the door, good-naturedly arguing about something and then they went silent.

"Ma, what's wrong?" Fred asked, with urgency.

"Your pa had an accident. Fell out of the boat. He's in a bad way—resting in the bedroom. I need you all to be quiet."

"I'll go to Medewin to find out what medicine we'll need."

Horace Ance, the local Medewin, answered the door. He could tell from the boy's face that something was wrong.

Fred was breathless. "Pa fell in the lake—he's terrible sick."

Horace put his coat on. He carried twine and a blanket. He gestured for Fred to follow him. They headed to the sacred spot in the woods where Fred and his father built the lodge earlier that year. When they got there, Horace broke the frame into smaller pieces and tied them into bundles. Then he laid out the blanket and placed the grandfather stones inside, tying it up for carrying. "Take the stones to your house. I'll come after I pray to the spirits."

Horace turned to the altar and laid out a few items. Fred had to stop a few times to rest—it was a burden for a young boy—but eventually he made it home.

Fred used his father's small axe to cut saplings, dragging each one to the yard. Once he had a dozen, he removed his father's knife from its sheath and used it to trim off excess branches, just as he had seen Albert do. Horace and Henry arrived several hours later. They bent the thin trees to the familiar shapes and covered it with blankets and furs.

Horace handed Fred a small piece of paper with the medicine written on it. Fred glanced at the paper, nodding solemnly. "You'll have a lot to do to get things ready—prepare the medicine, lay down wood for a fire and stack the stones nearby. I'll need an altar to lay out the sacred things. We'll be back tomorrow at early light."

That evening, Albert was laid up in bed, coughing. He fluctuated between a pasty pallor and intense sweats. John sat next to him, talking softly and humming when he ran out of words, willing Albert to get better. He had never seen his mighty father look so ill. John patted his chest gently when he coughed. "You gonna be okay, Pa?"

Albert responded in a weak, raspy voice, "I'm gonna try, Son."

John lay his head on his father's chest and eventually fell asleep.

Fred stayed up late into the night making tobacco ties according to Medewin's instructions. He also stacked wood for a large fire and laid out the grandfather rocks near the fire pit. He climbed inside the hut and chipped away an indent into the hard ground to place the hot stones in when they were ready. He had to scavenge his father's storage shack and the nearby woods to find things that he could use to build the altar. It was well after dark when he was finished with the outdoor responsibilities and went inside to do the most important thing.

This sweat was not planned. He was distressed to discover that his father did not have much tobacco on hand. He cut the requisite number of cloth ties in the right colors, but each one held only a few specks of tobacco when he was finished. He gathered them into his father's ceremonial pouch with disappointment. He prayed to the spirits that they would accept what he had to give them on behalf of his father.

The next morning, Fred had to be awakened by Henry and told that Medewin was waiting. Fred had not slept well and was riddled with anxiety as he pulled on his clothes. He went into his parents' bedroom and placed the ceremonial pouch on his father's folded hands, then helped Albert give the pouch to Medewin when the spiritual leader entered the room.

Medewin walked out immediately and Fred followed him. "You did good, Fred. I have everything I need." Medewin lit the fire and placed the stones in places where they would heat up as the fire built in intensity.

Horace prayed at the altar, offering sacred herbs to the winds. Soon a few other men from town arrived with food for the ceremony. When the stones were steaming hot, the men entered the house and carried Albert inside the sweat lodge. Fred followed.

The other men moved quickly into place so that the stones could be brought in to warm the air as soon possible since Albert's coughs echoed over the yard. Albert remained upright as long as he could, but eventually lay on his side. Fred curled up in the pocket of his father's legs and reached his arms up to hug him.

Medewin earnestly interceded with the spirits. When the ceremony was over, the group carried Albert back into the house and stood around his bed looking worried as they nibbled on wild rice, fish and apples.

The next day Albert was the same. At times, he shivered under his covers. He wheezed loudly and sometimes seemed to wince with pain if he took a deeper breath.

The day after that, Albert's color improved slightly but he seemed confused and mumbled under his breath.

The next day Albert's cough started to bring up thick mucus

streaked with blood.

The next evening, Albert died.

Albert Aslin was Ojibwe. When an Ojibwe dies, he cannot move on to the spirit world until his body is in the ground. The spirit of an Ojibwe does not leave this physical world at death. It lingers with family, reluctant to let go of the sweetness of this life. The body must rest below the earth in the cold darkness in order to encourage the spirit to begin the four-day journey to the happy land of the dead.

The Ojibwe bury their dead as quickly as they can to help them to reach the place of happiness as soon as possible. If the remains must be kept overnight, the community gathers at the home of the deceased, not only to keep company with the immediate and sorrowing relatives but also with the person who lies there. Because the ground was so cold, but fortunately not yet frozen, Albert's burial would take place the next day.

The Aslin home quickly filled with friends and neighbors who would stay all night. Albert was laid out on the table, which had been moved to the center of the front room. His hands rested on his ceremonial pipes. He was dressed in clothing that Frances had painstakingly decorated for him with small beads and shells for ceremonial events long past.

Each hour, the spiritual leaders sang one of a series of sacred songs meant to comfort Albert's spirit as he waited to leave. Frances would cover herself in Albert's wolf pelt and dance gently and quietly around the casket, holding the hide in such a way that had it been alive, it would have cast its eyes to the sky above.

She systematically pointed its face at each of her children and then the other people in the room. Each person would rise and join in the dance. When each song finished, the dancers would rest for the next round. It was in this fashion that the grieving widow and her children made it through that first night.

Eventually John was overcome with drowsiness. He dragged a chair in from the kitchen and pulled it up to the table, positioning it in such a way that he could reach his father's hand, which he pulled down to hold. John fell asleep with his forehead pressed to his father's palm.

A soft snow fell all night and continued to blanket the ground, creating a hushed world in line with the sorrow on the faces of those who had loved Albert dearly. His final resting place would be a small cemetery on the edge of town. Albert's cousin built a simple pine box for the journey. A horse-drawn wagon assisted the pallbearers by carrying their tragic freight much of the way. Frances and the children huddled together as they walked behind their beloved. They had declined the offer of a ride.

The gravediggers were still finishing up when Albert arrived. His immediate family circled his casket one last time as Medewin sang some prayers for Albert's departure.

Albert's uncle, the oldest relative present, said farewell on behalf of the clan in their native language. "My dear nephew, you are about to depart this world. We shall not be long parted, for it will seem like not much time has passed at all until we follow you. We are happy and proud to see your wife, who already misses you dearly, your loving children and countless friends and relatives surround the place where your remains shall lie. You have made a difference in this life. This world that you are departing is a temporary home for us all. When you reach that happy land of our forefathers, please continue to be to us what you were while living with us. Now that you will be with those that have the power to give to us knowledge and light, please assist us in finding the way to that happy land. Dear nephew…"

The elder's speech was interrupted by a clap of thunder—thundersnow was rare and everyone paused in wonder. Then the old man finished his speech. "We now bid you farewell. Even the heavens are saddened with emotion at your departure."

John was young, but he understood that his father would leave this earth soon, never to return. He was in the habit of giving his father beautiful things that he found in the woods when his father left the house. His pa always thanked him. "Now that I have this, I won't forget to come home. I'll remember that my John is waiting for me." This time—the most important leaving of his father's life--John had nothing to give.

The family walked back through town, headed to their home where people would gather for a powwow, to celebrate the life of Albert. John stumbled along near the back of the pack, weighed down by anxious grief.

As they passed a house, John spotted an evergreen with vibrant red berries—his father always admired Holly. They had often paused to admire the festive branches on their winter walks. John broke away from the crowd of mourners, flung open the gate and ran to the bush.

He frantically tore at the branches, leaving ragged gashes on the trunk.

His efforts were unsuccessful. Half-torn stalks hung limply, still attached. Suddenly Fred towered over him, picking him up and carrying him away. John sobbed to be let go so he could finish his task. "We need to hurry. If we don't get these to Pa soon, he'll have started his journey and he'll have nothing with him to remember me by."

Fred set John down and crouched to look him in the eye. "Let me do it. We need a proper bunch for Pa."

John nodded and remained still. Fred pulled his father's knife out. He had secured it to his waist with a belt so that he would feel closer to Albert when he said goodbye. Fred carefully cut a few branches, then handed them to John. They walked back to the grave.

"We made it in time. They haven't lit the fire yet, so Pa's still here."

Relief washed over John's face. "Here Pa. I got you these flowers. Don't forget me. I love you."

John was a big boy, but he let his brother carry him partway home. Being big was hard that day.

The purpose of a funeral powwow is to distract the minds of the mourners, so they won't be overcome by sadness. At dusk, Henry, Fred and Medewin drove to the cemetery to build a fire at the head of Albert's grave. They would repeat this activity for the next four nights in order to light his way on his journey to the spirit world. The path was long and it would take him four nights to get there. They wanted him to travel in light—not darkness—so he would be sure to find his way.

Fred lingered, warming his hands at the blaze. He took a few of John's holly branches and held them until they caught fire, thinking that it might make it easier for his father to take them with him. The men were patient, but eventually they coaxed him away, telling him he needed to eat, stay strong, as he was now the man of the family.

Back at the house, Frances thanked people and urged them to go home to rest. She was headed for bed, exhausted by all that had transpired. Fred looked for John, wanting to tell him that he had sent some of the holly along in the fire. John was curled up like a cub in Albert's wolf pelt, sound asleep.

The funeral ritual of the Ojibwe is a four-day process. On the fourth evening, after dusk, the mourners gathered for a final time to feast in celebration of Albert's arrival at the Place of Happiness.

It was Medewin's responsibility to dispose of all of Albert's worldly belongings by giving them away. He gave all of Albert's nephews an item of clothing. He set aside small decorative items for each of Albert's daughters. Fred was given his father's knife; Peter was given his gun; Teddy got his father's bow; Albert's pipe was to be kept for Baby George and John was given the wolf pelt.

Medewin invited those who had received a possession to make a bundle that would assure Albert's comfort in the spirit world. The bundle would contain a dish and articles of clothing. The clothing was to be supplied by those who had been given clothing that belonged to Albert and it had to be new. The dish was wrapped in one blanket, the clothing in another, then both bundles were given to Frances. She selected a recipient of the articles of clothing that she thought worthy of wearing them.

The bundle with the dish was given to Albert's oldest nephew to carry. For a year, it would be with him during any meal that he ate, at home or as a guest, and he would be responsible to place some food in it for Albert.

There were parts of the grieving ritual that Frances would continue for a year. She was not permitted to marry during that time. She would busy herself by making a single set of clothes for a man—moccasins, beaded shirts, and pants. At the end of a year, she would bring the clothing she made and the dish to a tribal feast and present them to one of Albert's male relatives; that would be the person she would marry.

St. Ignace, Michigan
December 1936

The state building was downtown. Frances hitched a ride with a neighbor to get there. She left John and George home, but she had the baby with her because she was still nursing. She sat quietly in the waiting room until a tall, well-dressed woman with light brown hair called her name. The woman looked at her with disapproval and did not introduce herself before turning and marching down the hall to an office. Frances nervously followed her.

The nameplate on the door said, "Mrs. Anderson." Mrs. Anderson opened a file on her desk. Frances took a seat across from her as Mrs. Anderson fired questions at her. "When did your husband die?"

"About two weeks ago."

"How many children do you have?"

"Nine."

"Are there any relatives who can take you in?"

"No, Ma'am."

"The state can provide you with money for food and a little extra but it's going to be difficult to care for that many children on your own."

"Yes, Ma'am. But my kids are good. The older ones can work on some of the farms round here come summer. We just weren't prepared for the winter without my husband. I have some food put up, but he kept us in fish and hunted up some meat."

Mrs. Anderson responded with disapproval. "There are grown men who can't get work on farms. Your children won't do any better.... Is Fred one of your sons?"

"Yes, Ma'am."

"That boy is out of control. He hacked up my holly bush a couple of weeks ago. I have a mind to report him to the police. He's on his way to becoming a criminal."

"No, Ma'am. He's a good boy. Who told you he did that?"

"I saw it with my own eyes. It just took me a while to find out his name."

"I'm sorry to hear that then. I'll talk to him, Mrs. Anderson. I'll tell him to stay away from your house."

Frances almost felt peaceful for the first time since Albert had gone. She could see snow falling through the large picture window in the front room. Christmas music played on the radio. Fred and Ted hung Christmas lights around the front window. There was a small tree in the corner with handmade ornaments. Doris, Alberta, Peter and Violet strung popcorn and made paper chains from newspaper.

Ted called out to his mother from the kitchen. "Ma, will there be any Christmas presents this year? Do you think Santa will come?"

Frances sighed. She didn't know if any charities would think of her kids this year. They had never needed help with that sort of thing in the past. She started making them gifts while they were at school, but the tragedy that had befallen the family ate up much of her time; none of the gifts would be completed by Christmas. "I don't know. I know you've been real good but Santa might not make it to every house this year. It's been a tough year for more than us. But I can make you your favorite cake for Christmas morning."

Fred saw several cars coming up the road. They pulled into the yard in front of the house. Six official-looking men and women in business attire got out. They talked to each other in the yard before approaching the house.

Fred watched them through the window, which was now hung with colorful lights. He bounced Baby Eva on his hip.

Ted joined him at the window. "Look pretty important. Do you think they're here about Christmas?"

Fred shrugged. "That or we're in trouble. See her? She's the one from town that Ma told me to stay away from. John and I tore up her bush."

"I hope Santa Claus don't know about that. I'd hate for him to skip you this year."

There was a quick knock at the door. Before anyone answered it, the people walked in. "Frances Aslin?"

A surprised Frances stepped into the front room from the kitchen. "Yes, Sir. That's me."

"I have an order from the probate court that allows me to gather you and your children. You've been determined to be feeble-minded and unable to care for them. We'll give you a few minutes to collect some things, but you can't take much."

At first Frances didn't comprehend what she was being told. Then she became frantic. "What? I don't understand. We're not feeble-minded. The teachers say my kids are real smart. We're fine. No one's going hungry here."

Mrs. Anderson sneered a response. "Your children are out of control. In a few years, they may even be a threat to the good citizens of this town. This is a problem that needs to be dealt with now."

Alberta stepped toward her mother. "Ma, what are they saying?"

"They say we've got to go with them. Doris, get the suitcases under the bed and pack up some things-- a set of clothes for each of you. Your Pa's picture."

The younger children, sensing something was very wrong, began crying. Somehow Frances was able to calm the children down. Soon they were all standing near the door with their things. Violet held a doll.

Mrs. Anderson took the doll away. She yanked the wolf pelt that John had wrapped himself up in away from him. "There isn't room for toys and this thing is disgusting." John lunged for his treasure, but Mrs. Anderson was very tall and simply held it above her head.

John melted into a tantrum. One of the men shook him, swatted him on the butt, then steadied him on his feet, grasping his upper arms tightly until he stopped struggling and was still. "There will be none of that, young man." John stood stoically, never talking his eyes off the eyes off the wolf.

Mrs. Anderson brusquely ushered the children outside. Frances, George and Eva were directed to one car. The other children were directed to another.

John broke away and ran back to the house, grabbed the turkey feather from the special shelf and tucked it in his pocket. A social worker burst through the door, roughly grabbed John's arm and pulled him outside.

John was forced into the car that held the five older kids; he scrambled to the back window so that he could see the house as they drove away. The Christmas lights made it look like the house was engulfed in flames.

None of the children ever met the guardian that the court appointed on their "behalf"—the one who told the judge that the ten people who Albert left behind were "feeble-minded." The Aslins were never examined by a doctor. Their teacher could have told the judge that the kids were whip-smart, among the school's best students. But that guardian probably never cared to ask. It was more important that the Aslins were newly poor, that they were Indians and that Albert's death put them on welfare.

The house that the family left that day may as well have literally gone up in flames—it would have mirrored the lives of its formerly happy tenants. It would be many years before Frances, George or Baby Eva saw the older children. Albert and Frances' offspring would have to reach adulthood and then fight like hell to get the state to set their mother free.

But that was way off in the future. For now, the car was headed into town.

Mrs. Anderson directed the driver to stop at a small store that bought pelts from local trappers. She went in with the wolf skin and was snapping up her purse when she walked out otherwise empty-handed.

The children didn't know that they should have grabbed on to their mother and never let go. They didn't know the peril they would face as the car carrying Doris, Alberta, Fred, Peter, Ted, Violet and John pulled on to the ferry to travel across the Mackinaw Straits to lower Michigan.

John usually enjoyed watching the ships pass by from shore and had always been fascinated with the idea of riding a large boat, but the fate of his father and the fact that the ferry was taking him away from home created a lifelong aversion to watercraft. Many years later, he chose the Army over the Navy for that very reason.

After the ferry left the shore, the children were allowed to stand on the deck. They huddled together, tearful. Fred ran to the back of the boat and watched the Upper Peninsula slowly recede.

John stood next to his brother. He worried over the feather in his pocket and checked it one more time, partially pulling it out. A gust of wind caught it and carried it down the deck. John chased it frantically, but he wasn't fast enough. It blew over the edge.

John looked as though he would jump in after it; Fred caught him and put a hand on each of his shoulders as they watched the feather fly away. John was inconsolable once it was clearly gone.

Charlotte, Michigan
1996
Fred Aslin

I wish I could reach back and tell those kids standing on that boat to run, run! Run as fast as you can. Nothing good is coming your way.

Michigan Home and Training School
Lapeer, Michigan
1936

The car disembarked from the ferry and headed south to Flint, then cut east to Lapeer. When they reached their destination, they were 250 miles from home. They had arrived at the place where each of them but one would spend the remainder of their childhoods.

The children were tired and hungry when the car pulled up to the gate. It was almost dark. They had driven all day, with just one stop to fuel up the car and relieve themselves. They had been given a sandwich hours ago but nothing else for the long ride.

A large building loomed as the car progressed down the driveway. It looked like a castle. Doris could not help but think that she was now a heroine in one of the gothic novels she loved to read. She hoped, contrary to appearances, that this gloomy scene would be the setting for a happy-ever-after.

The main building was an intimidating four-stories of brick with turrets on each end that looked like they were wearing conical caps. A porch spanned the front. Mrs. Anderson urged the children to exit the car quickly, pointing them toward the entrance. After the driver honked twice, a light came on in the vestibule on the other side of the door.

The Michigan Home for the Feeble-Minded and Epileptic had opened in 1895 in Lapeer, Michigan. There were three original buildings. It was designed to house 200 wards. By 1936, when the Aslin children arrived, it had grown into a self-sufficient complex with over 100 buildings sprawled across over 2000 acres.

The campus was a self-contained community comprised of enough "cottages" to house 4000 people, a chapel, school, library, hospital, nursery, dining hall, kitchen, bakery, woodworking and engineering shop, sewing workshop, laundry facility and working farm. The farm had a vast vegetable garden that spanned 450 acres and produced corn, potatoes, carrots, lettuce, squash, beets, tomatoes, cabbage, watermelon and strawberries. The orchard held 400 acres of fruit trees. A huge barn housed 120 Holstein cattle that produced 35 ounces of milk per resident each day. In addition to this, the farm had a vast brood of chickens and a drove of pigs. If nothing else, the residents were well fed.

But the Home had strayed from its initial purpose. Though it housed some developmentally-disabled residents, many of the people who lived there were castaways who had been sent there for convenience. There were women whose husbands placed them there when they hit menopause and orphans who had no family to care for them. Teenage girls were sent there for promiscuous or "wild" behavior. There were people who were not "feeble-minded" but did not fit the norms of the day—dwarves, epileptics or those with mild cerebral palsy. There were mixed-race babies and there were Indians, as the Aslin children referred to themselves.

By 1945, when the Aslin children started to leave the Home, the population peaked at 4,950. More people lived inside the walls of what was then called the Michigan Home and Training School than lived in the entire City of Lapeer. But that cold night in December of 1936, the children could not comprehend that they would be caught in this strange place until they became adults, separated from their mother and two youngest siblings.

Mrs. Anderson pushed her way in front of the children and was the first to reach the door. She waited for someone to open it. The hours in the car had not improved her disposition.

Doris reached out and tapped her on the shoulder. "Miss, is our ma gonna be here soon?"

Mrs. Anderson ignored her. John was practically falling asleep on his feet, so Doris picked him up. Mrs. Anderson turned to make sure the children were presentable and noticed Doris was holding her brother. Fury creased her crabby brow. "Put him down! He's too big for that."

A dejected set of children followed Mrs. Anderson into the building when a cheerful woman opened the door. Mrs. Anderson sternly directed them to line up in the lobby, forcefully moved those who were not standing in a straight line or looking forward into place.

Dr. Robert Dixon greeted the children a few minutes later. Mrs. Anderson handed him a stack of files. He took a moment to glance through them. Dr. Dixon spoke slowly, as if talking to someone who could not understand his words. "Hello. I am Dr. Dixon. I'm the director of this place."

Mrs. Anderson barked at them to say hello to the doctor and they chorused, "Hello, Sir."

"We're going to show you to your beds soon. You'll stay in the children's dorms, girls in one, boys in the other." He looked over his shoulder at the cheerful woman who had opened the door. "Lucy, can you please have someone prepare some food for these children?" He turned back to Doris. "Have any of you been to school?"

"Yes, sir. All of us but John." She pointed to John with her chin.

"Can you write your name?"

"Yes, sir. We all can. Even John and he's just four."

"Can you write your letters?"

"Yes sir. All of us can do that too."

Dr. Dixon picked up a reading primer and handed it to Doris. "Open it up to any page. Read to me."

Doris looked at the book for a moment and handed it to Ted, the youngest of them who had been to school. "Everyone of us has read this book. Ted is the youngest but for John. John hasn't been to school yet, so he can't read it, but Ted can. Go on, Ted. Read it for the doctor."

Ted read it easily, with a slight edge of boredom in his voice. "See Dick. See Dick run." He flipped to another page deeper in. "Father said, Run, run! One, two, three! Run to dinner. Run, run, run."

Dr. Dixon smiled. "Thank you, Ted." Dr. He walked over to a bookshelf and picked up "Anne of Avonlea," handing it to Doris. "What is your name, young lady?"

"Doris, sir."

"Doris, please read from the beginning."

Doris read easily, with fluency. "'Chapter One. An Irate Neighbor. A tall, slim girl, half-past sixteen, with serious gray eyes and hair which her friends called auburn, had sat down on the broad red sandstone doorstep of a Prince Edward Island farmhouse one ripe afternoon in August, firmly resolved to construe so many lines of Virgil.'"

"Thank you, Doris. Doris, what does irate mean?"

"Angry, Sir."

Dr. Dixon directed her to hand the book to Alberta. "Please continue."

Alberta continued easily. "'But an August afternoon, with blue hazes scarfing the harvest slopes, little winds whispering elfishly in the poplars, and a dancing splendor or red poppies...'"

Dr. Dixon held up his hand for Alberta to stop and nodded at Fred. "Let's hear you, Son."

Alberta handed Fred the book and pointed to where she left off. Fred picked up the story without hesitation. "'...red poppies out-flaming against the dark coppice of young firs in a corner of the cherry orchard was fitter for dreams than dead languages.'"

The doctor held up his hand and Fred paused. "What does all of that mean?"

Alberta spoke up. "She's trying to read, Sir, but the beautiful sights distract her."

"Very good. What type of marks did you get in school?

Doris answered with confidence. "We were all top of our class, Sir. Our teachers, especially, Miss Drummond, almost complained how hard it was to keep us busy. We were always borrowing books to read."

"Doris, what is your favorite book?"

"I couldn't really pick one, Sir. I love Jane Austen and Charles Dickens, but two of my favorites are Jane Eyre and Wuthering Heights. Pa used to say I'm a true romantic."

Dr. Dixon looked skeptically at Mrs. Anderson but was interrupted when Lucy walked back into the room. "Lucy, please take these children in to get a meal. I would like to have all of them attend school and participate in the music program. Mrs. Anderson, may I speak with you?"

Lucy gestured for the children to follow her. They walked single file deeper into the building.

Dr. Dixon led Mrs. Anderson into a private office just off the foyer. He made her wait as he sat quietly at his desk, looking over the files. When he spoke, there was an edge of displeasure in the mild doctor's voice. "These children do not appear to be feeble-minded."

Mrs. Anderson immediately became defensive. "Well, the judge who signed those papers had a different opinion. These Indians were planning to live off the charity of the state. Their mother couldn't control them or feed them. It is only a matter of time before they become criminals, or the girls get promiscuous and start spreading their inferior genes. Besides, their mother is feeble-minded and has already brought nine of them into this world. You know these defects can show up at any time once they're in the blood. Something had to be done."

Dr. Dixon sighed. "Well, there's no denying that they are Indians, and poor." He paused and a look of resignation clouded his face. Then he stood and pointed to the door. "Good day, Ma'am." He did not see her out.

Lucy led the children to the cafeteria. They had to pass through several walled-in walkways that connected the buildings on campus and made it look like a huge gerbil cage. The walkways had basements running under them so that steam heat could keep them warm in the winter. The purpose of this design was to limit the need for snow removal and outdoor clothing for the residents and provide them with a safe network to move around the complex regardless of the weather.

After the children ate, the girls were taken to their dorm by another adult. Lucy walked the boys to the laundry room and paused to hold up clothes next to each of them. She placed her selections in a basket.

"I think you all would feel better if you got cleaned up." She led them to a shower room and placed four sets of pajamas on a bench near the wall. She handed each boy a towel and washcloth, then pointed them toward the stalls.

"I'll wait for you here. Help the little ones, will you?" She gestured toward John and Ted. Fred nodded and urged his two younger brothers to begin undressing. "Give me the clothes you came with and I'll send them to the laundry."

Fred did feel better once he stood under the hot water for several minutes and soaped off the road grime. However, he was slowed and weighted by sadness as he realized they would be spending the night away from home for the first time.

Once they were all clean and dressed, he herded his brothers into the hallway where Lucy waited. "You poor boys look tuckered out." She motioned for them to follow her to the boy's dorm.

Dozens of beds lined the two sides of a large, open room. Many were occupied, some children already asleep and some watching their new neighbors intently.

Peter, Ted and John were given beds in a row. Fred was on the other side of the room. Lucy laid the clothing she carried on a bed, sorting sizes. She made a pile for each and handed the piles out. "There's a small box under each bed. Keep your clothes and personal items put away. You'll get two sets of clothes. We expect you to take good care of your things."

It took Fred a while to fall asleep, even though he was exhausted. Sometime during the night, he was roused by John, who was crying. He invited his little brother to climb in next to him. They settled in for sleep.

They were abruptly awakened by a guard standing over the bed, roughly shaking them awake. The man hit Fred in the center of his chest with a closed fist, then laughed.

Fred had never been struck before—Albert was a gentle disciplinarian who used words instead of blows. Fred could not catch his breath. The man yanked John up by the arm, then marched him over to his empty bed and roughly placed him in it. His voice was menacing. "You better not let me catch you out of your bed again. The rules is that you stay in bed until I give you permission to get up. You understand?!"

John wailed. The guard smacked him on the top of his head. Ted and Peter were awake, sitting up and looking at the guard. He turned to them. "All of you better go back to sleep."

The next morning, Fred lifted his shirt. A large bruise sat in the middle of his chest, a purple rose that had blossomed overnight.

Vernal Johnson, the night guard, was a small man, but he could do damage to a kid. He would be a continual source of menace to the "damn Indians" for years to come. A few days later, the boys long black locks were shaved off. The only good thing about it was that it was harder for Vernal Johnson to snatch them by the ear than by the hair.

LIFE THREE: AND JOHN ERIC'S CHILDHOOD WAS NO PARTY

VIGNETTES FROM JOHN'S FIRST DECADE

John Eric Aslin entered the world on April 30, 1963, on a cool and windy day. He had beaten the odds. The state had tried to cut off the Aslin bloodline and his mother had almost gotten herself recklessly killed in a car accident, yet he existed.

He nuzzled at his mother's breast. His future lay open, a vast constellation of luminous possibility. Time would form callouses on his innocence and lead him toward a tragic destiny, but neither mother nor son knew what awaited them as they gazed upon each other for the first time.

When John was born, Norma had not yet descended entirely into alcoholism, though poverty and disappointment nipped at her heels. She was simply happy to round out her family with a baby boy.

Norma had grown up in Beecher, an area that bumped up against the north end of Flint, Michigan, and that's where she chose to raise her kids. Beecher was working-class, more rundown than the suburbs to the west and south of the Vehicle City.

When Norma was young, her father owned the land bordered by Cass and Genesee Avenues to the north and south and Detroit and Chestnut Streets to the east and west. He sold the land off one parcel at a time during her childhood. The legacy was fully depleted by the time John came into the world.

Norma came in a tiny package, barely 5'2". She wore her brown hair short. By the time John arrived, Norma had developed a standard wardrobe—practical and inexpensive; her extra money went toward her kids, at least for the time being. She wore stretchy nylon pants in the winter and shorts of the same design in the summer. They all had a seam running down the leg. She wore white canvas shoes when she dressed up and blue canvas shoes when she had work to do. Make up and dress clothes were a waste of resources that she avoided.

John was a shy and sensitive kid. Though smart and talented, he rarely received the type of encouragement that would have bolstered him through his struggles and pointed him in a better direction than the one he took.

Norma was a mama bear, which was both good and bad. Bears are known to be fierce mothers, but they have also been known to abandon a cub here or there if the parenting is not convenient. Norma did not exactly abandon John as a child, but he ran wild in the streets and experienced trauma at home. At times Norma intervened to protect him; at times she was too drunk to care. She often directed her disappointment with life at him. John emerged from his childhood without a sense of how to put himself on a path that would lead to a good life.

"Beecher," Flint, Michigan
1967

They were at it again. Sam and Norma fought like siblings who didn't like each other. Sam started as her man-of-the-month but turned into husband number three.

Whenever they started up, John ran to his room. He had created a little burrow deep under his bed, filled with musty blankets and discarded pillows. He would scoot as far into the corner as he could, pull the blankets around him to blunt the noise and bite his thumb nail.

Because his nails were so short, he had to push hard against his teeth to catch the nail. The pain from the nail pushing into his skin distracted him; the distraction comforted him. He needed this comfort so much that his permanent teeth shifted, growing inward from the pressure. This resulted in a life-long habit of smiling in a way that hid them—his crooked teeth embarrassed him.

Rose City, Michigan
1968

Rose City was a tiny little place with some natural beauty but not much else to offer to anyone who was not a hunter or fisherman. It was the location of Sam's parents' cottage; they offered to let their son move his new family there while he was laid off.

Norma was bored, so she hustled up some cleaning jobs from the summer residents who wanted to relax in their home-away-from-homes and not worry about things like cleaning. Norma stretched the gig into a year-round thing by agreeing to keep an eye on the places when the owners returned to their "real lives" in Flint or Detroit.

John loved to fish. Sometimes Norma would take him to the edge of Sandback Pond. He got so caught up in the excitement of catching fish and examining them in his ma's bucket that he forgot that the purpose for catching the fish was to fry them up for supper. This reality would hit him on the walk back home and he would sniffle all the way there, trying to talk her into turning around and releasing them back into their freedom.

One day he decided to save the fish. He ran ahead of Norma and went straight for the bathroom. Those fish must be cold. They had been cool to the touch when he reached his hand in the bucket, trying to pet them. So he did something that seemed entirely logical—ran them a hot bath.

Norma left the bucket on the porch. It was bulky for a boy of five to carry, but he slowly dragged it through the doorway and across the family room to the bath. Norma was upstairs in the loft where she and Sam slept, changing into clean clothes after splashing herself with lake water as she carried the bucket. She did not see the little hero creeping though the house, intent on saving the fish.

John strained to lift the bucket to the edge of the tub. He was finally able to tip it far enough so that the fish flopped into the bath. He watched them with delight as they circled the tub, but his joy was replaced with confusion as their pace slowed and they eventually turned belly-up, one by one.

Norma stood in the doorway, laughing. "I see you decided to get a head start on cooking those fish."

Sometimes John went with his mom when she had a job. Other times he putzed around outside, walking in the woods that surrounded the cabin, examining bugs and stones and leaves. John was not allowed to go anywhere alone, so he didn't have any friends in this new place like he had in their Mt. Morris neighborhood, where wild packs of children roamed the streets until their parents came to their porches and called their progeny home.

Sometimes Linda would take pity on him and play a game, but Amy thought her little brother cramped her style. The cabin was within walking distance of town. The family had moved there a month before school would start. Amy, who was good with people and good at assessing every situation, rode her bike around for the first week after they arrived and gained a few buddies. She would have a ready-made gang of companions when school started—only a few of her friends were summer kids.

Amy left after breakfast, stopping back for a quick lunch and dinner if one of her friend's moms didn't feed her. She didn't come home for good until the fireflies were out.

Each day, John tried to get her to let him tag along. It became a ritual. He was sure this day would be different because he had a surprise. "I've been practicing. I can keep up with you."

She gave her usual response. "You can't keep up with me and my friends think you're a baby."

"I practiced. I'm good now. I can ride fast." He stood before her, trying to slow her down so that she would reconsider.

She easily moved past him. "We just do girl stuff. You wouldn't even like it."

"Staying here is boring." He sighed. "And I want to see the bear." The store up the road had a large black bear in a cage and John was fascinated by it. When he stared it in the face, he could almost hear it talking to him. He felt like it stopped and paid attention when he showed up, calming the frenetic pacing that caused it to bump up against the wires of the enclosure.

"Sorry Charlie." Amy loved to quote things off TV. She shrugged and walked outside. She got on her bike and started down the driveway but stopped to check something on her chain.

John had followed her out the door, hopped on his bike and whizzed past her. At least he felt like he was whizzing, though an onlooker might have chuckled at his wobbly handlebar skills and strained pedaling. "See. Told you I was good." He was looking back at her to see if she was paying attention. Then everything went black.

He woke up laid out on the ground looking up at a flustered woman. "Little boy, are you okay? You came out of nowhere and rode into my car." She turned and pointed at a tiny dent in her back door.

She got down on her knees and felt him, checking for blood and broken bones. John sat up, burst into tears and ran back to the house. When he turned to look back, he saw that the woman had picked up his bike and was rolling it up to the porch.

Amy was straddling her banana seat and, for once, was speechless as he ran by her. His mother stepped to the porch just before he got to the steps. "Johnnie, what's wrong?"

"I hurt that lady's car. I didn't mean to." Norma picked him up to put him on her hip and headed toward the woman.

"I didn't see him. I was driving by and suddenly heard something hit my car. Looks like he has a bump on his head."

Norma squinted at John's forehead. "You ok, Johnny?" He nodded and hiccupped at the same time, squeezing back the flood of more tears that threatened to escape. "He's fine. You have a good day."

Norma carried him inside and peered through the curtains. "Good. She's leaving. I was worried she was going to expect me to pay for that dent."

Norma felt the lump on John's forehead. "Yep, you've got a nice little robin egg. We better shrink it before a baby bird comes out."

"Really? A bird could come out?"

"Yes, but then you'd have a hole in your head."

"That's ok. I would have a pet bird and it could stay in the hole when it's tired."

Norma smiled and went to the freezer. She took out a bag of frozen peas and held it on John's head while she listened to him talk about his imaginary pet bird. John worried the spot on his forehead, but the egg never hatched.

(It is hard to say how the realities of John's childhood intersected and impacted his thought processes and decisions. He experienced several injuries to his head before he reached adulthood. John was an unusually accident-prone child whose mother was indifferent to most of his injuries. Did his mother's lack of focus and concern cause him to be distracted on his own behalf? He was injured many times throughout his first ten years and never receive medical treatment. Brain trauma may have been a factor in his decisions later in life, but the possibility of permanent damage from numerous childhood injuries was never explored by the court when he was sentenced to a life in prison. Studies show that a single concussion can cause impulsive behavior, but there was no nuance in court sentencing considerations in 1984, when John Eric Aslin was punished for his crime.)

Linda spent her days lying in the sun, reading. In the late afternoons, she'd walk John to town for an ice cream bar or a pop. She was friendly with Erika, a girl who scooped ice cream at a stand near the bear cage. A few teenaged boys took notice of them and showed up whenever Linda strolled into town.

John enjoyed watching her flirt with these shy, small-town boys who were nice to him. Sometimes they would whisper funny things in Linda's ears. If he caught some of the words and repeated them, it would draw a laugh.

"Your little brother is cute." Erika brushed John's hair with her fingers and winked at him. After that, John told everyone he had a girlfriend. He took a lot of razzing for "the older woman" but he didn't care. Erika was pretty and kind.

Sam was called back to work in early December, so it looked like they might have Christmas after all. It was easier for Sam to make the drive back and forth to Flint for a while than move the family closer to the factory. They decided to let the kids finish school before moving back to "the city" but eventually they left the idyllic woods of Northern Michigan and headed back to Flint.

"Beecher," Flint, Michigan
1969

Norma was at work and John was home alone with Princess, Sam's giant poodle. Sam had three modes of communication—arguing with Norma, yelling at his son, Billy, who came every other weekend and fawning over Princess. Other than that, Sam was silent. John wasn't even sure Sam knew the names of Norma's children who lurked around the house when he was home, trying to stay out of his way.

Fortunately for the kids, Sam worked a lot. Princess was John's best friend and often his only companion on the weekends, when everyone else had things to do. John loved to run his fingers through the poof of hair that stuck up on Princess' head.

On this day, his fingers got stuck on a knot. "Just a minute pretty girl. I'll take care of that." He ran into the laundry room and found the dog brush that Sam used daily to preen Princess. Then he noticed his mother's hairdryer. It was a small tank with a hose attached to a bag that fit over Norma's head when it was full of curlers.

John hatched a plan. An image popped into his head—of some

poodles at a beauty shop. He had seen it in a book. Wouldn't everyone be thrilled to come home and see Princess with her hair all fancy?

He tiptoed into Linda's room, not because anyone was home to see him but because he knew she would not approve. She had a box of curlers and some Dippity-Doo hair gel on her dresser.

"Princess!" The dog loved the attention that John gave her and came trotting into the family room. "Sit. Be still."

John gently brushed her hair, carefully working at the knot but letting up if she showed any sign of pain. It took a while, but eventually he could run the brush through without having it catch on anything. He twisted the top off the Dippity-Do and slathered it on a thick strand of hair, wrapped it around a small curler and snapped the latch.

Princess wasn't bothered, so he kept going. He repeated the process until the hair on her head was haphazardly twisted around a nest of curlers. Then he moved to the puff of hair that Sam kept long near her hips. Getting her to sit still while he put the plastic bonnet over her head was a bit tricky and he had to use all of his weight hugging her torso to stop her from running off once he turned the blower on. It probably sounded too much like the vacuum cleaner that she hated.

He turned the setting to low and calmly talked to her and stroked her side while the dryer buzzed. The smell of heated plastic filled his nostrils, but he was too excited to mind.

Once the top was dry, John moved the bag to Princess' back end and stretched it over her hips. The white bag puffed up and she looked like her tail had grown into a giant marshmallow. He had just gotten her to settle down when Sam bustled through the front door, whistling for Princess.

Sam, true to form, did not call John by name as his rage exploded. "You little brat!" Sam's face was bright red; a bullet of spit fired out of his mouth when he got to the "b" sound. He covered the space between them in two strides and lifted John off the ground by his shoulders, carrying him to the stairs and slamming him down on a step.

"Don't you dare move!" he said, threatening John with a finger close to his eye as he backed away and turned to check on his pet.

Princess, in the meantime, was circling with increasing anxiety. She had pulled the hose from the dryer but couldn't get the bag to release from her hips. Sam soothed her and gently stretched the elastic out to free her. Then he carefully removed the curlers and checked the damage. Her hair stuck out in all directions; some parts curled more than others.

Sam turned back to John, marched toward him, yanked him by one arm to a standing position and landed a half-dozen blows to his bottom and thighs. He wore out some of his anger and placed John roughly on the step again. "Not a word, not a sound, not a motion. You'll sit there until your mother gets home or I'll whip your little ass again."

It had been morning when John started his project. He hadn't even gotten himself a bowl of cereal yet. He tried to be quiet, but the crying he was trying to hold back morphed into hiccups and his stomach noises seemed very loud.

It was starting to get dark when his mother got home. She spotted his misery immediately. "What's wrong?"

Sam burst in from the other room, his fury reignited. "I'll tell you what's wrong. Your little brat ruined my dog." He stepped aside, exposing Princess, who stood behind him, to Norma's gaze. She took one look at the dog and laughed.

"It's not funny. When I came home, she was covered in curlers and he had that hair dryer of yours on her butt. So I laid hands on his butt and he's been sitting there all day waiting for you to take care of this."

"All day?"

Norma's tone changed. John nodded his head miserably in answer to her question. "Did you feed him? And where did you get the idea that you have a right to put your hands on my son?"

Sam gave her a disgusted look and turned to leave. Norma rushed at him and slapped him loudly in the middle of his back. "You son of a bitch! Don't you ever touch my kid. He didn't even do anything wrong. That'll just wash out."

He stopped abruptly when she hit him and weighed the wisdom of facing her, but he chose to keep walking.

John's mother picked him up, big boy that he was, and carried him into the kitchen. He laid his head on her shoulder and twirled her soft hair in his fingers, still hiccupping.

She sat him on the counter and chatted while she made him a sandwich. He felt a little better now that she had stuck up for him, but he would eventually learn that Norma wasn't necessarily against John getting hit—she just didn't think that anyone but her should have the right. And she mostly did it when she was drunk.

As her relationship with Sam deteriorated, Norma's drinking increased, as did her meanness. John heard the front door slam and watched through his bedroom window as Sam roared away in his car. Then Norma's rage travelled up the stairs.

"Johnny, get your ass down here." John tucked the comics he was reading under his bed. If Norma's rant led her up to his room, his comic books might become a casualty. When she drank, he kept the things that were important to him out of sight.

She was already holding a belt when he got downstairs—not a good sign. "I told you keep your bike in the garage." She pointed out the window at his bike, which was on the grass in front of the house. The angle suggested that she had tossed it there from the driveway. It must have been in her way when she pulled in.

"Take your pants off."

"Ma, I'm sorry. I forgot. I'll go put it away now."

"I said take your pants off."

John slowly unbuttoned and unzipped his jeans, then stepped out of them. Norma swung the belt at his legs and he reflexively moved out of its path.

She lurched at him, grabbing the waistband of his underwear. He tried to get out of the range of her swing, but the band of his underpants would only stretch so far. Her blows rained all over his legs and butt. They were both exhausted by the time she was done.

"Now put your pants back on and get that bike in the garage." No one noticed the marks that showed up on John when his mother's anger got the best of her.

Like other kids in the neighborhood, he preferred beatings to foster care, so he skipped school when the marks were too hard to explain. One of John's friends got punched in the face regularly by his father and his attendance was terrible.

1970

The snowbanks had grown high that John could only see the tops of the cars as they passed by, until they burst into full view at the break made by the driveway. Most of the tops were black or brown, so he made a game of it—guessing the color of the actual car when it flashed by.

The clouds had dumped eight inches on January 3, a day before he was to go back to school. This would make the walk to school a bit more challenging, but if he got there early enough, there would be time for a snowball fight.

John excitedly put on the brand-new bell-bottoms his ma gave him for Christmas and the Speed Racer t-shirt that matched his new lunchbox. "Bye, Ma!"

He almost made it out the door before Norma called. "John Eric, don't you dare leave here without boots and a hat."

"Nobody wears boots. Kids will make fun of me."

"Would you rather have a tongue-lashing from them or a butt-lashing from me?"

John begrudgingly took off his shoes, put them in a Hamady sack—the local name for a brown paper grocery bag in a town where everyone bought their groceries at Hamady's Market—and placed his new lunchbox on top of them. His second goodbye was much more subdued.

He walked slowly, without any joy, as he felt every heavy-booted step slowing him from getting to school in time for a snow battle. As he walked on his side of the street, he saw Mogie Samson on the opposite sidewalk through a driveway break. Mogie would never see the ambush that was forming in John's mind coming.

John giggled and dropped his bag to pack a snowball. He took off his boots and put his shoes on, so he could run up on Mogie without the clomping of boots giving him away. John had the snowball in one hand and the bag in the other as he sprinted across the street.

Suddenly he was airborne, twirling through an arc ten feet high and twice as long. Fortunately the projection had aimed him toward a snowbank. The snow was freshly plowed and still softly packed. He landed with a "woosh" instead of a "thunk" and slid down the snowbank to the slushy muck that was forming on the street.

His new jeans were a wreck and his lunchbox was bent in the middle. One of his boots was under the car. There would be no hiding this incident from his mother.

This time the lady who hit him was crying as she got out of her car. She leaned over with her arms straight out as she shuffled in his direction, as though she was corralling a hurt animal. "Oh my God, little boy! Are you okay? Don't move. Someone call the police! Call an ambulance!"

As soon as John heard the word police, he jumped up and ran to school, wailing all the way. All he could think of was that he was in trouble and the police were coming to get him. He heard the lady call after him but as soon as he hit the sidewalk, the snowbanks muffled her cries.

When he got to school, snot crusted his face and his eyes were puffy. The school peeled the story from him and called Norma as soon as they figured out what happened. The school nurse discovered that the right side of John's torso was bruised.

Norma arrived shortly after the call. "You okay, Johnny?"

He nodded solemnly. The nurse cooed over him and gently lifted his shirt to show his mother the damage the car had done. Norma nodded in acknowledgement. "You want to come home?"

The nurse was appalled. "Aren't you going to take him to a doctor?"

"He said he's fine. Let's go." John followed her out to the car and got in the front seat.

She gestured toward his seat belt. "You might want to put that on. You don't seem to have much luck with cars."

On the drive home, they spotted his boots and lunchbox perched on a snowbank. Inside the ruined lunchbox was a $10 bill.

"Johnny, run down and get the mail."

"Ok, ma." His mother tossed him a key ring from where she stood on the front porch. The post office was down the street and around the corner. John went inside and pulled out the mail. There were a few envelopes, but his attention was held by the K-Mart ad, which was covered with toys. He stuck the letters in the back of his waistband so that he would have both hands free to scan the pages and dream about the cars and superhero toys they contained.

He was distracted as he headed home. He heard the brakes screech seconds before he felt the impact. He had stepped into traffic and was laid out under the bumper and grill of a large car. He could feel the heat and smell the singe of the radiator. He rolled to his side and scrambled out from under the vehicle.

When he popped up and peered at the stunned driver, the man looked as though he was seeing a ghost. He jumped out of his car with a look of anguish on his face. John felt for the mail, which was miraculously still tucked into his pants. He held it as he ran home, crying all the way.

Norma was sitting on the couch when he burst through the door and tossed the mail at her on his way up the stairs to his room. He dove under his bed.

There was a knock at the door a few minutes later. He heard his mother speaking with a man. "He walked right out in front of me and ended up under my car. I'm so sorry. Do you want me to follow you to the hospital and make sure he's okay?"

"Did you see him hightail it in here? He's fine. That kid is indestructible."

The man mumbled something. John heard Norma say, "I ain't wasting time or money on no doctors. This is the third time he's gotten himself hit by a car. I'd be more worried about your car if I were you." Norma forced a laugh and urged the man to be on his way.

John crept out and looked out the window. The man's car was askew in the driveway. He glanced nervously at the house and caught John in the window before the boy had time to duck.

John gave the man a small wave. He watched as the man pulled out of the driveway and cautiously made his way up the street.

"Ma, Ms. Foster asked if I would I take a kitten. She said to tell you it's a Siamese, valuable."

Norma had her feet up as she enjoyed a cigarette. John dropped the tiny creature on her lap. He knew that Norma was a sucker for baby animals and wouldn't be able to say no once she saw it.

"Awe, ain't you the sweetest thing. You're a pretty one."

Pretty One became a part of the family but she belonged, heart and soul, to John. He never had to be sad on his own for the rest of his youth.

1971

Another dime! It was under the swing, partially hidden by a small rock. John spotted it as he floated over, leaning forward to pump himself higher. He jumped off, arms flailing, and pivoted toward the coin as soon as he landed. He lunged to snatch it up before some other kid saw it, then tucked it carefully in his pocket. John was saving every coin he found so that he could buy his very own Limited Edition Speed Racer Mach 5. This would up his total to 98 cents. *Now I only need one more penny and I'll have enough.*

John could barely wait to get home and recount his money to make sure he was only a penny away, but he stayed vigilant, scanning the sidewalk as he walked home. He spotted it in the distance, a shiny copper penny that sparkled like heaven was pointing it out to him. He checked before he picked it up. *Heads up. Good luck.*

The screen door slammed behind him as he called out to Norma. "Ma, can we go to K-Mart?"

Norma was in the front room and she had company. John heard the "beer laugh," the one that wasn't the kind of laugh Norma made when she was happy. He slowed down and cautiously entered the front room.

"Here's Johnny!" Norma cackled. The two women sitting on the couch cackled with her. John sort of recognized them but he didn't know their names.

The blonde had a high-pitched, squeaky voice. "Awe, he's so cute."

"Johnny, go over and give Trudy a kiss."

John tiptoed reluctantly over to Trudy and turned his cheek to her. He didn't like the smell of alcohol on her breath. She planted a slobbery kiss on his cheek. He wiped it off and saw her lipstick on the back of his hand.

Norma slurred, "What were you hollering about when you came in?"

John never knew what version of Norma he would get when the beer cans piled up next to her. "I have enough money to get a Speed Racer Limited Edition Mach 5. I want to go to K-Mart."

"Get down on your knees and ask me again."

John shook his head no, embarrassed by the extra sets of eyes.

"I said crawl over here on your knees." His mother had the tone in her voice that meant he had better do what she said or he would regret it. John dropped to his knees and crawled forward until he was in front of her. Norma was enjoying herself. "Say, 'Pretty please, Mother.'"

John looked at her with pleading eyes, but she did not smile. She meant it.

"Pretty please, Mother."

The women on the couch laughed enough to encourage her. "And kiss my foot." Norma stretched her bare foot out to him.

"Awe, Norma, leave him alone." John turned to look at Trudy. She made a motion as though she was calling a dog.

Norma picked up on the theme. "Go on, be a good little puppy and go see Trudy."

John started to stand up but Norma put an edge of menace in her voice. "I said be a puppy."

John crawled over to Trudy and waited on all fours. Trudy reached out and ruffled his hair. "Good dog," she said through her giggles.

"Hey, puppy, sit up and ask me again."

John stood up on his knees and held his hands out like he was a dog doing a trick. "Will you take me to K-Mart?"

"Ask me tomorrow. Now get out of here and leave us alone."

The next day, John counted out his money and put the coins in his pocket. He went downstairs, made himself a bowl of cereal and watched the Saturday cartoons. He was the only one awake. He waited for signs that Norma was up, hoping to catch her early, before she started drinking. When he heard her stirring, he ran to her bedroom door. "Ma, can we go to K-Mart today?"

"I need a few things. You can come if your room is clean."

John raced down the hall. He grabbed the clothes that were on the floor and threw them in his closet, along with a few toys; he pulled the blanket up to cover his pillow. He shoved a few things under his bed. "I'm ready, Ma." She was already out the door, halfway to the car. If he had taken any longer, she would have left without him.

As Norma pulled out of the driveway, John turned the radio on and twisted the dial. The Carpenter's "We've only Just Begun" sputtered through the speakers; he fine-tuned the station. Norma smiled at him. "I like this song."

She hummed along. Soon they were both singing loudly. *Sharing horizons that are new to us. Watching the signs along the way.* John pointed at a stop sign and Norma laughed. She affectionately patted his knee.

John skipped to the toy section. He knew exactly where the car was—he had longed for it for months, examining the package every time he came to the store. There was only one Speed Racer Limited Edition Mach 5 left. That penny had been lucky.

At the checkout, John counted his coins out one a time as he laid them on the counter.

The cashier checked the price and counted the change. She handed his car to him. "There you go."

He ripped the package open, removed the beautiful race car and handed the remains to the nice lady who was smiling at him in a friendly way. "Thank you."

He drove the car along the edge of the counter and flew it into the air. He was completely immersed in his joy over owning the Mach 5.

Norma must have called for him more than once because she was mad by the time her voice penetrated his play. "Johnny, where have you been? I've been looking for you. Get your ass out to the car and wait for me."

John subtly hid his car from view. Otherwise it would be just like his mother to take it away from him to teach him a lesson. Fortunately, she was too focused on herself to remember that he had come there to purchase the toy he'd been wanting for so long. The Mach 5 stayed in his pocket, safe from Norma's wrath.

The bike was a beauty, green with a white banana seat. It wasn't new, but it was new enough for John to feel excited as he rode across the street to the spot in the churchyard where all the neighborhood kids hung out.

The grass was slick with recent rain. He skidded to a stop with a flourish.

"Johnny, when'd ya get that? It's nicccce!" Adam drew out the last syllable in appreciation. The kids John hung out with came from homes where new bikes didn't show up except maybe on Christmas or a birthday.

"My ma brought it home yesterday." The wheels had kicked up mud on his way there, even though he had tried to avoid the largest puddles left by the overnight rain. He wiped it off the back bumper with his sleeve.

Richy Wells, who always had to be top dog, ran his mouth. "It looks cool, but I'll bet it's not as fast as mine. It probably won't do tricks." John didn't know. He'd never ridden a BMX bike like Richy's, but he wasn't going to back down from a challenge.

The churchyard was wide enough to allow them to gain momentum as they rode but they would have to slam on their brakes at the edge of the grass to avoid flying into the street. John rode to the edge of the parking lot and faced the grassy stretch. Richy lined up next to him. Adam waved his arm and slashed it down, yelling, "Go!"

John and Richy took off. Richy's bike was built for traction. He gained a lead right away. John pumped furiously to catch up. He wasn't focused on judging when he would need to brake. All that mattered was that the distance between him and Richy was shrinking.

Richy turned at the last minute at the edge of the grass and John realized it was time to stop. He jerked the pedals back to brake and they locked up. The slick grass made it impossible for his wheels to dig in. He slid. His beautiful new bike crashed into the side of a parked car and his head slammed into a bracket that had previously held a side mirror.

It did not provide a soft landing. He bounced backward onto his butt. Warm liquid trickled into his left eye from a robin-egg sized bump. His eyebrow felt like a caterpillar running across the top. John abandoned his bicycle and ran across the street to his house. "Maaaaaa."

His mother walked nonchalantly out of the kitchen, but as soon as she saw all the blood, she rushed over to him. "What the hell did you do? Come here." She knelt down. "Did you get hit by another damned car?"

John pointed to the old clunker on the other side of the street and nodded.

"You got hit by that car right there?" She was incredulous. "That thing hasn't moved in years. How in the world did you manage that?"

Richy brought the lawn darts to add variety to the churchyard activities. There were four darts and eight boys, so they all stood on the church steps and took turns throwing them up in the air, competing to see who could make the missiles go the highest.

John tried it a few times and was anxious to try again. He sprinted off the bottom step to pull a green-feathered dart out of the ground. Just as he stepped onto the "battlefield," Richy released the dart he was swinging.

It wasn't intentional, but the timing was bad. The dart flipped through the air, righted itself and dropped on John. Richy screamed a warning, but not in time. The metal point punctured John's skull. He dropped to the ground like a dead body.

The boys were in shock. Several headed toward John, Richy headed toward home and a boy named Mikey ran to get Norma. Her gait revealed her assumption that this was another of John's hapless but harmless incidents, but when the boys cleared away and she saw the tip of the projectile sunk into her boy's head, Norma showed an uncharacteristic display of concern. She pointed at one of the kids. "Go back to my house and call 911!" She knelt down on her knees and gently shook John. His eyes fluttered but they remained closed.

John would be fine, but the dart had punctured his skull. He would have a hole in his head, so to speak, for the rest of his life.

John gained a permanent "strawberry" patch on his arm that summer at a cookout. He loved roasted marshmallows but Norma said he was too little to roast his own. She was too busy socializing to do it for him.

"Come on, Amy! Make one for me."

"I'm doing my own."

"But I want one." John felt tears pricking his eyes.

Amy carefully toasted a marshmallow to a golden brown, then took her time eating it in front of him, licking her fingers one by one when she was done.

"Will you do one for me now?"

"Nope. I want another one."

"After that?"

"Maybe."

Amy put one on her stick but didn't carefully toast it brown. She lit it on fire. It looked like a ball of coal when she blew it out. "Still want it, Johnny?"

John nodded eagerly. Amy smacked the stick on his arm. The molten center stuck to his skin; his flesh melted underneath it. He ran screaming to his mother, but she barely interrupted the story she was telling. She wiped the remnants off and sent him on his way.

His only consolation was that a teenage boy hanging near the fire toasted three marshmallows in a row just the way he liked them and just for him.

1973

John graduated to a BMX bike on his birthday. He rode it with traffic along the edge of Detroit Street. He needed to cross the road. He looked back to see if traffic was clear. His bike drifted while his head was turned; his wheel slipped off the road. By the time he realized what was happening, he was crashing into a pristine Monte Carlo parked in front of a church. The impact sent him flying on to the trunk; he rolled off and landed on the sidewalk.

A concerned man exited the car as John hit the ground. Assuming he would be in trouble, John scrambled to his feet and took off running. After loading John's bike into his trunk, the man caught up to him as he turned the corner on to his street; the car tailed John and pulled up in front of the house just as John was flinging the door open.

John ran straight upstairs again and hid behind the curtains of the window that faced the street. He watched the man pull his bike out of the trunk, check that the wheels were working and make sure the frame was straight. Then he rolled it up near the porch, rested it against the railing and went out of view as he took the steps.

Seconds later the doorbell rang. John crept to the top of the stairs and crouched down to listen. "Howdy, Ma'am. Do you have a son, about so tall, maybe ten years old? Owns that bike right there?"

Norma was always skeptical, but she affirmed the existence of such a boy. "I'm afraid I might have hurt him. I pulled off to park and I might have been a bit quick about it. He ran into the back of my car, then took off running. I brought him his bike and wanted to make sure he's okay."

"Your car messed up?"

"No, I mean, I don't think so. But I'm not worried about that. I just want to make sure your boy's okay."

Norma called to him. "John, come down here and thank this nice man for bringing your bike home."

John reluctantly came halfway down the steps and mumbled a thank you.

"Are you okay?"

"Yes, Sir."

Norma laughed. "I swear, this kid had to be a cat in another life, as many times as he's thwarted death. I should keep him locked in the house for his own safety."

John realized he wasn't in trouble. He grinned, then meowed loudly until both adults were smiling at him in wonder. If he was a cat, he'd used up quite a few lives already. He wondered how many he had left.

LIFE FOUR: TRAUMA THAT CANNOT BE NAMED

Other things happened that are too painful to speak of during his mediocre-at-best childhood. John locked them away deep inside him, secrets he hoped would wither in the darkness. They lived below the surface, nipping at any fingers he poked them with during moments of distraction; he survived in spite of them, but they followed him into adolescence. They did not disappear.

Fred Aslin
Charlotte, Michigan
1996

Life at the Home was something out of Dickens. They fed us okay, but they beat us, knocked us around pretty good. Fists and belts. I tried to escape, but I couldn't. The administration told the community that we weren't prisoners—the fences were just there to look pretty—but anyone who ran away was hunted down. When they were caught, they were brought back and punished.

Maybe I could have gotten away for good, but I couldn't leave the younger kids behind. We learned to keep our heads down and do what we were told. I excelled in music. I could play anything on the piano. I was in demand for all the dances and musical programs. I got top marks. Eventually, I was sent to school in town. We all were. But that came about when I negotiated a deal with the Medical Superintendent that he couldn't refuse.

Michigan Home and Training School,
Lapeer, Michigan
Spring 1939

John Albert realized that he and his siblings were like Dr. Doolittle's monkeys. Somehow, they had become the weak ones that had to be kept away from the others so that the others could be strong. No one told him this, but there were sick children in the Home—sick in either mind or body—and he had been sent here just like them, locked away in this place surrounded by a fence, a place that was full of rules about staying inside the grounds. It was a "color inside the lines" kind of place and his inquisitiveness and stubborn streak got him in trouble.

The school at the Home was too easy for Doris, Alberta and Fred, so they were given jobs. Fred assisted the music teacher. Doris worked in the bakery. Alberta helped in the library, where John ended up most days after the teacher released him from class. He loved to look at the encyclopedias—to see pictures of amazing things that existed in the world that he might never see in real life.

He especially loved animals and would place a thin piece of paper over the ones that fascinated him the most and trace them. His box under his bed was a virtual Noah's ark of the variety of living things that he saw in those multi-volume pages. Soon, he didn't have to trace the pages. He could look at pictures and draw the creatures freehanded.

He drew pictures of the little home he remembered in the woods and Ma and Pa, lest he forget what they looked like—Pa proudly wearing his wolf pelt and Ma smiling into a book. The first time Alberta saw the pictures of their parents, she gasped in surprise. "John, you're getting really good. Can I keep these?"

Alberta and Doris had grown into young women. Fred was changing into a young man. The older three did what they could to strengthen the remnants of family that were left to them but finding private moments where all seven could be together was hard. Often, the best they could do was make the rounds and see each other one-on-one.

Of his sisters, John saw Alberta the most. Fred saw Violet. Doris kept up with Ted and Peter by getting them after-school jobs at the bakery. Sometimes they were able to sit together at dinner or meet secretly outside, but Vernal Johnson took pleasure in thwarting their attempts to stay connected. Doris, who was spunky, stood up to him, but then he would punish the boys in the middle of the night.

Fred had tired of the physical abuse he and his brothers suffered at the hands of Vernal Johnson. Vernal was not the only person who mistreated them, but he was the worst. Vernal was a small, wiry man. As Fred grew, he became less afraid of Vernal. He eventually had to tilt his head down slightly when he and the bully stood nose-to-nose.

Fred began a regimen of pushups, pullups, sit ups, running and stair climbing. Every strain against his arm muscles was overcome by his desire to reach a point where he could defend his family against the guard. Soon, Fred could do 43 pushups and 9 pull ups. His arms, though lean, became tightly muscled and his legs were strong.

He was ready for Vernal the night that Doris refused to move the girls to a different table at dinner. When she stood up and confronted the guard, Lucy intervened and talked Vernal into leaving the children alone. (It was no secret that Vernal was unkind to the residents, but his mistreatment was tolerated, though the late-night beatings may not have been widely known.)

Fred figured that one of his younger brothers would get the brunt of Vernal's terror that night. He kept himself awake to intervene. Vernal had been less apt to confront Fred now that the boy was taller than he was.

Soon Fred heard the door creak open. He cringed as the sinister whistle that Vernal emitted when he was about to strike floated through the room. For the boys in Cottage G, it was like the rattle of a snake.

Fred was a trained hunter and tracker. Albert had taught him from a young age how to sneak up on his prey, so Vernal did not see it coming when Fred slammed his fist into the middle of the older man's back as the guard was winding up to smack John awake.

Vernal fell forward and lost his balance. Fred kicked his leg out from under him and Johnson hit his head on the edge of John's bed as he fell to the ground. The guard rolled over and recovered from his shock quickly, jumping up to defend himself. He wound up to strike Fred until he noticed that they were surrounded by several other big boys, some of whom held baseball bats.

Fred leaned over the guard who had terrorized him and his little brothers and many other kids for three years. "This ends now. You come back here, you're going to have an accident much worse than this one."

Vernal Johnson cussed at the boys as he stormed out of the dorm. The boys had won that skirmish, but the war was not over. A new guard patrolled Cottage G the next night. He was stern and strict, but he did not engage in late night mischief. Fred relaxed a bit but should have known that the reprieve was short-lived.

A week later, the new guard, Danny Boyne, announced that the older boys would move to a different cottage in a week. Fred and Peter would be forced to leave Ted and John to handle Johnson on their own; Fred had no doubt that Johnson was behind the change and would be back to terrorize the younger kids when their protectors were gone.

The Aslins were not the only Indian family at the Home and so they were not the only ones who had been singled out for Vernal Johnson's special attention. Fred approached his friend, Charlie Kequom, with a plan.

Fred was the captain of the Home baseball team and held the position of catcher. That Saturday, they were scheduled to play in a game against a team from the town of Lapeer. The game was an annual event that was well attended. The field was set out in a pretty spot at the edge of a thick patch of woods. Of the nine starting players, five of them were Indians—Fred, Peter, Charlie and Charlie's twin brothers, Sam and Stan—and the other four were up for an adventure.

Charlie could throw a burner that was hard to get a hold of and the team from the Home was winning the game as only one of the townie batters had made contact with any of Charlie's lightning-fast pitches. In the seventh inning, the townie batter strutted up to the plate. Fred gave Charlie the signal to lob a soft pitch so the batter would be able to get a piece of it. The ball soared well into the outfield and landed beyond the tree line.

As the unwitting townie accomplice to Fred and Charlies' plan rounded the bases, the entire Home team but Fred turned toward the outfield and ran into the woods. They paused briefly to pick up the bags of food that had been surreptitiously stashed there by the Aslin and Kequom sisters, then kept going. The homerun hitter thought that all the commotion was due to his fabulous hit, but it was coming from the crowd of people who initially stood staring silently after the escapees with their mouths wide open, then erupted into cries of shock.

Fred met with superintendent Dr. Fred Hanna when he returned to the Home with the bewildered coach.

"Fred, were you a part of this?"

"No sir. Would I be here if I was?"

Dr. Hanna studied him carefully. "The sheriff will be here soon. I expect you to tell him everything you know."

Fred put a serious look on his face. "You know, I got a brother out there. I'm mighty worried. The sheriff's not gonna find those boys. Most of them are Ojibwe born and bred. They know how to cover their tracks. You need an authentic Indian to find an Indian. You need me. I'm the only one who'll be able to track them down."

Dr. Hanna was surprised by Fred's pronouncement, then intrigued.

Fred continued. "If you want me to help you, I'm gonna have to ask for a few favors. Nothing too much, considering how much is riding on getting those boys back. Just imagine how embarrassing it will be for the sheriff when he can't find them and the whole town knows how they run off."

Dr Hanna developed a twinkle in his eye. He saw through Fred's ruse, but felt respect rather than annoyance. "What are your demands, son?"

"I've got five of them. First, none of those boys gets in trouble if they come back with me. Second, we get to go to school in town. Third, the housing changes get cancelled—older boys get to stay with their little brothers. Fourth, Johnson gets moved to an adult unit. And finally, Indian boys get to do their Vision Quests."

"Vision Quest?"

"It's how we become men in our tribe. All our ancestors have done it. It connects this world to the spiritual world. It'll prepare me to find the purpose for my life." Fred could hear the words his father had spoken to him in the past flowing out to touch the doctor and stir his compassion.

Dr. Hanna was moved by the boy's earnestness, but the last demand gave him pause. He frowned. The Home's policies prohibited anything that supported Indians' retention of their culture. Indians were not allowed to speak their language or engage in rituals. They were required to assimilate. "You've really thought this through, Fred. I can meet demands one through four, but I'll have to think about number five."

Fred figured he'd have time to work out the Vision Quest issue and needed to lock in the agreement on the more urgent concerns. He held out his hand and looked the doctor in the eye as they shook hands.

Fred borrowed a bicycle and returned to the ball field. He whistled twice. Ted responded. The missing boys stepped out of the woods and met him on the pitching mound. "Dr Hanna said we can stay together and he's moving Johnson. Nobody's getting punished for what we did. They're keeping supper warm for you." The boys whooped in victory and jogged toward the Home.

Charlie climbed on the back of Fred's bike and they rode alongside their team. "I threw in a couple of extra things."

"What's that?" asked Charlie.

"We get to go to the real school in town come fall. And I asked him to let us Indians do the Vision Quest." The boys cheered and patted Fred on the back.

"Hold on. He didn't say yes about that one yet. He's gonna think on it."

The night before the fire, Fred dreamt of Fox. He should have known to be on the lookout for trouble. There were many residents who had been dumped at the Home in Lapeer who were not "feeble-minded"—and quite a few had musical talent.

Fred and his friend, Arnie, started a band. They needed something to pass the time and music brought them happiness and normalcy. The group practiced in the basement of the chapel. They had to stick to church music when the minister was there but played dance music when he was gone. He was gone most days.

The Home had a marching band that performed in town on occasion and participated in all of the local parades, but Fred's band was a smaller, more intense group of musicians who made up their own material; they crossed over into the realm of artists.

Arnie wasn't really a musician, but he could sing tolerably well and was a good organizer. He was the oldest member at the ripe old age of 17. He managed the group and filled in on male vocals in a pinch. The band had fifteen members. Their official name was the "Kellogg Band" after the source who paid for their instruments, but they secretly called themselves the "Ojibwe Blues Band."

Just like the Big Bands of the day, they had three trumpets, three trombones, three saxophones, a rhythm section of guitar, piano, double bass, and drums, plus a female vocalist. Many band members had already graduated from the on-campus school and held jobs at the Home or in town. They met for band practice when their work was done, squeezing in a few hours between responsibilities and dinner; they were often late to eat because they got carried away with the excitement of pushing themselves to perfect the popular songs of the day and make up original tunes.

It was 1939. They were intently practicing for a performance at the

Spring Fling dance. Fred played many instruments; he was playing piano when the fire broke out.

Arnie was listening intently as Millard played a riff on his saxophone. "I like it. I like it. Let's get some bass in there too, Oggie."

Oggie, who stood belly to belly with the bass that towered over him, plucked enthusiastically and creatively along with Millard. Violet Aslin confidently joined in with the drums.

"Fantastic!" Arnie cheered. "Again!" Arnie tapped his hand on the post that he was leaning against. Without looking behind him, he hollered back over his shoulder at Pony, one of the trumpeters. "Pony, I told you to stop smoking in here."

Pony had a job in town and kept himself stocked well in cigarettes, which he generously shared with his friends. Arnie constantly harped on him that the smoke made it hard for the horn players to blow. "I'm not smoking. But I smell it now that you mention it."

The odor became more intense. Fred walked toward it. When he opened the door to the stairway, it was blocked with a mass of chairs and other furniture that he couldn't budge, furniture that wasn't there when band practice started; smoke quickly filled the stairwell, as well as heat and the flicker of flames.

Fred slammed the door and yelled at the band members to take the other stairs that led to the chapel itself, but when Arnie reached that door, it was locked from the other side. Arnie battered his body against the door. He was tall, but he only weighed 99 pounds. The door was not concerned with his efforts.

Fred was almost as tall but sturdier, even at thirteen. He yelled for everyone to clear the door. He ran at it with a chair and smashed the wood against the thick pine surface. Nothing happened. They would not escape that way.

Fred focused on a small window high on the wall. It would not be easy to reach—the basement walls were taller than one would expect. "Pony, help me lift Violet up." They lifted Violet, paused as she struggled to unlock the window, then pushed her up through it. Fred yelled at her to go get help as her legs disappeared into safety.

Fred and Pony lifted their friends, one by one, up to the window. After a few were out, things went faster as those on the outside grabbed hands and pulled their friends through the window. They were teens and children, but their adrenaline kicked in.

When Pony and Fred were the only two left, Pony locked his hands together to give Fred a stirrup that he could use to catapult himself high enough to reach the window. Fred shook his head. "No, you go first."

"We don't have time to argue. Get your butt up there so I can follow you." Fred stepped into his friend's hands and pushed off, glancing the edge of the window with his fingertips, almost losing his grip but then latching on. All of the pull-ups and push-ups he had done to fight off Vernal Johnson came in handy and helped him pull himself high enough through the window that the people on the other side were able to grab him and pull him through. He turned back to check on Pony and saw the older boy sliding a couple benches over to the wall and then setting a chair on top of them. Pony easily reached the window and pulled himself up, making the whole rescue look like it was no big deal.

Everyone was safe, but the chapel was not. Smoke billowed out of the window they had opened, then flames peeked out through a hole that had opened in the roof. The glow passed over the rest of the building like the rising sun, and when the sun set, the entire scene was dark and smoldering.

Vernal Johnson watched it all from a window of the Castle, arms crossed against his chest. He did nothing to help.

The sheriff ruled the fire arson, but no one was ever charged with the crime.

After Fred and Pony saved the band, Dr. Hanna called Fred into his office. "I interviewed a couple of the kids you and Halbert saved."

"Pony's name is Halbert?"

"I'm impressed with you, Fred. I've checked into this Vision Quest request. I can't give you permission to do it. It's against the rules of this place. So if a young man decided to leave on his own for a few days and come back, I'm not sure what would happen to that young man—who just decided on his own to go off and do what he felt he needed to do." Dr. Hanna stared Fred hard in the eyes to see if his message was received. Then he smiled.

Fred nodded and planned his journey. The Vision Quest was a way for Fred to recapture his past and connect with his father. If he made contact with the spirit world, he could learn more from the ancestors about being Ojibwe and build on the things that his father taught him.

His father had not been able to pass along everything, but Fred played key memories over and over in his mind; he remembered them in great detail. Albert told Fred that dreams and visions are an important part of Ojibwe spiritual life. Dreams build a path into the spiritual world. As with all Indian children, Fred was taught to remember his dreams so they could be interpreted by tribal elders. The dreams would reveal his guardian spirits and they would guide him to wisdom.

If Fred did not complete this otherworld journey, he risked the chance that he would travel through this life unmoored from his true self. His father told him of the Ojibwe belief that human beings have two souls. One soul travels at night and lives the dreams and the other soul walks the earth with him. Having two souls allows humans to communicate with both spirits and animals. Going on his Vision Quest would free his second soul and open up a channel to the spirit world. It would help Fred discover the kind of adult he was meant to be.

There was an old Indian at the Home. Herman Bazenet had lost one leg and one eye after volunteering to fight in World War I, then ended up at the Home. His body was beaten up, but his mind was sharp.

Fred pushed Herman's wheelchair around the grounds and practiced his native tongue when they were out of earshot of staff. Fred did not want to lose his ability to speak to the spirits and hoped to communicate with his father some day in his dreams. "I'm going. Bawajigaywin." *On a Vision Quest.* "Soon."

Herman inhaled in surprise. "When?"

"Ingo-anama'e-giizhik." *One week.*

"Minwaabamewizi." *I wish you good luck.*

"I remember some things my father told me, but he didn't know he needed to teach me everything before he went to the spirit world. Gimikwenden ina?" *Do you remember?* "Bawajigaywin?" *Your Vision Quest?* "Can you tell me things I need to know?"

"I know a little. You must walk until you find a quiet place where no one will disturb you. Once you arrive, you must not eat. You only pray. Pray to find your spirit helper, the animal that will be your lifelong aide and guide. This may not happen for days. If you have not prepared well enough, it may not happen at all. When you return, come talk to me about it. If you have seen things, I will try to help you understand them. But know that I was cut off from our people too and did not learn everything from my elders that I wish I could know. I will say this. You may see a vision of what you might do with the life that you have been gifted, but it is just a possibility until you find your purpose. It is your moral responsibility to bring that revelation into existence."

John's Neighborhood Friends
Provide Unfortunate Guidance
1974

"I gotta be ma and pa to you. You're a boy, so I gotta whip you harder." Norma was breathless as she spat the words out; beating John was more challenging as he got bigger and stronger. The combination of drinking and ass-whooping exhausted her. She still made him strip down to his underwear, but this time the waistband tore off in her hand and he took off to his room before she could catch him. She was too drunk to walk the stairs, so the fact that they lived in a two-story house was a blessing on nights like this.

Still, he locked his door. Later on, John tiptoed to the bathroom before he went to sleep. It was quiet downstairs.

The next morning, he was awakened by a punch to his bicep. It was Saturday. Most kids looked forward to the weekend, but for John, Saturdays meant that Norma had a chance to start drinking earlier.

John swung out with his arm before he thought about it and knocked his mother's arm away. She lost her balance and fell back on her bottom. He took the opportunity to run downstairs, grab money off the table on his way by and fling himself out the door, wearing nothing but the shorts he had been sleeping in.

John left the neighborhood and headed for the main road. His anger fueled him; he moved at a swift pace. Saginaw Street reached all the way from his community, Beecher, to downtown Flint. He walked for hours.

When he reached downtown Flint, his stomach was rumbling. Eventually the smell of Halo Burger drew him to the local hamburger joint's doorstep. He snuck in and took a seat at the counter before anyone could use the excuse of his bare feet to keep him out.

John ordered a burger and fries. He lingered at the restaurant because the waitress was nice, calling him sweetie, ignoring his bare feet and refilling his pop. He slowly dipped each french-fry in catsup, licking the drips that ran down his fingers.

When he stepped back to the sidewalk, there was a plane flying over, headed toward the airport. John had nothing better to do, so he followed the path of smoke.

Bishop Airport was on the edge of the city. John had to walk past the Chevrolet Truck and Bus Plant to get there, down industrial roads that didn't often carry pedestrians. No one seemed to notice or be bothered by a young boy walking along these truck routes in just a pair of shorts.

When he got to the airport, he leaned against the perimeter fence and dreamed of boarding one of the planes and being transported to a new life.

John arrived at his aunt's house just after dinner, but she still fixed him a plate. His feet were filthy and he didn't look much better. She didn't ask questions, but he was worried she would call Norma and tell her where he was. The last thing he needed was a drunken drive home with his mother swinging at him the whole way, so he slipped out after using the bathroom. He was only a couple hours walk from home; he would be in familiar territory just as it was getting dark.

Mr. Pacheko, his neighbor, shook John awake. John had snuck into the elderly man's screened porch to avoid mosquitos, then fallen asleep on a couch. The Pachekos lived close enough to hear all the yelling that came from John's home. Mrs. Pacheko commented to her husband on the fact that John seemed to stay outside as long as he could. They knew something wasn't right in John's house. Still, Norma had been worried when she knocked on the elderly man's door the day before, asking if he had seen her son. Besides, a family's business was its own.

"John, your mother's been sick with worry. Can I walk you home?" John was resigned to the fact that he had to go home eventually. Being escorted by Mr. Pacheko would give him a chance to assess the situation before he was alone with his mother. If she was still violent, he would just leave again. And this time he wouldn't come back.

Mr. Pacheko put his arm around John and talked about the most recent Detroit Tiger's game as they walked up the block. When they reached his house, John hung back. Mr. Pacheko walked unsteadily up the first porch step and John rushed to help him. They did the next three together, then Mr. Pacheko knocked on the door.

Norma showed concern on her face when she breathlessly opened the door, just before she turned her face neutral. She nodded at John as he walked past her and up to his room. "Thank you, Steve."

It had taken John thirty miles to walk off his hurt. He had landed back at the same place but maybe something had changed. Norma never said she was sorry—it was a word that wasn't part of her vocabulary—but worry and sorry were almost spelled the same.

It was a piece of junk really. Yet, when Norma unloaded it from her trunk, John could not believe the yellow minibike was his.

The little two-and-a-half horse-power engine could only be started by pulling a rope with a piece of wood tied to the end. John had to wrap it around the crankcase and yank with all his twelve-year-old might. If it didn't work, he would have to start all over. The throttle was broken too, so another piece of string with a make-shift wood handle was tied to the carburetor. When John pulled to get some gas, he would have to hold it steady or the bike would slow down. It was a death trap, but it was freedom and a quick path to coolness.

The minibike had a steep learning curve. The starter rope was tied to a wheel that spun. If John wasn't careful, it would grab his pant leg and keep chomping until a chuck was taken out of his leg. After losing three pieces of his leg, he developed the instinct to avoid that hazard.

The chain guard was missing too. Getting his pant leg caught in the chain didn't result in pieces of his body being eaten by the bike, but it would cause his leg to be slammed back into the foot peg, catching his foot and causing a wipeout. But when the stars were aligned, he could get the machine up to 20 miles per hour.

"You can go down to the corner and around the field, but don't let me see you riding it anywhere else."

"Thanks, Ma!" John hugged his mother around the waist and gave her a peck on the cheek. He barely had to stretch on his toes. They were almost the same size.

The dirt bike made John the center of the neighborhood social circle. He was an immediate "chick magnet" for the twelve-year-old set and all of the boys wanted to be his friend with the hopes of getting a chance to ride.

John ran home to gas up his bike. Some friends were going to meet him in the field. His minibike had been leaning against the tree when he left for school, but now it was gone. It had been raining earlier. Maybe his mom put it in the garage. He checked but it wasn't there either.

He crashed through the kitchen door, grabbing an apple on his way through. "Ma, do you know where my motorcycle is?"

"Nope."

"It's gone."

Norma came outside with him. "Where did you leave it?"

"Under that tree." Norma walked over by the tree trunk and tracks came into view. They led away from the tree, across three yards behind the house and ended at the Boman backyard. The Boman's had a teenaged son named Ronnie. Things often went missing when Ronnie was around. "That little thief, Ronnie. He took your bike. Get in the car."

Norma marched into the house and came back carrying a shot gun. She backed the car out quickly and drove around the block to the Boman house, whipping her car into their driveway. She threw it into gear, grabbed the shotgun and marched up the steps. She leaned the gun against the house and knocked.

Ronnie answered the door, a cocky expression on his face. "Can I help you?"

Norma casually picked up the shotgun, resting it on her hip. "Sure can. Get out here."

Ronnie's face turned pale; he had a blank look on his face as he slid through the front door. He stood nervously on the porch. Norma barked at him like a general. "Where's Johnny's bike?"

"I don't have it."

"You really think it's a good idea to lie to me?"

"No Ma'am. I know where it is, but I don't have it."

"Take me to it." Norma handed him the keys and got into the back seat behind him. They drove for fifteen minutes.

Norma poked the gun into the back of Ronnie's seat a few times as he drove. "You mess with my family again, I'll blow your nuts off." Ronnie started crying.

The buyer was fiddling with the dirt bike in the yard when they pulled up. Ronnie barely put the car in park. He jumped out and ran up to the kid in the yard. "I'm sorry man, but I gotta get that bike back."

"No way, man. I bought it fair and square."

"She's gonna kill me if I don't get it back. It belongs to her kid."

"What about my money?"

"You'll get your money. Just help me load this thing into the trunk."

Norma drove home with Ronnie in the passenger seat. She was not done with him. "You best be at my house at 9:00 tomorrow morning or I'll track you down."

Ronnie knocked on the door at 8:45 am. Norma came out and pointed him toward the passenger seat. "Get in!"

Ronnie didn't dare disobey; he shakily opened the door and got in. She drove to a lawn-mower repair shop. She pointed out several items to the shop owner—a motor, some new cables, a throttle, a cover for the chain and a can of fire-engine red paint. "Got any tips for him?" She nodded toward Ronnie. "He's gonna be working on my son's motorbike today."

The man asked Ronnie if he knew what he was doing. Ronnie asked a few questions, then Norma drove him back to her house. It took him all day to install the new parts and paint the bike, but it looked great when he was done and ran even better.

Norma, with her rough, wild-west ways, made a difference for Ronnie Boman. He was so relieved that she didn't call the cops or shoot off his nuts that he straightened up and stopped taking things that didn't belong to him.

The new and improved minibike was faster than before and exponentially more fun. More kids hung out at the end of the street. Having a large group of spectators made the riders a bit reckless as they strove to impress each other. John, as the owner, felt invincible. The improvements gave the bike an unwarranted appearance of safety; everyone rode it with less caution.

Tim, the kid next door, pointed out a circuit and timed each kid with his stopwatch to see who was the fastest. When it was his turn, John revved the motor, barefoot and helmetless, and took off. The second goal on the route was to loop around his mother's car. He whizzed by the sedan, feet sticking out, and caught one foot on the rusty fender.

The pain was shocking. Three of his toes had been almost peeled off. In spite of the excruciating sting, his immediate thought was that he had to hide the injury from Norma who had already commented about the risk of riding the now-faster bike. The current state of his foot would not bode well for the likelihood of future dirt bike riding.

John left a bloody path from the yard to the bathroom; red footprints traced a path up the stairs and the blood shone starkly against the white tile bathroom floor. It looked like someone had been butchered. He turned the faucet on and gingerly stepped into the tub, running cool water over the cut, hoping it would staunch the bleeding. As he stared down at his feet, looking for signs that the flow was lessening, he was startled by a scream.

Amy stood in the doorway, observing the blood, a look of horror on her face. "Maaaaaaa!" was the only sound she was able to make.

The water didn't stop the blood but it did make the extent of the damage clearer. Norma wrapped an old towel around John's foot and helped him hobble to the car. She broke a lot of traffic laws on the way to the doctor's office. John fought the needle, not wanting to cooperate with having his toes stitched up. Every employee of Dr. Adam's office was called in to hold him down and Norma had to pitch in. Amy sat in the corner, laughing at his tears, panic and screams.

Two weeks later, the motorbike disappeared again, but this time it was Norma's doing. She sold it to a neighborhood dad for $50, a third of her recent investment. John sat in the window, morosely watching the new owners ride his pride and joy while he had been forbidden from ever sitting in the seat again. He was reduced to "the kid who used to have the cool red minibike."

His misery in seeing the bike in action didn't last for long. One of the kids wrecked the bike a week later and it went to the curb.

"Johnny, it's your turn."

"I know. Give it to me." Peter handed him the empty Coke bottle.

Empty bottles could be turned in for ten cents each. John whistled as he entered the store.

The man behind the counter had a heavy accent when he said hello. John didn't say anything, just put the bottle next to the cash register. The man placed a dime on the counter, walked to the back of the store and disappeared. John grabbed a pecan pie and ran outside.

Their scheme had worked again, or so he thought, until he hit the corner of the building and felt his head yank back. The store owner had him by his long hair.

John scrabbled backwards to keep up with the force that was dragging him into the store. The man whipped a chair around and slammed John into the seat. He removed a chrome gun from his waistband and set it roughly on a ledge. "I should tell your mother."

John stared at him. The threat felt vague.

"You think I don't know Norma? She's a good customer." He nodded toward the wall of alcohol behind the register. John's mouth went dry. The shop owner really did know his mother. "You come to my store tomorrow after school. You better show up. I have some things for you to do."

The next day, the owner, Sam Badel, handed John a broom and pointed at the parking lot. "Clean it up."

John swept and swept and swept, too afraid to say the job was done. He finally walked into the store. "I swept it good for you."

Sam gestured for him to come closer to the counter. John braced himself for whatever he had coming. Sam held out two crisp dollar bills. "Look kid, those pies are $1.99. You can keep these moneys or you can have a pie and a penny."

John enjoyed that pie.

As he was leaving, Sam called out., "You come back tomorrow, and I give you more work." John had found a rare thing—a friend and mentor who extended him grace and tried to steer him away from trouble. Unfortunately, it wasn't enough.

Norma worked second shift at the Fisher Body plant, building parts for the shiny cars that were pumped out by the General Motors assembly lines sprinkled all over lower Michigan. John would be in bed when she got home.

By the time she made it up to his room to say good night, she would have already been slammed with the list of his sins for the day that Amy had collected for her. He could hear murmurs of "John did this," and "John did that," floating up from the first floor.

The fact that he was already in bed and that Norma was exhausted prevented him from being punished much of the time. She would threaten to deal with things in the morning, but if he laid low for the next day, all would be forgotten.

Sweet Linda, who lit up any room she entered with her bubbly personality, may have lightened up the atmosphere of John's childhood, but she moved out to begin her own life. She was a newlywed, living across town.

The family member who John saw the most was Amy who, as a teenager, understandably resented being yoked with the responsibility of a little brother who simply got on her nerves.

Amy was laser-focused on her friends and cultivated an image designed to attract people to her. The hippy-chic styles of the day suited her because she could put together an impressive wardrobe by taking a small amount of cash and sprinkling it with a dose of ingenuity. Many of her bell-bottom jeans were enhanced with extra swaths of material added to a seam that she ripped and then sewed additional fabric into herself. These flowing creations would be topped by a tight, short jean jacket and a decorative leather belt.

Amy concerned herself with "cool" and John wasn't cool in her adolescent eyes. John lingered at the door, yearning to hang out with his sister but knowing he wouldn't be welcomed. Amy laid on her bed, stomach down, waving her legs in tune with the music streaming through the large headphones on her head. It took her a few moments to notice him.

He smiled hopefully.

"Ewwwwww! Get out of my room. I told you to stay out."

"I'm bored."

She raised one eyebrow, staring John down, but did not remove the ear pads so that she could hear him. "Get!"

John was drawn downstairs by the doorbell. There were three boys and a girl on the porch. Some of Amy's friends had driver's licenses and John's house was a popular destination because Norma worked evenings. The lack of adult supervision was reliable.

"Your sister home?"

John nodded and pointed up toward the stairs.

The tall boy laughed. "Can you get her for us? Tell her we'll be in the garage." His words came out slowly, like he was talking underwater. He already wreaked of the funny smell that the kids acquired once the garage door was closed.

John ran upstairs and stood in Amy's doorway again. "I told you to beat it."

"Some people are here."

"What?"

John pointed out the window, toward the garage and right on cue, the stereo in the garage blasted the Bee Gee's "Jive Talkin'." He did some of his best disco moves and made Amy smile. He mouthed "Steve" in an over-exaggerated way.

"Go tell 'em I'll be right down."

Steve and a muscular short kid had already set up a game on the pool table in the garage; the other boys were playing air hockey. A girl was running the music; she danced trance-like in between changing the disks.

When Amy got there, Steve lit up a joint to share with her. Amy noticed John in the doorway. "You better get out of here, Johnny, or you won't like what I do."

John went into the house and turned the TV up loud enough to drown out the sounds of the party going on in his backyard.

There was no one in John's life who made him feel loved, like he mattered. But he could find something that felt close to that with his peers. He could become accepted and respected, someone who took care of the people close to him.

The problem was that most of the so-called friends in his orbit did not offer much in the way of good influences. There would be a few, but they didn't make enough of a difference to change the outcome that his life was propelling him toward. His decision-making was all jumbled, driven by insecurity, the need to belong—it was driving him toward disaster.

1975

The Caravellis lived across the street, a huge Italian family squeezed into a tiny house. This meant that the kids were usually outside. The twins, Peter and Pauli, were smack dab in the middle of the Caravelli pack but they ruled the twelve-year-olds in the neighborhood. The fact that their perpetually pregnant mother was overwhelmed and therefore inattentive gave them free reign. No one wanted to be on their bad side as Peter was known for concocting devious retribution that would be carried out with the backup of Pauli's brawn. They were chaos in two twelve-year-old packages.

A typical day spent with the Caravelli twins and their crew would involve serious risk to life or limb. John became an accepted member of their ramshackle gang by syphoning some of Norma's liquor into his bottle of Coke and walking across the street to share it.

Peter spit his latest scheme out with a gleam in his eye. "Let's blow some shit up." He produced a bundle of M-80s from his pocket. John didn't quite know how the boys acquired their amateur pyrotechnic supplies and weapon-making skills, but he could count on feeling a mixture of excitement and terror in their presence.

Pauli laughed. "What you got in mind?"

Peter pointed at the street drain.

John tried to redirect him. "That's boring. Those things aren't gonna do any damage to that." He had seen a mother raccoon with a trio of babies disappear down the same spot the night before. He didn't want to divulge his reason for wanting to steer the twins away from the drain though, fearing that messing with the raccoons might make that target more attractive to their anti-social brains.

The handful of kids hanging out at the Caravellis' followed Peter into the garage. He pointed at a plastic garbage can. "Let's send this thing up like a rocket." Pauli emptied the can and carried it to the back border of their yard. He lit an M-80, threw it on the ground and put the can upside down over it.

Everyone ran for cover. John peeked out from behind a tree, eager to see what would happen. Suddenly there was an earth-shattering boom and tiny pieces of plastic rained down all over the yard.

Peter and Pauli laughed so hard that they fell on the ground. Afterwards, everyone was giddy, deciding what to blow up next. A red-headed kid who lived around the corner came up with their next target. "The Vicarios put a toilet out at the curb."

Peter nodded, a devilish smile on his face. The pack of boys took off running, stopping at the end of the block to peer at the toilet that teetered on the curb. The seat was up. "Pauli, get the bike."

The twins' favorite mode of transportation was a dirt bike—Pauli drove and Peter stood on the pegs in the back. Pauli returned and Peter climbed aboard. No words were needed. Pauli pedaled. When they got close, Peter lit the fuse, dropped the M-80 in the toilet and closed the lid. They sped up to make their escape. When they got far enough away, Pauli locked the brakes and spun the bike around so they could watch the show.

A loud boom erupted; shards of white porcelain sprinkled the street, sounding like mechanical rain. The spectators cheered. Peter bowed like a king as Pauli drove the chariot back to their house. The other kids ran behind them, high fiving each other, already building the legend of the exploding toilet with exaggerated claims of what they saw.

Old man Caravelli was in the garage. He had beaten a man to death in his youth and served a lengthy prison sentence. Everyone in the neighborhood was terrified of him, including his much younger wife and kids. Peter and Pauli often missed school while black eyes and bruises healed up, preferring their dad's temper to foster care. "You boys seen the garbage can?"

The kids struggled to keep a straight face as Peter and Pauli helped their dad look for the missing receptacle, all traces of toughness stripped from their faces.

John thought he was being nonchalant as he walked out the front door of K-Mart. He even whistled. He had the flawed mindset of invincibility that a kid who had gotten away with petty theft many times might have, believing that he could continue to avoid any consequences.

This time he shot too high. He was pretty sure he would have gotten away with stuffing the shirt and shorts under his clothing. It was the three comic books that probably gave him away. Just as he stepped on the sidewalk, thinking he was home free, he felt a vise squeeze the back of his neck. He jolted to attention and tried to run; he looked like a cartoon character, legs flailing but no ground gained.

A deep voice boomed, "Son, you need to come back in the store."

He tried to turn, wanting to see his captor. The man allowed him to spin and face him, relenting the grip on John's neck but locking John's arm in his meaty hand. The security guard was an older man with iron grey hair; his age had not diminished his strength. He towered over the boy, who only reached his chest.

"Let's go to the office, Son." There was no meanness to the man, but John did not dare disobey him. John kept his eyes pointed at his feet as the man marched him to the back of the store where a small office was tucked out of the view of customers. The guard pointed to a chair. "Sit. And don't move."

The man left. John examined the room. It held a dingy metal desk. The walls had once been white, but they were now covered in a light-yellow film. The only colorful item in sight was a framed photo of a younger version of the guard with his pretty wife and two small children sitting on a picnic blanket.

John envied the tableau. It might have been nice to be raised by such a man, who had a deep, firm voice that was still patient and somehow kind to a bad kid like John, a man who seemed to have a clear sense of what was right. The man returned, filling up the small room. He carried a clipboard. "Okay son, what's your name?"

John thought about lying then said, "John."

"How old are you, John?"

"Almost thirteen."

"What's your dad's name."

"Don't know. Never met one."

Sympathy washed into the man's eyes. "Who do you live with?"

"My mom."

"What's her name?"

John hesitated then released the lie. "Linda." John gave the guard Linda's number and held his breath as the man slowly dialed the phone, hoping she would not give anything away. He felt respect for the guard and regretted lying to him, but he couldn't risk having his mom find out that he had gotten caught stealing. Her beatings were getting more severe.

"May I speak to Linda?" he paused. "I work security at K-Mart. I have your son, John, here... yes, he's fine but we had a little issue with him taking some things that don't belong to him. I need you to come in and talk it over with me." He hung up the phone. "Your mom is on her way. Would you like a Coke?"

John nodded.

"Can I trust you to wait here until I come back?"

"Yes, Sir."

John and the guard talked about hunting while they sipped their Cokes. They agreed that they could never shoot an animal. A stock boy knocked on the office door and showed Linda into the room.

The older man raised his eyebrow at Linda's youth, but he did not insult them by calling out the lie. "I caught John outside the store with these items." He pointed to the things he had laid out on the top of his desk. "I could have called the police, and I still can, but I wanted to size the both of you up before I make that decision."

Linda played the part of a disappointed mother very well because she truly was disappointed.

The security guard continued. "As much as I've enjoyed getting to know John, I have to insist that he not come back to our store unless he is accompanied by an adult. He messed up those comic books, so those are going to have to be paid for today."

Linda nodded. "How much do we owe you?"

He gave her a number and she opened her wallet and placed the money on his desk. "Give those comics to someone who's following the rules. And don't worry—he won't cause trouble up here again."

John followed Linda silently to her car. His bubbly sister was clearly upset. "You better not come back up here, Johnny."

"I won't."

"And you'll have to do chores at my house to pay me back."

"I will. Are you gonna tell Ma?"

"Course not. But don't make me regret it."

Pauli called from across the street. "Johnny, get over here and make your gun." The project of the day was to assemble a "spoke gun" from bike spokes by screwing the threaded end of the tire spoke out, packing it with gun powder, sealing the end up with a carpet tack and then heating it up with a lighter to shoot the tack at the other kids running around the yard.

The day before, they had taken turns riding their bikes in front of the house while Peter and Pauli shot bottle rockets at them.

And then Peter got his hands on the BB gun that his dad used to shoot dogs who came into their yard, along with a fresh CO_2 canister. They went deep in the woods and set up targets to test their aim.

John hit three pop cans in a row off a log and Peter only hit two. So Chucky O'Donnell, an insecure kid who always tried to cull Peter's favor, bragged that Peter could shoot anything. He pulled a pack of gum out of his pocket and put it on the top of his head. "Peter's such a good shot, I'll even let him shoot this off my head."

Peter, without hesitation, motioned for Chucky to stand in a certain place, took aim and fired. The gum flew off Chucky's head, not because Peter hit it but because Chucky buckled over in pain, clapping his hands to his face. When he stood up, blood dripped between his fingers, gushing from a hole at the top of his nose, between his eyes.

Chucky took off running, screaming at the top of his lungs, back toward civilization. Peter nodded toward Pauli, who chased Chucky down and tackled him, pinning him to the ground by sitting on his chest. Peter bent down and felt the BB, which he was able to roll around with his finger. It was lodged just under the skin. He pulled out a pocket-knife and opened the blade.

"Chucky, we're going to have to get that thing out." He nodded at the other kids. "Grab his arms."

John took one arm and Al took the other. Chucky screamed bloody murder, but the only thing he could move was his head, which he whipped back and forth. Peter knelt down and slid forward so that his knees locked Chucky's head firmly in place, then he cut out the BB. He held the bloody ball up when he finally got it out. "You want to keep it?"

Pauli and the others released Chucky who sat up and crab-walked himself backward until he was sitting against a tree. He panted frantically and glared at the boys who surrounded him.

"When they ask you what happened, you tripped and fell on a nail, got it?" Chucky nodded, anger practically lighting up his face.

John realized that Chucky had not gotten the memo when he heard Peter screaming from across the street, the sickening sound of a belt striking him echoing through John's window. John's own beating came later that night, when Mrs. Caravelli walked over to catch Norma as she was getting out of her car after a full shift.

At least Norma was sober when she struck him over and over. Her aim was better when she was sober, less likely to strike him on the head or face.

From all appearances, things had returned to normal. The neighborhood kids assembled to pick teams for a friendly game of baseball. Peter was captain of one team and Pauli was captain of the other.

Chucky whined at Peter, "Come on. Pick me."

Pauli intervened. "I'll take you." Chucky shuffled over to stand next to Pauli. After the teams were picked, Pauli's team took the field. "Chucky, you're the catcher."

Peter was first at bat. He lined up to face the pitcher and Chucky started his chatter in a squeaky voice. "Hey, batter, batter. Hey batter, batter. Swing—"

Peter took a slight step back and swung his bat low as though he was revving up to hit the ball. The bat connected with Chucky's face; he howled in pain. Peter didn't even turn to look; he finished his swing and ran for first base.

No one rushed forward to comfort Chucky, who was again catching blood with his hands, along with two teeth. The other kids weren't in on the plan, but Peter's lack of concern had sent a clear message. Don't mess with the Caravelli twins and don't befriend anyone who does.

John learned to drive on Mr. Cavarelli's car, but not with his permission. The old man's drinking habit lended itself to deep sleep. Once the twins could hear his snores from the family room, they took the keys and walked outside.

John would listen for the whistle and sneak out, equally safe from detection once Norma was also in a drunken slumber. John was the smallest, so he steered the car until the twins pushed it down the block, then started it up as they jumped in. They were off!

"Jenny said to pick them up at the gas station. What time is it?" Peter exuded a nervous energy. Jenny had long blonde hair and could blow smoke rings. They met her at the skating rink. Peter claimed her. John liked Debbie, who had short, dark hair, brown eyes and had to look up at him. Pauli usually latched on to whomever else came along for the ride.

The girls were sitting on the curb, sharing a Pepsi, when they pulled in. Jenny leaned into the open window. "Hey, boys. What took ya so long?"

Peter was shy around Jenny. He directed Debbie and the other girl, Brandy, into the front seat and nudged Jenny toward the back. Pauli leaned over the passenger seat to talk to Debbie and Brandy as he lit up a joint. They passed it around the car. Debbie held it for John to hit while he drove, then rested her hand on his knee. He could see Peter and Jenny making out in the back seat. They went to the park and played music from the car radio while they danced and laughed. Debbie was John's first kiss.

Even though they had to sneak out and break the law to be with the girls, the nights they cruised around, laughing and carefree, were some of his best memories.

John got off the school bus and spotted his best friend standing on the sidewalk at the edge of the parking lot. He hollered as he approached him. "You got any?"

Jeff nodded enthusiastically, a huge smile blossoming across his face, his long hair flipping back and forth to cover and then expose what John could now see were blood-shot eyes. "The good stuff."

"You started without me, you prick."

Jeff laughed too hard at the joke, the weed expanding the humor he heard in John's words.

"You feel like praying or playing today?"

Now Jeff was doubled over. John pulled him away from the school grounds. "Let's go to church. Katie and Tina are going to meet us there."

When Jeff and John skipped school, they usually took the city bus to the mall. They would head directly to the dumpster that was far out at the back of the mall parking lot and sit behind it while they smoked a joint. Then they would play video games at the arcade, eat at the food court and occasionally enhance their wardrobes with a five-finger discount. They were careful to catch the city bus back in time for school to let out so they could take the school bus back home.

St. Frances Catholic Church was a good alternative on nice days. There was a huge tree way in the back. They could hang out there, share their weed with any cute girls who tagged along and flirt to their heart's content.

John and Jeff got to the tree and lit up the half-joint that Jeff carefully pulled out of his jean jacket pocket. John's head was just starting to get that pleasant hum when he spotted Father McKeon heading straight for them.

John fumbled to put the joint out, licking his fingers and squeezing out the smoldering embers. He stood up and waited for the priest to arrive.

"Morning boys."

"Good morning, Father."

"You've been coming around quite a bit lately. It's hard for the Lord to rub off on you way out here though."

John laughed at the elderly man's attempt at a joke.

"We just like how quiet it is back here."

"No school today?"

Jeff answered quickly. "No, Sir."

"Well, I certainly don't mind you boys spending time out here, but I can't let you keep smoking that stinky stuff and not say anything. Cigarettes are okay, but no alcohol or marijuana in the Lord's backyard. Understand?"

"Yes Sir."

"And you can always come inside. I've got a good ear for hearing problems and figuring things out with folks."

"Thank you, Father."

They watched Father McKeon make his way across the uneven grass with his firm step and didn't starting giggling until he was well out of earshot. The old man was pretty cool.

They continued to skip school and smoke weed, and sometimes they got drunk, but they never again did any of this in the Lord's backyard.

1976

Norma loved Jeff. John could always count on his best friend's ability to talk John's way out of his house, even if Norma was in a bad mood or riding a mean drunk. His easy-going spirit drew people of all ages to him.

This was a good attribute for the sidekick to a low-level junior-high drug dealer specializing exclusively in high-quality weed. John had been tapped by a young guy who lived on his block to expand his market to the junior high set and business was good.

So, he brought Jeff in on the action and Jeff grew his customer-base. They were soon flush in cash—at least it felt like that to two poor kids who were only in eighth grade. John's new job improved his attendance, but it didn't do much for his grades.

Peter and Jenny had broken up, so there were no girls to pick up. The boys drove around without purpose and then Peter settled on a plan for the night. "Stevens mentioned that he was feeding his neighbor's cat while they were out of town. Let's go check out their house."

They parked up the street and tiptoed to the small brown house. Chucky stood lookout while Pauli, Peter and John prowled around the place, looking for a way in. The windows on the first floor were all locked, but Pauli hoisted John up on the roof above the large covered porch; a second-floor window opened when he pushed it up. John climbed in and walked downstairs to unlock the side door for the others.

The boys walked around inside the house, oddly respectful. They were more curious than anything, opening drawers and closets just to see what was inside.

They were hungry, so they made some bologna sandwiches for the road and took a six-pack of beer. Pauli swiped a cool knife he found in a drawer. They locked the door behind them and left as quietly as they came.

This was the unfortunate start to a bad habit that would ultimately ruin John's life. It would have been better if they had gotten caught.

The Lincoln Continental was just sitting there for the taking. It was a beauty, the keys were in it, the engine was on and there was even a good song playing on the radio—*My Maserati does 185*.... John jumped in, threw it into drive and hit the gas.

The problem was that he needed to throw it in reverse. When he crashed through the front wall of the restaurant, glass shards flying everywhere, he gave up the element of surprise. An irate man, probably the owner of the car, took a running jump, stepping on the table of the nearest booth, and flew through the space where a window had been just a moment ago. He landed spread eagle on the hood of the car but failed to grab anything solid. He slid off, fury turning his face bright red, as John finally got the gear he needed, whipped the car backwards and spun around to rocket out of the parking lot.

Luckily, the cars on the street saw him coming and screeched to a stop, clearing his path. He looked back to see if the man who had just fizzled off the hood of the car was following him. Feeling like he was home free, he accelerated down the street, whooping and singing along with Joe Walsh, though life had never been good to John Aslin.

The cops caught up with him down the road. They must have been set up to catch speeders and he gave them their chance as he flashed by, going at least 20 miles over the posted limit. He was forced to a halt by two cruisers parked across the road. He was a decent driver but not good enough to get out of that mess.

The nickname of the youth detention center was the Pasadena Playhouse but very little fun went on behind the tall fences that surrounded the place. John was overwhelmed when he arrived. It was his first time in juvie. He ran in a rough neighborhood, but things had gotten to the point that people left him alone because he had proven himself fierce and loyal over and over again.

"You're John, right?"

John nodded just a little, trying to be tough. The female guard smiled and motioned for him to follow her. They walked down a hall; boys, much larger than him, stood behind the iron bars that served as doors to their rooms, sizing him up.

Every last one towered over him. He wondered which one would be his bunkmate—they terrified him equally. But the guard kept going, all the way to the end of the hall and up a flight of stairs. She talked over her shoulder. "The younger kids are up here." John was still challenged by a few kids upstairs, but they soon settled into a truce.

All he dreamed about was escape. During free time, he could watch TV or go to the gym. He and one other kid always chose the gym. They shot hoops, played two-man dodgeball and burned up energy and anxiety.

The pretty guard, who was always kind to him, took them outside one day. Once John got to see the lay of the land, his escape plan was hatched. The yard was surrounded by a tall fence with razor wire at the top, but John spotted a place where, if he could get up on the roof, he could run along a brick wall and jump above the other fence. He would just need to get outside by himself.

He had been casing the female guard for weeks. She had a routine. After lunch, she let the older boys out of their cells, turned on the TV and opened the gym. The younger boys had free reign during this time. Once everyone got settled into their activities, she would go back to her office, put her keys in her desk drawer and disappear into the bathroom for fifteen minutes. This gave John the opportunity he needed.

I'm getting out. John was too ramped up to sleep. Where would he go? Would his friends be able to hide him? Would he camp out in the woods, catching his own food? Would he hitchhike into a new life?

At first, things went smoothly. The guard did exactly what she did every day. John sat in the hall, pretending to read a book. As soon as she turned the corner and was out of sight, he bolted into her office and grabbed the keys. His basketball buddy was still upstairs.

He shook with adrenaline as he tried each key in the gym door. He finally found the right one and gently positioned the door so that it looked closed but wasn't latched. He casually slipped back into the office, replaced the keys, then sat in the middle of the gym, waiting for the other kid to come, shoot his baskets and leave.

"Wanna play HORSE?"

John didn't respond. He sat in the middle of the circle at the center of the basketball court, cross-legged, staring straight ahead and silently urging the kid to get the hell out so that he could be on his way. When the same Joe Walsh came on the radio that was propped in the corner of the gym, still singing about living a wild life, John took it as a sign, and maybe it was, but he read it wrong.

The kid awkwardly bounced the ball, staring at him. "What's your problem?" The kid was getting irritated. He bounced a few more times and then bounced the ball off John's head. "Asshole."

John watched him leave. He was halfway to the door when the guard leaned in. "John, I need you to come with me."

Shock flushed the nervous energy out of him. How did she know? He had been so careful.

Out in the hall, she scrutinized his face. "You feeling okay? You're kind of pale." He shook off the hand that was reaching for his forehead.

A line of girls came into sight at the end of the hallway and filed by him, headed for the gym. A dozen of them carried dodgeballs. The guard smiled at him. "You can have the gym after they finish their game."

Hope sparked. He sat outside the gym door, planning to sneak in and slip out the door during the chaos of the end of the match that the girls were engrossed in. Then he heard a deep voice scream, "Get back in here." Apparently one of the girls had fallen against the door when she was trying to avoid getting hit and the door flung open.

Someone told him how the guards had been lined up and lectured, threatened with their jobs, if anything like that ever happened again. All the leniency and kindness of the female guard evaporated; she became stricter than the others. John felt bad that he had betrayed her kindness, but he felt worse that he was still stuck in lock up, unable to run.

After he was released from Juvie, John went back to school. He and Jeff were finishing their morning smoke when an old Buick Electra 225 roared up the street, screeching as it slowed enough to make the turn into the school parking lot.

A giant emerged. His curly blonde hair added a few inches. The new kid, Randy Gunderson, had enrolled a few days before. He and John had a class together, but they hadn't talked. Randy was the only student at Summit Junior High who drove himself to school. He was a Swedish kid from the Upper Peninsula.

Randy would have had to shave at least twice a day if he cared about taming his facial hair, but he did not. John would later learn Randy was smart but various circumstances put him behind in school. John nudged Jeff, then headed over to inspect the car as a way to break the ice. "Nice wheels."

The blankness that John had seen on the new kid's face broke into a smile. He was just shy. Randy popped the hood so they could appreciate the 455 engine, the biggest one that Buick made. He answered John's questions with enthusiasm. "Oh, ya, it's fast alright. Meet me after school and I'll give you a ride home. We'll take the long way, open her up on some back roads."

John was amused by the iron-range flavor of the kid's speech. Randy was just so damn nice, not worried about playing a tough like the kids John was used to, who constantly struggled for status as a means to survive the world that they orbited.

Before he started hanging out with Randy, John went to Skateland most Saturday nights. He would drink and smoke pot in the parking lot, then go in with his friends and hit on any girls that the uppity boys from Clio, a slightly wealthier nearby town, would ask to skate.

The main purpose of these tactics was to instigate a fight in the parking lot. John had come out of these fights with fat lips, bloody elbows after rolling around on the concrete, and even adjustments to his nose, but he was proud of the fact that he'd never had a black eye.

He usually squared up with a larger opponent, typically seeing a mocking glint in the other guy's eye that would turn to shock once John threw his first punch. He was small, but he was quick and hit hard, before the other guy had a chance to expect it. He became a bit of a hero in his crowd.

The same scenario played out over and over. "Hey, John, that guy over there is bothering me. Could you take care of it?" He definitely could and he did.

Fighting gave John a sense of purpose. It made him feel needed. He belonged, a good feeling that had not been common in his life.

Randy Gunderson was a big teddy bear, but his size was intimidating. The sea of kids that filled the school halls parted with each turn he made. John always beat him to the cafeteria. Randy would suddenly appear as the crowd of kids would evaporate upon his approach. He dropped the brown grocery bag that carried his lunch on the table and pulled out three sandwiches, a banana and a Twinkie; he could hold his three cartons of milk in one hand. This was all in addition to the free lunch he would get once the line went down.

"Got a job for you." John raised his eyebrow in a question mark.

The answer came out in between Randy's bites and chews. "My dad's bringing me into the family business." Randy laughed. "The Swedish mafia. We got the newspaper racket nailed down."

Randy's dad worked full-time at the Buick plant but he had the contract to do overnight deliveries all over Genesee County for the Detroit Free Press. On Monday, Wednesday and Friday nights, Randy would relieve one of his many brothers who was tired of delivering papers in the middle of the night. He wanted John to help him.

Randy offered John his first steady opportunity to earn an honest living. "Go home. Get some sleep. I'll pick you up at 11:00 and get you home around 4:00."

"Norma's never going to go for that."

"Just leave that up to me."

Randy was waiting on the porch when Norma got home from work. Somehow he talked her into letting John work with him by sprinkling in words like "responsibility," "honest income," "he can spend the night at my house after so we won't wake you up" and "it will keep him from running the streets on Friday nights."

They developed a routine. John sat in the passenger seat, folding the papers and watching for the reflective stickers that Randy's dad put on the customer mailboxes. Each time they turned down a street, they saw dozens of little beacons calling for the nightly news. They had to keep the windows open and the cool night air helped them stay awake.

Soon John was spending the whole weekend at Randy's. They slept until afternoon and raided the refrigerator, demolishing unopened boxes of generic cereal in a single day. They practiced a bastardized version of karate, mimicking moves they saw in the kung fu movies they both loved. They hung boards from the ceiling, attacking them with kicks and punches, the giant Swede and under-sized John locked in good-natured pissing contests fueled by their burgeoning masculinity.

After they wore themselves out, they drove to Randy's uncle's house and helped him fix transmissions. He gave them a little cash that they spent at the movies or the roller-skating rink, where they worked on their disco skating skills and flirted with girls.

Though Randy was just two years older, he was a good influence on John; he took John under his wing. As long as he hung out with Randy, John stayed out of trouble. Randy provided the yin to the yang of the Caravellis and their gang of hoods.

Many things pulled John toward darkness—drinking, taking drugs, breaking into houses, fighting, and stealing cars—but Randy provided a glimmer of light. It just wasn't bright enough to overcome the shadows.

John came of age in a blue collar, rough and tumble town that was dependent on the auto industry. Just as he reached the point where puberty was pushing him toward independence, he was left to fend for himself while his mother was either at work, taking as many overtime hours as she could at the auto factory, or passed out drunk.

John ran wild on the streets, seeking to define himself through the eyes of his friends, the only people in his life who were paying attention. When his Uncle Fred was the same age, he took a different path in his quest to figure out who he was.

Somewhere in the Thumb of Michigan
Late-Summer 1939

Fred left on a cool summer morning, so early that he didn't encounter a soul. He was contemplative as he slipped away from his cottage and retrieved the supplies stashed in a hollow tree deep into the copse that grew on the outer edges of the main grounds.

It was a bundle of sacred objects tied up in a blanket, Gishkibidagunnun, hundreds of brightly-colored medicine ties prepared with tobacco from Pony, matches, a knife, a small cup and some herbs that Doris had taken from the kitchen as well as a tube of lipstick, bundles of sweet grass, small branches of cedar and somehow, sage that Herman had squirreled away—as well as a pipe that Fred had done his best to make without traditional materials. The blanket was a dull grey, unlike the beautiful blankets that his mother made.

Once he began his prayers, it might take as long as four days for them to reach the spirit world. Herman instructed Fred not to eat or drink until his communication with the spirits was complete. The Vision Quest would be physically demanding; he would be in a weakened state when it was done. He carried a small amount of food, mainly nuts and apples, so that he could eat a small meal before he began his fast.

Fred slipped through an opening in the fence and quickly crossed the road, dissolving into the heavy tree line on the other side. After a few minutes, he paused to pray to the spirits, and to his father, that they would guide him to a proper place.

The walk remained cool as he journeyed through tall Michigan pines. Fred felt a peace return to him that he had not felt in several years. The constant noise at the Home covered the hums of the natural world. He identified the calls of individual birds and whistled at them as he followed instincts that the ancestors sent him.

Fred was not in a hurry. He headed northeast, pausing periodically to check in with the wind. He noticed a crow with a white patch circling its eye slightly ahead of him. It cawed, then moved forward once Fred took a step in its direction. The animal's call sounded like, "c'mon, c'mon, c'mon" and Fred quickened his pace to keep up.

The other animals went quiet. The world shrunk to Fred and his winged guide. It was well past noon when he found himself in an open space near a brook. The crow hopped from branch to branch, circling, and Fred understood that he had arrived at his sacred place. The physical leg of the journey had been accomplished. He would begin the spiritual piece the next morning.

If Fred were living among his people, the elders would have lit a fire for him when he left and kept it burning until he returned. That part of the ritual was not possible under the circumstances, but Pony vowed to keep a candle burning until Fred returned.

Fred prepared the site for the next day. He gathered stones and built an altar to hold his pipe and herbs. He scoured the nearby woods and found a birch tree. He cut some of the thick bark off, thanking the tree for assisting him in his quest. Fred had not fished since arriving in Lapeer, but he relived his childhood success and caught several perch. Soon they were roasting over a small fire.

Fred sang the songs of his childhood, softly at first and then with gusto, as the fish crackled in the flames. He ate them carefully, enjoying each sumptuous bite. If he were at home with his father, they would have entered the sweat lodge for several days before he began his quest.

Fred improvised as best he could by gathering stones and placing them in the fire. When they were hot, he rolled them away from the flames with a stick. He tented the blanket over himself and the stones, then poured water on them. The steam that he caught was not as intense as the sweats of his childhood, but it paid homage to the tradition.

Fred lay down on the ground, catching the last moments of heat from the sun. As it went down, he reviewed all the loss that had been brought to the surface by this journey. Would he see his father? He stared at the flames until the fire faded and he fell asleep. He did not dream.

Then it was morning. Fred was awakened by the spotted crow. He restarted a small fire, then laid out the sacred items. First, he folded the blanket in quarters and placed it in the center of the clearing; the altar sat between the blanket and the water's edge. Fred circled the blanket with 400 tobacco ties, creating a sacred ring that only he could enter. He walked to the water's edge and found a calm spot that could serve as a mirror and painted his face red from the lipstick tube that his sister had provided. He softly chanted the prayers he had heard his father sing. He made offerings of the sacred medicine—the tobacco, sweet grass, cedar and herbs—to the four directions and then burned each in the fire as he thanked the spirit world for guiding him on his quest.

After the medicine was consumed by the flames, Fred stepped into the holy loop and sat facing the altar. He had practiced sitting still for long stretches, even taking a couple of beatings for staying out all night when he had been overcome by the meditative calm and lost track of the stars. He crossed his legs, rested his hands on his thighs, closed his eyes and prayed silently for the vision to come.

Fred's request was granted late into the second day, as he moved beyond hunger and thirst. He lost track of the outer world; he had not opened his eyes for so long that the space behind them had darkened to nothingness. He did not feel the breeze, did not hear the forest sounds, did not feel hot or cold. Several hours before, a hum had started forming in his mind, soft like a whisper and then slowly building into a chorus of ancient chants.

It was background noise for an eternity; eventually it had meaning. The voices sang the history of the Ojibwe and confirmed Fred's place among them. A pinprick of light like the north star pushed the darkness to the edges. A dream world opened before him with a path of brightness leading him forward. He walked toward a glowing blue orb at the bottom of a rocky path.

Fred climbed to a ledge that floated above him. The ledge led to a cave. Figures sat around a huge fire; the flame shadows danced on the walls. Bear stood in front of the fire, facing Fred, obstructing Fred's view of the others. She was fierce, rearing up on her hindquarters, then lowering to all fours and gesturing with her snout for Fred to approach.

Bear's cubs played behind her, then ran out of sight. "You've done well protecting your cubs. Sometimes it is good to show your power. Don't forget that power comes from knowledge."

Bear lumbered off after her cubs and Fred could see Fox warming his paws. Fox waved Fred toward the fire. "You've done well, Aseban. You've gotten my messages."

Aseban. So my spirit animal is Racoon.

"We have watched you get what you need to escape danger. You have protected the less powerful from the shadows. You may be small, but like Aseban, you are fierce when cornered. You have outsmarted your enemy but there are many enemies and more danger coming. Aseban and I will visit you in the dreamworld to bring you our wisdom. Heed our warnings."

"Thank you, Waagosh, for helping me learn the ways of the spirit world."

Raccoon emerged from the shadows holding a bowl and painted Fred's face. She dipped her paw into black paint and drew a line from Fred's forehead to the tip of his nose. She drew wide circles around Fred's eyes and filled them in with white paint.

Aseban led Fred to a pool. Fred saw a raccoon looking back at him—it was his true self. Raccoon pointed to an open seat by the fire. Fred sat down and looked to his right. He reached out and stroked Wolf's arm. "Pa."

"Son, I've been waiting for you."

Fred was overcome with emotion. Just as his father began to speak, Fred was pulled out of the dream world as though he had been sucked into a vacuum and spat back into the world. He opened his eyes to a terrifying sight—a man on the other side of the stream held a rifle.

Fred realized the man had fired a warning shot; now he was lowering the muzzle in Fred's direction. "Get off my land, you dirty Indian!" the farmer spat.

Fred backpedaled on all fours toward the nearby woods, then turned and fled. A bullet whizzed past his shoulder. He ran until he felt the man was far behind him, then caught his breath as sobs emerged from deep inside him. He roared at the universe in frustration and despair, then collapsed.

It was dark when Fred awoke. This time it was a bat, with a white ring around its eye. Apakwaanaajiinh. Fred followed it, jogging lightly. He was weak from hunger but driven by the fury of disappointment that he had missed what his father wanted to say to him.

The bat swooped through a clearing that opened to a copse of wild fruit trees. His guide circled, lapping up mosquitos and moths as Fred gorged on ripe peaches, the juice dripping down his arms. He wiped his hands on the damp grass. The bat hung upside down from a branch, watching him closely.

"Thank you, Apakwaanaajiinh. Are you going to take me home?" The bat took off through the woods. Fred struggled to keep up. He was focused on his mind, not his surroundings, and suddenly he burst through the trees across the street from the Home.

It was still dark. He stealthily entered the cottage, went to the bathroom to wash his hands and face, then went to bed. He shed a few tears as he fell asleep. There had been circles of dark brown earth around his eyes.

Fred was harshly awakened by the sensation of flying. He was in fact flying as the night guard, Larry Daniels, picked him up and flung him on the floor. The man bent over him, red-faced, eyes bulging as he screamed, "Where the hell have you been? You trying to make me lose my job?"

The other boys circled them, awakened by the commotion. John wrung his hands. Larry was a huge man with a hair-trigger temper who could be counted on to lash out with a punch or a slap whenever the spirit moved him.

Fred curled up in a protective position as Larry kicked him on his thighs and buttocks. The difference between Larry and Vernal was that Larry wouldn't hold a grudge. Larry would run out of steam soon and Fred's transgression would be forgotten. It was John's high-pitched scream that stopped the attack.

Larry turned on him and raised his hand to strike him, but Ted and Peter stepped in front of their little brother, diffusing the outburst. Daniels pushed roughly past them, sputtering and muttering unintelligible things, then turned. "Don't none of you better be late for breakfast—or missing." Then he stormed out, slamming the door.

As beatings go, that one had not inflicted as much damage as Fred expected. He sat up, grabbed John by the shirt and pulled him in for a hug. One thing he knew for sure from his journey—the ancestors expected him to protect his brothers and he would not be deterred from that task.

Herman listened carefully. Fred limped from a bruise on his thigh but persisted in pushing Herman's chair. They spoke in their native tongue. Fred told him everything. When he mentioned the crow, Herman interrupted him.

"The presence of the crow is complicated. Crows have life magic, the mystery of creation. They can point us toward our destiny, urge us to be fearless and adapt to our circumstances. But they can be a bad omen and trick those who follow them. They are powerful prophets. Did the crow speak in your dream?"

"No, the crow was not in my vision. He led me to the spot. It seemed like a good spot." Fred described how he had prepared for the ceremony.

Herman laughed when Fred told him about the improvised sweat lodge. "You did your best to make the medicine right. I'm sure the ancestors were pleased. Tell me about the dream."

"I climbed a path of stars to a cave. Bear was waiting for me. At first I was afraid that she wouldn't allow me inside." He told Herman what bear had said.

"You need to go to that school in town. Learn everything you can. Bear wants you to be powerful. In this world, getting an education will make you formidable. What happened next?"

"Fox told me he would warn me of danger."

"Fox is a strong ally. He will help you be clever when you need to avoid trouble."

"He told me that my doodem totem is Raccoon."

"Awe. I should have seen that coming." Herman smiled. "You are Raccoon. Look at how you made the plan for the baseball game and got Dr. Hanna to meet your demands. Raccoon is smart at making sure he gets what he wants."

Fred was quiet as he mulled that over.

"As Raccoon you will likely face danger in your life and need to use your wits to save yourself. Raccoon will help you survive."

"Raccoon painted my face, gave me his mask." Fred paused, because the next part still made him emotional. "My father was there. Wolf. He had something to tell me, but a hunter woke me up. I didn't get to hear my father's wisdom." Tears streamed down Fred's face. He was glad he was behind Herman and did not have to look him in the eye.

"You can do many vision quests. This was the first, but not the last.

Your father will be there for you. If Wolf is not threatening you in your dream, it is a good sign. Your father will guide you. Wolf is telling you to trust your instincts. Your father will be beside you, helping you along life's journey."

"I told you before, the vision quest can show you the possibilities of your life. You didn't get to see everything that the spirit world wanted to show you, but the ancestors have pointed you toward your path. Continue to lead and protect. Learn everything you can. Be on the lookout for danger. Be ready to outwit your enemies. The ancestors have spoken this."

Fred waited for Dr. Hanna outside his office. The doctor had summoned him. "Hello, young man. Just wanted to check on you. I hear you were missing for a couple of days and then you came back. Did you do what you needed to do?"

"It didn't go exactly as I planned, but I started something that needed to be started."

"I'm happy to hear that."

John Eric Almost
Becomes an Orphan
1977

It was snowing hard. They probably should have stayed home but there wasn't much food in the cupboards. "I'm going to the store. You want to come?" Norma was in a slightly good mood because she was low on booze and fairly sober. John expected they would be stopping at the liquor store too.

Their large Chevy Impala dared the roads to mess with it as it steadily navigated toward their destination. They almost made it. Norma pulled into the center lane, waiting to turn left in the parking lot. Then they were struck head on. John felt his head whip back, then snap forward. His forehead slammed into the dash and everything went black.

"You okay, kid?" A man shook his shoulder. John lifted his head, trying to figure out why this stranger was so close to his face. When he looked at the man full on, he saw him wince and reach out to brush shards of glass off John's face. John touched where the stranger's hand was headed and felt warm blood on his fingers.

Straight ahead, a truck was wedged into the hood of the Impala, the shocked driver staring at John, close enough that they could have been sitting in a restaurant, sharing a meal.

John turned toward his mother. She was wedged under the steering wheel. She looked like she was dead. He shook her shoulder frantically. "Ma, wake up, wake up." He pleaded with her, but she gave no response.

He shakily pushed past the man who was leaning over him and ran to the driver's side, trying to pull his mother's door open. Several strangers gently tried to talk him out of his panic. "Son, the ambulance will be here soon. Let's wait for the professionals so we don't hurt her more."

John shook off their words when he locked eyes with a young man who was now standing outside his smashed truck, the person who had caused all of it. John lunged at him but was tackled by another man on the scene. He wanted his fists to hit the man, but his words would have to do. "You bastard! You killed my ma!"

They wouldn't let John ride in the same ambulance as Norma. When he saw himself in the bathroom mirror at the hospital, he assumed his face would be ruined forever. He had dozens of cuts, blood like war paint on his face. It had dripped down and soaked his shirt. The sink filled with weak red water when he washed his hands.

The next day, John looked even worse. He had the black eyes that he had been so proud of avoiding in the fights of his youth. The cuts on his face were angry; his right ear was sliced. His body was bruised and sore.

Norma was in another coma. John listened as the doctors gave Linda an update. "She has extensive internal injuries. Her pancreas is damaged and she has swelling on her brain. We've stabilized her, but we'll have to wait and see about her long-term prognosis."

"When will she wake up?"

"There's no way to know."

John visited her every day. The doctors told Norma's children that she might be able to hear them, so they talked about funny things. She looked so fragile, hoses, tubes and wires surrounding her, a broken bird in a medical nest.

Linda liked to fix her mother's hair and put a make up on her. Sometimes she painted Norma's nails. One day, without even opening her eyes, Norma was back. "Dammit, leave me alone. Just get me a damned cigarette."

The doctors said that the fact that she was back to her mean old self was a good sign; it signaled that she would recover.

John went back to school. He still looked like he had been in a fight with a cougar. Some of the kids acted like they were seeing a ghost. "Aslin, I heard you were dead." One of his classmates had witnessed the scene—John covered in blood and carted off in an ambulance. When he didn't show up for school for several weeks, his schoolmates had assumed the worst.

John laughed. "My ma says I must be a cat—I've gotten hit by cars so many times that I must have nine lives. I can't be killed."

Norma came home, but she could barely walk. She still had tubes attached to her as she shuffled around the house with difficulty. She slept in an easy chair, parked in front of the TV. She was given a special diet to follow while they waited for her pancreas to heal; booze was not supposed to be on the menu.

Norma tied a red ribbon over her whiskey bottles to hide the shrinking contents. John was worried that if she didn't stop, she might die. Linda lectured their mother over and over that she had to stop drinking.

After observing the lowering levels in the bottles, John took action. He was in the middle of pouring the first one out when Norma appeared in the kitchen doorway. "Stop! Don't you know that's the only thing keeping me alive?

John stopped emptying the bottles down the sink but shifted to another strategy. He drank from the bottles himself, then added water to bring the level even with the ribbon. Norma didn't notice but his dependence on alcohol grew.

The highlight of Sundays was the teen dance at the Mikatam lounge. Saturday Night Fever showed up on Sunday nights. John and Jeff spent as much time in front of the mirror as his sisters did, feathering their long hair with plastic combs that stuck out of their back pockets when they weren't using them.

They practiced the Hustle in a corner of the cafeteria during lunch at school and did the Bump with cute girls. They spent their money on flashy chains that they displayed by leaving several buttons of their wide-lapelled polyester shirts undone. This complimented their flared pants and platform shoes.

John was a good dancer. It was the best thing he had going in his life. He went with Jeff, the Caravellis and a loose group of boys who called themselves the "Beecher Bums" in private but the "Beecher Warlords" on the street. He still fought, if necessary, but he didn't like messing up his fancy new clothes.

Norma's words ran on a loop through his mind. "You're a no-good little bastard, just like your father." John felt like he had risen up from the dirt, not from a man—whoever this supposed father was, he had never met him, never even seen a picture. He hit the sidewalk running. His mom had just gotten started and the booze would fuel her ravings for a while—she probably didn't even realize she was screaming at an empty house.

John turned toward Jeff's house, slowing to a walk. Jeff was on his porch, looking uncharacteristically miserable. He glanced up when he noticed John on the sidewalk. "I hate this fucking place."

"Yeah, it sucks balls."

"I'd be happy if I never had to step back inside that prison." He gestured back toward his house. John waited quietly as Jeff muttered to himself for another moment, something about his asshole of a father.

They walked without purpose, then hitchhiked to Meijer's Thrifty Acres. They watched a woman go in to pay for her gas with a $20 bill. She left a flawless Cutlass parked at the pump. They walked around it, admiring its newness. It was the automotive equivalent of what they dreamed of for themselves and it felt unattainable.

At first they just wanted a closer look. It was burgundy, shiny new, with a plush black interior, black vinyl roof and sparkly chrome rims. Someone had splurged on this beauty. A large chrome key chain caught the light and John noticed that it hung from the ignition key, like a big bow wrapped on the present of an escape ticket. John whistled at Jeff and nodded toward the keys.

Jeff grinned and climbed into the passenger seat. When John turned the key over, it felt like a fresh start. The engine roared as John, in his fourteen-year-old nervousness, cranked the key and pushed the pedal a bit too hard. He peeled out on to the street and immediately took the on-ramp to the highway, driving down 1-75 with a sense of freedom he'd rarely felt in his short life. The car responded as he firmly pressed the gas, accelerating to over 100 mph as he weaved around slower-moving drivers.

Jeff rolled down the window, pumping his fist and squealing, "Yes!" into the wind. It wasn't long before John spotted Bishop Airport. He veered off the freeway and drove along Torrey Road, watching a few planes take off. The he went to a distant cousin's house.

"Hey, Auntie. Is Cindy home?"

"Nope. She's at a friend's."

John was concocting an explanation for why he had a car yet no driver's license, but his aunt never asked. The boys wound their way through side roads. They spotted a trail and pulled in, out of sight from the main road. Jeff rummaged through the groceries in the back seat. He grabbed a loaf of bread, sliced ham and cheese. "You want a sandwich?"

They each ate two, loaded thick with meat and several slices of cheese. They cracked open cans of warm Pepsi and leaned back, enjoying their full bellies and sense of adventure. Then they took off again.

John felt bliss at the helm of a fast car on the open road and pushed the motor to 120 whenever the highway cleared out. Soon they were in Ohio. When they tried to cash in a bag of empty pop cans that they found in the trunk of the car at a party store, they were told there were no deposits in Ohio. John poured the bag on the store floor, angry to be denied the five dollars or so he was anticipating. He left without paying for the gas.

They stopped at a rest area to use the bathroom and examined a map posted in the lobby. "Where should we go?"

John thought for a moment. "California." Their blue jean cut-off shorts, tank tops and flipflops would fit in well if they lived at the beach.

They had the rest of the cash from the lady's purse, a carton of Virginia Slims and a few more groceries in the back seat. There was also a TV back there—something they might be able to sell.

John turned back west. Jeff climbed into the back seat to take a nap and John chain-smoked to stay awake. He heard the back door open and a loud crash off to the side. He checked his rearview mirror in time to see the TV bouncing behind them. He noted they were going 80 mph. "You idiot. I was gonna sell that."

"It was in my way. I couldn't get comfortable."

They stopped in a sleepy town in Indiana, pulling behind an old church to get some rest. A loud pounding startled them awake.

"You okay in there?" A tall police officer peered in the window.

John was scared to death that their adventure was over, but he played it cool as he cracked the window open. "We're driving to see my dad and got tired. Thought we should pull over, get some sleep."

"Well, you can't sleep here. You'll have to move on."

"Sure thing, officer."

Neither boy could believe it when the officer walked to his car, whistling loudly, and drove away.

They were headed to California in a beautiful new car. Life was already better. The purse on the passenger seat was the cherry on top that provided them with an unexpected resource—they were flush with cash.

They stopped for breakfast. Both boys felt lighter, relaxing into a booth in a diner and ordering mounds of eggs, hash browns and bacon. They topped it off with milkshakes. They wolfed down their food, eager to get on with their plan.

Neither of them was particularly good at geography—in their minds, all roads led to California, but they ended up in Indianapolis. It was the biggest city either had ever seen. John parked the Cutlass on a side street.

They wandered, stumbling upon the newly-constructed Indianapolis Museum of Art. John walked its halls in wonder. Jeff made crude jokes about the nudes, but John was lost in the beauty of it all. He stepped close to the paintings, trying to see how they were put together. An older woman started to scold him for getting too close, but when she saw the look on his face as he turned to meet her voice, as though he was being pulled out of a dream, her voice softened. She simply told him to be careful not to touch anything as the oils in his fingers could hurt the masterpieces.

John lingered until closing time. Jeff had grown impatient. They found the car and headed in the direction of California, at least the direction that a gas station attendant had pointed them in. He also told them to stop at the Rock-Cola Café.

John slipped a little liquid fun into their cokes and they were flying high by the time they were on a highway. They might have made it if the booze had not unlocked John's discretion. When the fuel light lit up, he drove to a gas station near the exit.

An attendant trotted out and cleaned the windshield as he filled the tank. When he finished, he tapped on the window for payment. The buzz made John feel like an outlaw. He threw the car into low gear, punch the pedal and slid sideways as he exited the parking lot and shot back on the highway.

A cruiser was soon drafting them—he must have been on the highway already because they were driving fast enough that no one should have been able to catch up. John veered to an off ramp at the last second, brakes squealing as he slowed enough to make the turn.

Another cruiser drove toward him and stopped in the road; he swerved around it. Eventually he found himself at a dead-end road. He turned into a church parking lot, gravel flying as he passed an officer who was still inside his car, frantically trying to roll down his window, waving his gun as he locked eyes with John.

John drove over a decline at the back of the parking lot and the car stalled. He threw it into neutral and it started up. He was back on an open road. He accelerated to eighty. Two cruisers tried to keep up with him as he flew down a narrow lane. He could see a small bridge in the distance where he would probably meet the state trooper who was headed in his direction.

Instead of hesitating, John doubled-down, accelerating even more and pointing the nose of the Cutlass directly at the trooper, who ultimately veered off the road and hit the concrete embankment on his side of the bridge. John turned on to another road and pushed the car to a speed that was too high to negotiate the S-curve he encountered further down. The brakes screeched as he tried to slow down, then the car shot into a cornfield, rocking violently.

He and Jeff hit their heads on the ceiling several times as the car protested and slowed to a stop. This was clearly the most excitement these police officers has seen in a long time as they huffed and puffed their way out into the cornfield, yanking the boys out of the car and pushing their faces into the cold dirt as they cuffed them and dragged them to a waiting cruiser.

They were booked at the jail in Shelbyville wearing nothing but shorts, filthy, hungry and slightly hung-over but did they have a story to tell when they got back home! Two Shelbyville police department vehicles had to be towed away that evening and the state police trooper, who showed up later with a bandage on his head, couldn't believe he had been run off the road by a fourteen-year-old. He did not appreciate the razzing he got about Mario Andretti Jr. dominating him, so he stood outside the cell and screamed at the boys for a solid ten minutes.

Their cellmate reeked of alcohol, but it was a smell that John was unfortunately intimate with. He was not, however, intimate with the smell of vomit that soon pervaded the small space.

The boys didn't know that they shouldn't have been locked up with adults, but they knew they were scared. They huddled together on the top bunk, getting very little sleep. The next morning, they heard a female officer who was not happy. "What the hell, Joe. You can't put these kids in with adults."

She murmured comforting sounds as she moved them to their own cell, but the scent of puke followed them because their cellmate had splashed it on their feet. Their private cell would be their home for weeks, until they went to court without any parents to oversee their case.

"We should have just left you down here to rot," Norma sneered.

"You better hope your dad has to work a double tonight when you get home," was Jeff's mom's greeting, delivered with a heavy dose of disappointment.

"You're gonna pay me back," was the last thing Norma said until they got home seven hours later. John's stomach was rumbling. Norma refused to buy him any food on the way back. He climbed into the front seat after they dropped Jeff and his mom off. John was stunned, though he should have expected it, when Norma rained punches and slaps on him.

No matter what she did, he never hit his mom back, but he did try to grab her wrists to stop her flailing. She was breathing hard when she decided to stop the attack and drive the car. Her final pronouncement was, "You're just like your father."

When they got to the house, he was out of the car door before she had it in park. He ran in, grabbed bread and milk, and raced to his room, locking himself in before she could get to him. He moved his dresser in front of the door just to be safe.

John tiptoed around the house for the next couple of weeks. As he was leaving to wander the streets for the tenth day in a row—anything to escape the smoldering hostility of that house—his mother blocked him. "I can't deal with your shit anymore. I think you should stay with your aunt for a while."

They had to wait until John went to court for stealing the car. The judge agreed with Norma's idea. Aunt Vera lived outside of Los Angeles. John was headed to the west coast after all.

John and Norma drove for several days. The trip was dull through the Midwest and the flat plains of Nebraska, but the scenery got interesting in Wyoming. The mountains of Utah blew them away. Norma was excited at the sights I-80 offered—they hadn't traveled much.

John examined pamphlets in a diner in northern Nevada while Norma paid the bill. She joined him. One caught her eye—the Redwood Forest in Crescent City, California. "I've always wanted to see these." This made sense to John. Looking back, his mother was her most relaxed when they went up north. She made time to walk in the woods and came back to the cabin with a dreamy look in her eyes. She seemed to have an affinity for trees.

Visiting the Redwoods added a full day to their trip, but it was worth it. They cruised through the deserts of northern Nevada and on to California, turning north instead of south.

The Redwood Forest transported John to another world, where his challenges seemed, for a moment, inconsequential. He was surrounded by happy families. The campers were chatty, inviting strangers to join their cookouts, sharing cold cans of pop or beer.

I could just stay here. I could run away. No one would even notice. There were showers, water fountains. Norma would never find him. He would be free and could start over. He could live in nature, like the animals he admired. It would be a purer existence than the one he had lived to date.

The Redwoods became John's happiest memory of his mother, yet it took place during a trip where she was dumping him off to live with someone else. The irony.

Los Angeles was a big change for a kid from a small city. John's Aunt Vera didn't live in L.A. proper, but she lived close enough.

Glendora was in Orange County, butting up against the foothills that bled into the Angeles National Forest. John gazed in wonder at them—they sure looked like mountains to him.

John was nervous when he realized that his aunt was a drinker like his mom, but his fears were misplaced. Vera was a happy drunk, smiling and laughing as the alcohol kicked in. She was hard on her own kids, but her rules were different for John. She had a soft spot for him and let it slide if he skipped school, smoked cigarettes or weed in his room or got drunk.

All of that changed when he took her car and wound up in Yuma, Arizona. John had been at Vera's for several months. He was doing well, but the pressure built—the hurt and the anger of never feeling truly loved didn't change with new scenery. He got drunk and made an unfortunate, rash decision.

He was homesick for the friends who had known him all his life, who knew of the reputation he had already built. At home in Flint, he didn't have to recreate himself from scratch. If he had just been honest with his aunt, she would have sent him home. She was trying to help a foolish kid, not hold anyone hostage. But nothing in John's life had ever taught him that he could be honest and say what he wanted or needed. He was a broken young man who was programmed to run.

When he walked out of his room, melancholy and lonely, her car keys shined like a beacon. When he grabbed them off the table, he saw cash peeking out of her open purse. He grabbed both.

The El Camino hummed. He drove straight to the 210 and headed east, back to his old habits, his old mistakes. He drove until he started to nod off. He stopped at a gas station in the middle of the night, getting sleepy as he came down from his buzz. He bought No-Doze, took four and got back behind the wheel.

The desert was mesmerizing. The empty roads called to him to drive like he was free, so he pushed the car to 105. The cacti flew by, sometimes tricking him into thinking that they were friendly people waving hello to a fellow traveler. But the momentum was so lulling that he closed his eyes for just a moment—he was so tired.

When he woke up, he was so far out in the desert that he couldn't see the road. Somehow, he had driven all that way without hitting anything that jolted him awake. He was unsure if he could even find his way back, so he closed his eyes until morning.

John woke up sweaty and disoriented as the sun warmed up the car. After taking a piss in the middle of nowhere, he turned the car and carefully followed his tracks back to the highway.

There was a hitchhiker standing near the spot where he reentered the road; he picked the guy up. "Thanks for the ride. I thought I was going to be there for a while. Where you headed?"

"Kingman." At least that's where the road signs told him he was headed the night before.

"Cool. Name's Ben." The young man hesitated. "You got any food? I haven't eaten in a while." He laughed uncomfortably.

"I'm not sure. Check the glovebox."

Ben rummaged around and pulled out a pint of vodka. He held it up and looked at John to see if he could take a sip.

"Go ahead."

Ben took a swig and winced as he swallowed. He held the bottle out to John, who also took a nip. The alcohol loosened Ben's tongue.

"Where you coming from so early? The desert? Did you drop a body out there?"

"I was hunting cactus. And scorpions." John gave him a sinister look for as long as he could hold it then broke into a smile.

"How fast can this thing go?"

"Had her up to 105 yesterday."

"The cops are probably still in bed. Open her up. See if she's awake."

John pressed the accelerator and the needle hovered just over 100. Ben rolled down his window and whooped at the sun, like Jeff had on the first wild ride, but he quickly pulled back inside the car. "State Trooper going west." Ben squinted in the side mirror. "He just whipped around."

John was cocky. "No problem." He accelerated even more, until the car started shaking a little, then he pulled back.

The trooper caught up to him as though he was coasting, pulling even and giving him a look that said, "Son, please, why are you being so ridiculous."

John pulled over. Trying to outrun the cops on a lonely highway surrounded by desert was more challenging that when he had the winding roads of Indiana or the streets of Flint at his disposal. Soon he and Ben were cuffed and in the back of the cruiser.

As they drove to the nearest town, John made sure Ben would not suffer for John's foolishness. "Officer, I just met this guy. He was hitchhiking and was unlucky enough to get picked up by me. He didn't have anything to do with anything."

Relief washed over Ben's face and his breathing quieted. "Thanks, man. I ain't never been in trouble before."

"Take it from me. You want to keep it that way."

John spent a few days in an Arizona facility for youth offenders, most of whom were Native Americans. A small kid with long braided hair walked up to him at lunch. "What tribe are you?"

"Huh?" John was ignorant of his Ojibwe heritage. He was surrounded by kids that had so much in common with him for the first time—survivors of genocide and poverty—and he didn't even know it.

Vera picked him up in Yuma, Arizona and drove him directly to the Glendora Police station. It was a quiet drive. Vera ordered him out of the car. "Let's go, Johnny."

His cousin leaned over and gave him a peck on the cheek. "You'll be okay."

An officer passed them on the sidewalk on their way in and Vera stopped him. "This is him."

The officer looked him up and down. "Turn around." John turned and held his arms away from his body so that the handcuffs could be put on. He knew the drill. He stood stoically as the officer patted him down, then guided him into the station.

Vera turned back toward the parking lot and did not look back. The officer motioned for John to sit on a bench. An hour later he was on his way to Los Padrinos. The car radio was turned up loud and classical music was playing. The officer drove silently, even when he stopped to buy breakfast at a McDonalds. He indicated that he would switch John's cuffs to the front, then handed him two Egg McMuffins, hash browns and an orange juice. It was the tastiest meal John would have for a long time.

California Youth Authority was a world away from juvie in Flint. Los Padrino's was a walled city, with housing units that went on as far as his eye could see. The inmates shared the grounds with chickens, roosters and peacocks. The grid of covered walkways and the silent escorted juveniles in their orange jumpsuits gave the place a bizarre quality, like a futuristic outpost, where only birds were allowed to talk.

The first night, John huddled in a freezing cell with a mattress on the floor and only a sheet as a cover, waiting for someone to come take him for a bathroom break.

When he couldn't hold it any longer, he relieved himself out a screened window. He heard a blood-curdling scream. Eventually he got used to the peacocks' nocturnal screams, but the bird he had startled with the warm yellow shower proved to give the loudest protest. He was awakened early by a chorus of roosters, before being taken to a mess hall that served the worst institutional food he had encountered to date.

Los Padrino's was full of gang members—the 18th Street Boys, Bloods, Crips and a variety of Mexican crews. John was thrown into a dangerous, alien world with no experience that allowed him to understand it. He thought Flint had made him tough and hip, but he was out-toughed and "out-classed" by his peers at Los Padrino's when it came to being a juvenile delinquent.

He was a terrified stranger from another state, an outcast, but he couldn't show it. If anyone picked on him, he fought back hard and fast, the same way he had built his reputation at home.

After six months, just as he was earning the respect of the other boys, he was moved. When the counselor drove out of the parking lot of Los Padrino's, the sky was clear and the sun was bright. Later, the sky turned dark; soon they were surrounded by fog. They drove up eerie mountain roads, thick with vegetation. John felt like he was being driven into the belly of the beast of his "badness"—a cave of punishment.

Suddenly their path was blocked by foreboding metal gates—he was delivered to Camp Rocky, a bootcamp for bad boys. The counselor drove him to the front door and walked him in without cuffs. After processing, he went to the yard and took in his new home. The place was encased by high brick walls, but the dark mountains that surrounded him in every direction made the barriers feel redundant.

John was led to the open dorm where he would sleep with a couple hundred other boys. Everyone hovered around the TV, watching Sugar Ray delivered a rope-a-dope punch and knock out Roberto Duran. The room exploded with cheers. The intimidation John felt was momentarily tempered by the sense of camaraderie he felt amongst the excited young men. Their celebration was quickly cut off by the aggressive screams to be quiet coming from the guards. The guards enforced total silence.

John was led to his space—a three-foot tall wooden locker and a bunk bed. He had never stayed in a place where everything was so out in the open. Each row of bunks was named after a professional sports team. He was put with the Chiefs.

Everything at Camp Rocky was coordinated. The entire group was totally responsible for what any individual did. The boys called out chants as a group and marched single file everywhere they went. If an individual did not attend a meal, the group would not be able to eat. If anyone didn't follow the rules, the whole group got punished. Anyone who caused anything bad to happen to the group got their asses beat after-hours.

At Camp Rocky, fighting was a double-edged sword.

"Chiefs, listen up." The group leader called out commands. He slept in the last bunk and was responsible for everything the young men in John's group did. He was the only one who could talk and that was only when he was ordering his troops around.

"Chiefs, move out." Stomp, stomp, stomp. Clap, clap, clap. Every move was synchronized. They marched to the chow hall and silently took their seats. If the guards saw anyone speaking, the group would be sent back to the unit and be the last to eat. Anyone who caused a late dinner would be soundly beaten by his peers after the lights went out.

Once they sat, they had to wait until the pitcher of Koolaid was set on the table. Only then could they engage in any conversation. Camp Rocky was segregated, probably to cut down on infighting in the groups themselves.

Groups were sorted by gangs—18th Street, Crips and Bloods—and race. The white kids were divided into bikers and surfers. John didn't fit in anywhere as a Michigan kid, but he knew how to fight. He struck out at the drop of a pin. Eventually everyone stayed clear of him. It started when he showed his fighting skills one day in the yard.

John laid on the grass, enjoying the sun on his face and listening to the music playing over the intercom. A rock hit him in the side of the head. He jumped up, ready to attack. "Whoever threw that rock, your mother sucks dick."

A little guy named Hefner walked toward John. John tackled him without hesitation and pummeled him once he had him on the ground.

The guards rushed in and dragged them apart, hauling them both to the hole for 24 hours.

Hefner was behind him. John heard him whisper, "I didn't throw the rock, Johnny. I was coming to tell you that Gosha threw it and then you just jumped me."

John felt foolish. His temper caused him to attack someone who was trying to help him and caused that person to suffer a night in the hole. "Man, I'm sorry."

John was sent back to his unit on movie night. Everyone would be in the Chow Hall to watch the movie, "Tommy." He maneuvered so that he was sitting behind Gosha. When the lights went out, he leaned in and whispered, in a menacing voice, "So you threw the rock, huh?"

Gosha turned, a shocked look on his face and John landed the first punch. John was able to land several more before the guards figured out what was going on and turned on the lights.

John went back to the hole but Gosha was in a world of hurt. After getting into five or six fights in a few months, word spread that the Michigan kid would scrap. All harassment stopped. No one bothered him.

The guards liked John. Still, he ended up in the hole on the night when he and his friend, Keith, planned an escape. Keith's parents belonged to the Hell's Angels. Keith had taken a shining to John and brought John in on his scheme to escape—his parents arranged for a dirt bike to be left near the wall and for a rope to be tied to a tree and thrown over.

Unfortunately, someone picked a fight with John that day. He heard dirt bikes all around the place from the hole. The next morning, the guards found the rope and a motorbike in the bushes, so they closed the place down.

Somehow, they figured out that Keith was the culprit; he ended up in the hole too. But John was now obsessed with the idea of escape; he came up with a plan that successfully got him beyond the walls.

The classroom building butted up against the enclosure with a gap of only a few feet to get outside. There was a sturdy set of wooden shelves made by the wood class teacher in the classroom. In John's eyes, they were ready-made ladders.

Several days later, a substitute teacher sat at the head of the classroom. John got up periodically and took books off the shelves, casually spreading them around the room and handing them out to other students. John watched the teacher carefully. She placed her emergency beeper in the desk drawer. When she left the room, he saw his chance. He threw the beeper in the trash. He carried the empty bookshelf toward the door.

She didn't spot him until he was halfway out. "Hey, stop! Oh my god! Where are you going?"

John ran down the steps, placed the shelf against the building, climbed up and ran across the roof to the wall. He jumped like he was flying, landed hard on the ground, but took off running down the mountain. He didn't evade detection for long—a mass of cops waited for him at the bottom and he was back in the hole soon after.

His counselor was not happy. "John, you could be out of here in a month if you would straighten your ass up. I'll give you another chance, but you better fly straight. You're going to be on work crew outside the fence. You better not run, boy, I'm telling you. If you don't, I'll let you go home in thirty days. Be smart!"

The first day John was on work crew, he mowed the side of the mountain. At the edge, he had a view of the city below. He hadn't realized home was so close, but there he stood, looking over Glendora. He could see the 210 and the exit for Sunflower Avenue, near Aunt Vera's house. His heart ached to be back with family; he decided to make it through the next month and then home.

He did it. He was a group leader for a few weeks and then he was free.

When he walked through the gate, his aunt was waiting for him. "Here pothead." She handed him a pack of cigarettes. "Don't smoke pot anymore, got it?"

"Deal."

It was 1979. John turned 16 at Camp Rocky.

"I'm gonna let you come back, but your neck is going to be under my foot. NO drinking. NO smoking weed. You'll get your ass up and go to school every day unless I decide you're too sick. And you're going to get a job. I want you too busy to do anything stupid. I'm trying to save you from yourself."

His uncle resented him, but his aunt didn't hold a grudge. John cleaned up. He flew straight. He paid almost half of his paycheck to his aunt, not because she asked him to, but because he wanted to show her that he was sorry for what he had done and appreciated her. The first time he handed her cash, she was shocked and burst into a genuine smile.

John felt proud to be contributing financially to the household from a legitimate source. But he was still a damaged kid who occasionally made bad decisions. One of them was punching his cousin in the mouth. Shock washed over Seth's face. He touched his lip, checking for blood, then he took his protest to his mom.

A few minutes later his aunt was on the porch. "You hit Seth in the mouth?"

John felt nervous, like he was about to be in trouble, but he owned up to his choice. "Yes, Ma'am, I hit him."

His aunt laughed. "He needs it. He's a big pussy." She handed him the beer she had just opened. "But you kids have to live together so try to get along. Got it, bully? And just because I gave you a beer doesn't mean that you get to start drinking again. I'm holding you to our deal."

When John got out of juvie, he went to a local charter school. In spite of his ability, he was far behind his classmates. The principal called Aunt Vera in. "I don't think your nephew is Charter Oaks material. He wears chain belts and leather coats. He doesn't fit in. He would be better served at the school down the road."

John immediately recognized Arrow Continuation for what it was—the burnout school. He felt more comfortable there. He wasn't getting much of an education, but the charter school principal's bias proved John's blessing. His classmates at Arrow were nice.

They went to gym class from 8:00 am to 11:00 every day. Several volleyball nets were set up next to the baseball bleachers. The monitor would play catcher for the baseball game, which made it hard for her to monitor the kids who chose to play volleyball. She looked the other way while they hung out under the stands, drinking and smoking pot. Surely she could smell it, but she never bothered them.

The same woman taught health class in the afternoon. John got certified for CPR and learned how to fill out job applications that the teacher gave to owners of local businesses. That's how John ended up working at a health spa restaurant.

He soon experienced the benefits of a job well done when he used his wages to buy a moped to get around town. It topped out at 38 mph and was completely rusted out, but he felt like he was flying.

Norma came to visit at Christmas. She decided that John wasn't so bad after all, maybe because she was getting good reports from his aunt. She asked him to come home. He told her he wanted to stay. He was just starting to feel a part of his new town and starting to make real friends. He had a job that he liked, and his boss appreciated his hard work. But the fact that Norma seemed to genuinely miss him was a powerful pull.

He finally relented. Her nostalgia was all dried up by the time the four-day bus ride was over. *Damned no good kid… you stole from my sister… you're just like your no good father… you little bastard.*

Her rejection and abuse drove him back out into the streets, running away, getting in trouble. The vicious cycle that had faded into the distance in California was back with a vengeance.

It might be tempting to write John off after hearing about his troubled teenage years. He was selfish in his youth. He made terrible decisions. But there were failures on the part of the institutions that he butted up against that contributed to the path his life took.

When he stopped going to school in junior high, no one at his school raised a red flag. His situation was never brought to the attention of Child Protective Services, though neighbors and probably school personnel, knew that he was regularly beaten by an alcoholic mother.

When he stole the first car, the authorities never investigated his home life. No one asked why such a young person was stealing so many cars. No one worried what kind of opportunities John would have later in life if he only had an eighth-grade education—no one encouraged him to come back to school.

John's juvenile cases were punished by a system that was outdated by today's standards. The facilities that he was sent to engaged in methods that have been exposed by current research to significantly increase recidivism. These programs did not deter kids who completed their curriculums from committing crime; instead, they functioned like finishing schools for future outlaws.

Bootcamp programs and "scared straight" ideologies have been shown to produce results that are the exact opposite of the outcomes they claimed they would achieve. These programs, designed with purely punitive goals, did not deter youth from developing a permanent criminal lifestyle; they solidified youthful offenders into adult offenders—making young people see themselves as career criminals and nothing else.

Some states have eliminated detention and incarceration for non-violent youth offenders, but John was locked up multiple times before he became an adult, without any therapeutic intervention or organized compassionate component in the institutional programming. These systems could have mentored him—could have helped a troubled teen like him turn a corner to a more positive path. He simply got pushed further along the destructive path that he was already on.

Another relevant factor to John's behavior is what is now known about brain development. Research shows that the human brain does not fully mature until the age of 25. Abuse, neglect and brain injury can impact brain development and delay the maturation process. John Aslin was subjected to the first two and his multiple car/bike/lawn dart accidents likely resulted in the third.

Research about brain development has caused many states to modify their treatment of juvenile offenders to align with realistic expectations for young people based on their age. Science-based projections of maturity levels have greatly improved the effectiveness of the juvenile justice system in many states, but this was not the case in the 1980s, when John was cycling through detention centers. The California legislature was so compelled by recent brain research that it mandated that all life sentences handed out to anyone under the age of 23 be reviewed.

Other states, including Michigan, have fought against reviewing cases where actual juveniles—those under the age of 18—were handed out life sentences. In Michigan, someone like John, who was 21 when he committed his crime, does not have an opportunity to have his case reviewed to see if his brain was mature enough to hold him accountable for murder that carries a life sentence.

Another factor that cannot be ignored is that John became dependent on alcohol at the age of fourteen. John was intoxicated much of the time when he stole cars. Consuming alcohol to the point of chemical dependence when his brain was still developing must have had an impact on the health of John's brain.

The impact of John's childhood experiences—physical, emotional, social, chemical and otherwise—must be taken into account when judging his behavior and the choices he made as a young man. He grew up in the badlands of childhood in almost every way. His upbringing did not provide a solid ground upon which to build a basis for making decisions that were moral and just. He developed into a moral and just man later, but too late to save himself from himself.

Big Shoes Do Not Get Filled
Lapeer, Michigan
October 28, 1942

Lapeer County Press

The community was shocked this morning to learn of the sudden and unexpected death of Dr. Fred R. Hanna, medical superintendent of the Lapeer State Home. Dr. Hanna suffered a heart attack last evening at about 11 o'clock and died shortly afterward. He was only 42 years old. Dr. Hanna had capably administered the affairs of the Lapeer State Home, the largest institution of its kind in the world, for the last five years. His death will be keenly felt by all who knew him and scores of friends mourn his loss. There was always a feeling of cordial cooperation between the Home and downtown Lapeer under Dr. Hanna's administration.

Michigan Home and Training School
Lapeer, Michigan
Spring 1943

"Pony and I are leaving tomorrow." Alberta found Fred alone in the library doing his homework. She whispered so softly he could barely hear her. He packed up his books and followed her outside. They walked away from the buildings, where they could be assured of privacy.

"Is Doris going with you?"

"No, she won't leave Violet. Violet won't leave the boys—so Doris is staying. Are you sure you won't come?"

"You know I can't leave the younger kids here with no one to protect them. Where will you go?"

"Pony's been saving up. Doris gave us a little that she had. I've got some money too." Alberta had an evening job in town at a store. "We've got enough to get to Detroit and get a place. Pony's a hard worker. He'll find something. Me too. We'll be okay. I'll write you. We'll figure out some way for you to write me back."

"Do you need me to do anything?"

"No, we've planned it all out. Pony's got a friend in town who'll drive us to Flint and then we're taking a bus. All I need you to do is keep looking out for everyone until I figure how to get you free. They can't keep you here forever. I'll get you out and I'll build something for the rest of you for when I do. And I'll try to find Ma." Alberta had worked herself up—the declarations came out in a stream of determination tinted by anguish.

Fred pulled bills out of his pocket and peeled off four singles. It had taken him a long time to save it, but for now, Alberta would need it more than he.

Michigan Home and Training School, Lapeer, Michigan Spring 1944

Fred noticed the car parked on the street a half block down from the school. As he turned the corner, walking in the other direction, he heard the engine start. The car crept behind him for several blocks before he turned and faced it. The sun glared off the windshield; he couldn't see inside.

The passenger's door opened and a set of high heels stepped to the pavement. A young woman was attached to them and her head was tipped forward as she exited the vehicle, a hat obscuring her face. When she stood up, Fred was overcome with joy. "Albie, you did it!"

Doris had received one post card from their runaway sister in the past year and all it had said was, "I'm alive." It carried no return address and had been sent to Doris' job in town.

"They sent all of my letters back to the post office. I'm sorry that you all must have been worried. But Pony and I are doing real good. They tried to make him join the army, but there was something about his back that kept him out. We both got factory jobs. I'm saving up to get you a lawyer."

The day Fred turned 18, Doris brought fresh cream sticks home from the bakery. The Aslins met near the pond. She spread out a blanket from the laundry. Fred laid in the middle, content in the rare family moment as his siblings sat around him. They enjoyed the fresh pastries that Doris had overstuffed with the cream filling that oozed down their fingers; they took care to lick every drop.

"That was so good. Thank you."

"You're welcome…. you remind me of Pa today"

Fred sighed with contentment. "That makes me happy."

John sighed and pushed out his words in sadness. "I can barely remember what Pa looked like. If I didn't have my drawings from when I was little, I would completely lose him. And Ma."

"Violet looks just like Ma. Just look at her." Violet made a noise that sounded like a smile.

That night, Fred had a dream. Fox ran behind Raccoon, barking frantically. Fred thought he was chasing her, but he realized Fox was trying to get her attention. The scene shifted to slow motion and the view spun until Raccoon was facing Fred with Fox behind her. She cradled her children, but they fell out of her arms and dropped into a pool of water. She tried to grab them as they sunk under the surface, but they were out of reach.

Fox held her tightly to stop her from jumping in after them. "You can't swim," said Fox as he struggled to hold her. As Raccoon thrashed around, trying to break free, an owl burst out of the water, with Raccoon's babies hanging from his claws; it flew off into the night sky.

Herman had a lot to say about that dream. He was fervent in pressing his conclusion on Fred. "You gotta be alert. Something bad is stirring up. That dream is telling you that people are going to deceive you, trick you into making a bad decision. The ancestors are trying to warn you. Be on guard, son."

Superintendent Randal Cooper ran things by The Book. The Book had been written by John Harvey Kellogg. The Book said that residents of the Home were to be sterilized upon their 18th birthday. He reviewed the file of a resident who turned 18 a few weeks before.

Fred Aslin had done well at the Home. He was set to graduate from the high school in town with high grades; his behavior was outstanding and he was a talented musician. In spite of all that, there was a court order in place that judged him feeble-minded. Under policy, he had to be prevented from fathering any offspring. According to The Book, there were enough Indians in the world already.

Fred Aslin waited in the hallway until Dr. Randal Cooper arrived. The young man had an intelligent air about him and a solid handshake as he greeted the doctor. "It's been a few years since I've been in this office, Sir. I used to visit Dr. Hanna."

"Come on in and have a seat." Dr. Cooper picked up Fred's file and looked it over, commenting on a few things here and there. "I have some paperwork here that I would like you to sign."

"What is it?"

"It is a consent form for surgery."

"Surgery?" Fred waited for an answer.

The doctor dropped his eyes down to the file and avoided looking at him. "We just want to make sure you don't get any girls in trouble—in the family way. It's just a simple procedure."

"Can I see the paperwork?"

The doctor handed him a piece of paper. Fred read it carefully. "I'll need to think on this."

"Well, you need to think quickly. We have rules and regulations—we need to get this procedure done quickly."

Fred made mental note of the procedure listed on the form: "Vasectomy." He headed to the library and pulled out an encyclopedia. He was horrified. They wanted to cut him in an area that no one should ever be cut, as far as he was concerned. "Doris, look what they want to do to me." He pointed to the illustration in the book.

The Home didn't offer any education on issues of reproduction, but there was talk among the residents. He thought he understood the basics.

"Why do they want to do that?"

Fred was distracted as he read further. "Dr. Cooper said they don't want me to put any girls on the nest. This says that vasectomy causes sterilization. Do you know what that is?"

Doris shook her head and grabbed the volume that would hold that word. She found the right page. "It says that it's a process that kills life forms." Her face turned white. "Are they trying to kill you?"

"Let me see that." She handed him the book and he read it carefully. "There's another meaning here—intentionally making it so someone can't reproduce." Fred had already grabbed a dictionary and opened it up the page that held that word. He skimmed numerous meanings and found the dangerous one that was coming for him—produce an offspring or breed. "They want to stop me from making any kids."

Doris was alarmed. "Don't you sign those papers!"

"I won't. Dammit. I sure won't."

Fred knocked on the doctor's office door the next day. "Are you here to sign the papers?"

"No Sir. I won't be signing them."

"Well, I guess we'll have to get your mother to sign them."

Fred's felt anger rise in him like a flash of fire. In all these years, no one had ever told them if their mother was alive or dead. "What do you know about my ma?" he said defensively.

"I know where she lives. I know that she's a ward of the state. I know she'll sign these papers, so why don't you just make it easy for everyone and sign them yourself."

The mention of his mother threw Fred off-kilter. He usually kept his head down, didn't sass back or draw attention to himself, but he was awash with indignation, outrage. "I guess you waited too long. I'm a man now. Don't need a parent to decide what I will or won't do with my life."

"Well, I guess that's the end of it then. I'll make sure your file reflects that you're refusing treatment."

Adulthood The Eighties

Disco was dying or maybe it was dead. John rode the New Wave, trading in his platform dance shoes for Adidas and his audacious disco apparel for peg-legged jeans and leather jackets. John's nights were full of girls and fighting, hanging around bars and dancing his pain away. When he was tired, he crashed at a friend's house, not far from where Norma lived.

During the day, he attended adult education, hoping to get a GED and possibly a legitimate job. Sometimes he went across the street to hear his neighbor's band. Jeff Bland, or "Blando," who would go on to sing and play lead guitar for Slaughter, held concerts for his local band, Black Satin, in his basement. John would show up with a case of beer and be welcomed in.

That was where he met Carrie Murphy, the sweetest girl, to this day, he has ever known. If only he had been equipped to hold on to Carrie—it might have saved his life.

Classes were over for the summer. John felt buoyant. He spotted several long thin boxes that were stacked outside the door of the classroom building. He kicked them lightly. They seemed empty and looked abandoned. They were a perfect size for some things he wanted to organize in the garage, so he took them.

When he opened them later, they were full of carnations. He had inadvertently stolen the flowers for the graduation ceremony that was scheduled later that evening. He put them back in the car and thought about driving back to the school, admitting his mistake, but as he turned up a nearby street, he saw Carrie's house. He made a rash decision and pulled over. He scooped the flowers into a single box and walked to the porch.

"Hello, Mrs. Murphy. Is your daughter home?"

"Hello hoodlum."

John never knew if Mrs. Murphy was joking.

"Carrie's not here."

"Could you give her these?"

Mrs. Murphy peered skeptically into the box and then a look of surprise came over her. "I guess you're not so bad after all."

Carrie called him the next morning. "What were those flowers for?"

"Nice people deserve nice things."

They made plans to see a movie that night. Old Man Bland rented out his Cadillac, so John was able to arrive in style. Night after night he came back; he would pick Carrie up (without a Cadillac but she didn't seem to care) and wouldn't bring her home until the night was spent.

Carrie was a spot of light in his life. She was kind; she loved to laugh. Being with her made him content, but he really had no idea what it meant to be in a relationship. For him, it was spending time with Carrie, but the time was filled with sex, drinking, smoking a little pot and keeping things light.

He and Carrie developed a pattern—after he picked her up, they would smoke a little pot as they drove to the party store to pick up a case of beer. They went to somebody's house, where a group of freeloaders, whom he called friends, would be waiting for the beer that John could be counted on to provide.

Being the big shot who provided nightly liquid entertainment to all fed his insecurity. If he failed to bring booze, would he still have friends? Little did these "friends" know that he paid the tab with the proceeds from a steady string of break ins.

They were out of beer. The crowd for Blando's basement show was bigger than usual. John stayed across the street with his friend, Roy. He knew Roy had tapped a keg earlier. He rinsed out some 2-liter pop bottles, hoping to bring them back to Blando's full of beer.

Roy was passed out on the bathroom floor in a pool of vomit, so it took longer than expected to get back to the party across the street—he called another guy to help him lift Roy into his bed. He took some time to take Roy's shoes off and clean him up, but he was eager to get back to the party—to be the hero who brings beer and to see Carrie. She was supposed to show up.

By the time he got back to the party, the numbers in the basement had dwindled.

"Hey man, where's Blando?"

"Upstairs with Carrie."

Fury washed over John. He sat on the couch, stewing. *You assholes— you think this is funny?* He felt betrayed by both of them. No one was paying attention when he took Blando's Les Paul guitar and Peavey amplifier and walked out the door. John drove straight to a pawn shop and traded them for cash.

He went back to the party. Blando and Carrie were making out on the very couch where he had hatched his revenge plot—but it wasn't his Carrie. His Carrie had been home all night with a fever.

John was awakened from his hang-over by a heavy knock at the door. He was groggy until he opened up to a pissed-off detective. Then he was wide awake. He hung his head and admitted why he had taken the guitar.

"I'll tell you what, you get them back to me within 24 hours and we can pretend this whole thing never happened."

He didn't have all the money anymore, so he had to steal to make things right with Blando. John apologized, but their friendship was never the same. He had lashed out at a friend, with no regard to the damage it would inflict. He felt ashamed by his inadequacies. He moved back to Norma's house. Seeing Blando across the street on the regular was awkward as hell.

Summer flew by. Starting adult ed slowed John's partying, but he wanted nothing more than to see Carrie every night. Usually, they would pop rented movies in the VCR but never see the ends as they made out deliriously. Sometimes they went to a bar to dance.

Things came to a crashing halt when Carrie climbed into the car one night, tears streaming down her cheeks. "I'm pregnant. My dad wants to meet you."

John turned the car off and solemnly walked up to the house. Mr. Murphy wasn't home from work yet. Carrie went to her room to fix her make-up. John sat on the couch, twisting his shirt in his hands. Mrs. Murphy made small talk. "John, you go to adult ed, right?"

"Yes, Ma'am."

"My friend goes there. Funny story I heard. Someone stole the graduation flowers. Isn't that a funny story?"

John's face went blank.

Mrs. Murphy laughed. "You thug—don't worry. I won't tell my daughter you stole her heart with stolen flowers."

A few minutes later, Mr. Murphy came in the back door. "He's here?"

Mrs. Murphy pointed John to the kitchen. He nervously walked toward the deep voice. He had only seen Mr. Murphy from a distance, but the man always looked mean. John's heart pounded as he waited for an attack, verbally or literally. Carrie's dad turned and went back outside.

As John followed him, he wondered if he was stumbling into an ass-kicking. Mr. Murphy sat in the driver's seat of his van. John tried not to be obvious as checked the back seat for an ambush before he got in.

As Mr. Murphy backed out of the driveway, he tossed John a bag of weed. "So you're the infamous Johnny Aslin. Roll us one. I guess we should get to know each other now that there's a baby on the way."

John's hands shook as he rolled a fat blunt and handed it to the old man. Mr. Murphy took a deep hit. A smile washed over his face. He handed it back. "Go ahead."

"I stopped smoking a few months ago."

"Sure you did. I don't care if you smoke in front of me."

"No thank you, Sir."

"You still drink?"

"Unfortunately."

"If you can quit smoking, you can quit drinking. That's what you need to do from what I hear. Buckle down. Get your GED. I might be able to get you into the shop." Mr. Murphy worked at the Buick plant. Working there would be boring as hell, but all John's money troubles would be over.

People who worked the line, especially with overtime, could afford to drive nice cars and buy second homes on lakes in Northern Michigan.

John nodded in agreement but giving up drinking was much more complicated than giving up marijuana. He decided to stop smoking pot and that was it—he hadn't even been tempted to take it up, even under pressure from his friends. But drinking was an itch that needed to be scratched on a daily basis.

This was the first of many words of encouragement John received from the older man but they came along too late to sink in. John's life patterns had been solidly set by years of emotional neglect and the lack of a male role model.

John would learn that though Mr. Murphy looked like a ball-buster, Carrie got her sweetness and kindness from her dad. Mr. Murphy treated John with respect; it grew to be mutual, the more that John got to know him.

When Norma found out that there was a baby on the way, she blew up. "You stupid bastard. I feel sorry for that kid." She kicked John out and took back the car she had loaned him.

As he careened toward fatherhood, his life became more unstable than ever. Though Linda let John stay in her spare room and borrow her car to see Carrie, she lived on the other side of the county. John's life was disrupted. He could have buckled down, gotten his GED and focused on transforming himself into a man who held a legitimate job and took care of the baby that was on the way.

Instead, he spotted Linda's wedding ring on a dish in the window above the kitchen sink—she must have taken it off when she did the dishes—and he took it. He didn't plan to steal it—he just wanted to show it to Carrie, make her see that he understood, in his limited way, how serious things had become. He wanted her to think that he had gotten it for her, but he planned to put it back in the dish before Linda even knew it was gone.

John was meeting Carrie at a party. A kid that he didn't know well gave him a ride. On the way, John was giddy with excitement about the ring. He pulled it out, put it on his pinky and waved it so that it caught some light from on-coming headlights. "Look what I got my girl."

"That's a nice one. How much that set you back?"

John shrugged and put the ring back in his coat pocket. He had been at the party for about an hour and Carrie hadn't shown up yet. He went into the kitchen to call her. "I didn't know how to get ahold of you. I've been throwing up."

"You want me to come see you?"

"Sure." John grabbed his jacket and looked for his ride. The kid was gone and, he soon discovered, so was the ring.

John avoided Linda the next morning as long as he could, but she stopped him as he was sneaking out the door. "John." She waited until he looked her in the eye. "You seen my wedding ring?"

"No."

"Oh, John, how could you?" She knew him well enough to know that his denial was fake. "I can't let this go."

This led to John's first stint in the adult system—a 90-day stay in jail for stealing from Linda, the only family member who had always been there for him. He felt like a failure and a jerk.

"Aslin, wake up. I got some good news and some bad news." John was groggy, but he sat up and tried to focus on what his probation officer was saying. "The good news is that you've been cleared to go to New Paths, a halfway house, so you're about to get out of this cell. The bad news is that your son was born last night and you were here instead of there."

John already felt like a failure as a father and his kid wasn't even a day old. His probation officer took him up to the hospital on the way to New Paths. He came, empty handed, and held his child for a little while before the officer told him it was time to go.

He didn't have much to offer that baby. He had never had a dad of his own and no man had stepped up to fill that gap for him. He knew how to drink—he was pretty good at that—and he knew how to steal—though he should have grasped sooner that he wasn't very good at that at all—but he didn't know how to love and cherish the baby he held, how to help that child become a better person than his father was.

Maybe he could have learned, but he never got the chance to test himself on that measure. So he bought some diapers, helped Carrie sign up for welfare and thought he was stepping up to fulfill his duties. Carrie soon realized she wanted more for herself, for her son, than John was able to give. She moved on and John spiraled.

"Johnny, Pretty One isn't doing so good. You have to take her to the vet." John drove to his mother's house in a borrowed car, worried about his oldest friend.

Pretty One had lived a long time. He thought about all the times when he would lay in his bed, miserable over a beating or scared by one of his mother's drunken rages, and Pretty One would comfort him until he fell asleep. She would still be there, tucked under his arm, when he woke up.

Now the regal, Siamese cat couldn't walk and had stopped eating. He gently knelt down to pet her soft fur and a flicker of recognition perked up her ears. He gently placed her in a box lined with a blanket. This would be their final adventure together.

After he left the vet's office, alone, he sat in the car and cried like a baby. That cat had always made him feel loved, a rare experience for John Aslin.

When he got out of New Paths, John stayed with Amy, but when he "borrowed" her sports car and smashed it up, he lost that landing spot. The State of Michigan gave him a place to stay for two years after he got caught stealing a truck.

His selfishness and uncaring attitude finally caught up with him. His first stint in prison happened after John's ride ran out of gas just as they were arriving at a party. Some guys that John had recently fought showed up, so he left on foot. He was drunk, walking home in the cold, and decided he wanted to get home faster.

He slipped through an open side door of a random garage, looking for a bicycle. Instead, he found a nice truck with the keys in the ignition. He couldn't find the garage door opener, so he threw the truck in reverse and drove right through the garage door. The large aluminum door stuck to the back of the truck as he screeched down the driveway. It didn't fall off until he backed into the street, then accelerated forward down the road. The sound must have caused quite a fright to the owners, asleep in their bed.

John drove the truck into a swamp near his destination; he threw the keys in the water. It was a short walk to his friend Eddy's house. They split a six-pack of Budweiser, then Eddy was ready for some fun. "Man, I wish we had some wheels. I met these girls that we could pick up."

"I've got wheels. Let's go." They were a bit of a mess after they dug around in the swamp to find the keys, but soon they were on the road. John honked when they pulled up to a small house.

Two pretty blondes came out. "Hey guys. We need some smokes. Can you take us?"

The four of them squeezed into the front bench seat. One of the young women said, "Wow. It's about time someone had a nice ride. Let's go get some refreshments."

When they were leaving the party store, John looked back over his shoulder to tell a joke as he walked to the parking lot. He had no time to run from the officers standing next to the truck. He wasn't a kid anymore so his antics were punished more severely—that's how he found himself in prison when he should have been taking care of his son.

When he got out of prison in the spring of 1984, John was only 21 years old and all of his bridges had been burned. No one who had a blood connection to him was willing to let him crash at their house, so he was sleeping on a friend's couch—actually a friend's grandmother's couch. He tried to stay out as much as possible to keep from being under foot. But it wouldn't be long before he had another place to stay—with the State of Michigan—for good.

Adulthood: Permanent Damage
Lapeer, Michigan
1943

They came for Fred in the middle of the night. Vernal Johnson placed a hand over his mouth to muffle Fred's cries and laid across

Fred's chest, pinning him to the bed. Two other men held his arms. A nurse stood by with a needle and plunged it into his leg. The room went black.

When Fred woke up, he was sore in places where a person shouldn't be sore. He laid in bed with a vague sense of dread. Dr. Cooper entered the ward but was down at the other end of the room. Fred felt the rage of every indignity he had suffered at the hands of the Home boil up like molten lava in his throat. He spewed it out in a scream of rage. "What did you do to me?"

Dr. Cooper didn't react to the outburst as he finished examining a patient several beds away. Then he sauntered down to where Fred lay in anguish, an admonishing look on his face. "Just that simple procedure we discussed."

"I never signed those papers."

"Your guardian is responsible for your welfare. He went to court and asked the judge to sign them."

"What guardian? I've never met any guardian."

"He doesn't have to meet with you. Your file establishes that you're feeble-minded, so all he has to do is tell the court you're unable to make your own decisions. The law allows the judge to make them for you on the guardian's recommendation."

"It ain't right, what you did. If that guardian met me, he would've known I wasn't feeble-minded."

"It's all for the best. There isn't a place for your kind anymore, so it's better if your line stops now."

Michigan Home and Training School,
Lapeer, Michigan
1947

Fred stayed. Ted, John and Violet were still minors. He could not bear to leave them behind, though his anger toward the Home was banked like hot coals across his soul and he yearned for a new life. They had cut into his physical body, but the powerlessness he felt when it was over cut deeply into his psyche. He was not willing to play by the rules in the same way that he had before.

As long as he was there, the guards would leave the Aslins alone because they sensed the new threat that he posed to anyone who meant his family harm. The staff knew something in Fred had shifted; he could not be pushed too hard unless they were willing to risk the consequences.

When Fred returned from his second vision quest, there were no beatings. He sought out Herman and took him for a walk. They stopped out near the pond and Fred placed the older man on the grass so they could talk.

Herman detected a sliver of peace in Fred's demeanor that had not been there for a while. "Did you see your father?"

Fred nodded. "Tell me what you saw."

"It was the same cave as before. When I got there, Bear was digging around in the ground outside. She told me she had found me some strong medicine. She asked me to open my hands and my heart, then she did a smudging."

"Did you smell it?"

"It was sage."

"That's good medicine."

"After Bear cleansed me, I walked to a fire deep in the cave. Snake was coiled in my path. I tried to step around him, but he bit my foot. Fox shooed him away. The wound swarmed with dragonflies. Snake caught some in his jaws. They looked dead until Wolf stood up from behind the fire. He was fierce. He howled at Snake. Snake opened his jaws and released the dragonflies. They came back to life and landed on my shoulders. Hummingbird came and asked me to follow her. She flew straight up. When I looked up, there was an open sky and I floated above the ground. Wolf leaped over the fire and grabbed my foot, where Snake had bitten me. Wolf licked the wound and it healed. I floated back to Earth and followed Wolf to the fire."

Herman had been listening carefully. "The ancestors had a lot to say. This is what I can tell you. Don't be afraid of Snake. Snake is telling you that you have been ignoring something important. Snake bit you to get your attention. He's telling you to take care of your business. Dragonfly represents change. They start out living in the water and then become flyers."

Herman paused to think. "Something is going to change for you and at first it might seem like a bad change, but it will turn out good. Whatever it is, Wolf will be watching over you. Hummingbird was telling you that soon you will be free, but Wolf didn't think it was time yet, so he called you back."

Fred was quiet. It was a lot to consider.

Fred at 21
Michigan Home and Training School,
Lapeer, Michigan
1948

Dr. Cooper left at the end 1943, but nothing changed since his right-hand man, Adolph Rehn, took his place and oversaw the sterilization of two Aslin men and one Aslin woman. The Home refused to release the siblings, who were now adults, but Dr. Rehn couldn't argue with paperwork issued by the US Army.

Fred was released without fanfare. Leaving John behind was hard for Fred. In a few years, Doris, Violet and John would quietly walk away from the Home to Alberta's waiting car. Before that, Peter would follow Fred into the service and Ted would become a marine.

But Fred didn't know any of that when he left. A few days before he was scheduled to go, Fred led his three younger brothers to a small clearing deep into some nearby woods. Fred and Peter had set up an altar and built a small sweat lodge. The older boys focus was to create protection for John.

John carried his medicine bag—it held hundreds of colorful tobacco ties. Fred conducted a ceremony that held a mishmash of traditional elements. Fred laid out a ring of tobacco ties, smudged John with burning cedar, placed hot stones inside the hut and poured water for a sweat.

Then John stepped into the medicine ring and his brothers prayed over him, singing to the ancestors to come to his aid, watch over him and protect him from evil intents. The brothers were solemn as they returned to their cottage.

Fred was given a bus ticket to Detroit, compliments of the U.S. Army; from there he was processed into the service. The recruiter asked him if wanted leave to spend time with family before he reported for duty, but what he really wanted was to see the ocean. He stayed at Alberta's home for a couple of days before presenting himself to the office in downtown Detroit. Once he was processed, Uncle Sam gave Fred a bus ticket to Fort Benning, Georgia and permission to delay reporting for two weeks.

He traveled far from everything he knew—he had been born across the water from the beginning of US-23 in Mackinaw City and traveled that highway all the way to its southern end before he began this new phase of his life so that he could feel warm sand between his toes and dip them in the sea.

Fred was too excited to sleep as the bus headed south. The land swelled in gentle curves. For a boy who had been confined to Michigan his entire life, and to a Michigan institution for half, in a single long bus trip, he added Ohio, Kentucky, Tennessee, Virginia, North Carolina, Georgia and Florida to the list of places he had seen.

When the bus rolled across the Ohio River and picked up a new driver, Fred got to hear some music that was a perfect soundtrack for his journey—Hank Williams, Gene Autry, Tex Williams and Earnest Tubb made him feel the potential of the open road.

The accents got slower and twangier as he moved south; he never imagined that he would be met with kindness from total strangers again and again—a sandwich from an elderly woman heading south to see some grandkids; at a stop near the Virginia state line, a soldier who had served in Italy during the last war purchased him a Coca-Cola. The same man slipped him a few dollars when he disembarked in Georgia and wished him luck.

These strangers could not see what Michigan had claimed he was. Life in the outside world might be okay. Fred's army ticket did not get him all the way to his destination, but his luck continued as he hitched a series of rides until he found himself walking in the dark toward a subtle roar that grew louder and louder.

He didn't even have to see where he was going. His body knew where he needed to be. When he got to the end, he sat on the sand and waited for the sun to peak its nose over the edge of the world. He was treated to the most beautiful sight he had seen since he was a boy.

No one was around. Fred sprinted to the water line, stripped down to his undergarments and jumped into the foamy wetness, whooping with joy. He dove under the water and came up, his eyes burning. He wasn't sure if it was due to the salt water or tears.

After he spent some of his excitement, he floated on his back completely at peace for the first time since he was a boy swimming in Lake Michigan with his father. When the sun was high enough in the sky that he feared being seen and possibly chastised for not being properly clothed, he returned to the beach, dressed and found a small restaurant where he ate a breakfast that he would not soon forget— thick bacon, buttery grits, fried eggs, homemade toast and coffee thick enough to eat with a spoon.

He spent the rest of the day snoozing on the beach and repeated his routine for a few days before heading back to real life. He was armed with a pocket full of shells and a large shark tooth that he intended to turn into protective medicine. He felt ready to face whatever lay ahead.

John Eric at 21
The Trial

December 11, 1984 was a cold day. The fog outside matched the fog in John's brain. He was taken from his cell at the city lock up and walked to the Genesee County Circuit Courthouse across the street.

Before the jury was brought in, John's attorney made the Honorable Philip E. Elliott aware that Glenn Stephens had given unsubstantiated testimony at the Preliminary Exam; he wanted to prevent that same thing from happening in front of the jury. The assistant prosecutor handling the case agreed that Glenn Stephens needed to be kept on a short leash.

The legal professionals also discussed the jury instruction for Felony Murder. "Jury instructions" refers to the information given to jurors to help them decide guilt or innocence. John's attorney warned the court that he would be quoting the "standard instruction"—language that had been written for statewide use in an effort to standardize outcomes.

The judge said something that would come back to haunt John. "I don't usually read verbatim any of the standard instructions. I give my own instructions peculiar to a case." Would the judge's misguided idea that he knew better than the legislature, who had commissioned panels to carefully craft the language of jury instructions, be John's undoing? Would his arrogance cost John in the end?

The judge read the instruction for murder to the lawyers. "For murder you must find that the defendant either intended to kill or that he intended to do great bodily harm or that he committed a wanton and willful act, the natural tendency of which is to cause death or great bodily harm. There must be strong and plain likelihood that death or serious bodily harm will result and the defendant must have willfully and wantonly disregarded the knowledge of the possible consequences of death or serious injury."

"The theory of the prosecution isn't that Mr. Aslin intended to kill Mrs. Stephens but that he committed a wanton and willful act, the natural tendency of which is to cause death or great bodily harm." The judge paused. "I'll read that and give an example. The best one I can think of is based on the recent train station bombings in Montreal when the Pope was visiting." He explained some details of that scenario. "Now that we've got that settled, let's bring the jury up."

Eight men and four women soon sat in the jury box, listening to the judge explain the case. He told them that John was being accused of killing or murdering Ella Stephens while perpetrating a robbery, that she died as a result of a fright or excitement when her home was broken into.

He explained that murder requires a certain state of mind that can be broken into three types: intent to kill, intent to inflict great bodily harm where death results or the commission of a willful and wanton act, the natural tendency of which is to cause death or great bodily harm. The judge explained that the third type was the one most applicable in John's case, but he worded it in a confusing way, mixing strong probability with mere possibility.

"There must be a strong and plain likelihood that death or serious bodily harm will result and that a defendant must have willfully and wantonly disregarded the knowledge of the possible consequences of death or serious injury." He said "possible" when he should have said "probable."

"Perhaps you've read that shortly before the Pope visited Canada somebody, a terrorist I suppose, planted a bomb in a locker in a railroad station and set it off. Three people were walking close to the locker when the bomb went off and they died. Even if the person that planted the bomb did not intend to kill anyone or even to cause great bodily harm to anyone, the deaths would be the result of a willful and wanton act, the natural tendency of which is to cause death or great bodily harm—by setting off a bomb in a public place."

"Another example of this type of murder is setting fire to a building, knowing that people were in it, although they expected the people would be able to get out. If someone was asleep in a building that was deliberately arsoned and died because they were unable to get out, that could be another example of this sort of murder."

On a statewide level, the standard jury instructions were meant to stand alone—no examples need be provided for the jury. The examples that the judge added likely confused the issues of the case; the jury may have thought that he was lumping the circumstances of John's case in with these more serious and extreme scenarios rather than drawing a distinction between them.

He added a single sentence to present John's side. "It's the theory of the defense that this death in this case was accidental."

The court conducted Voire Dire of the jurors, a process intended to weed out anyone out who may have preconceived ideas or biases about the case. Jurors were asked to disclose if they knew any of the witnesses or had personally been a crime victim. They were asked if they had a family member who had been robbed or killed or if they had close connections to any police officers. After they sorted through potential candidates and dismissed everyone who had a reason that they could not serve, the jury was seated. The show began.

The assistant prosecutor told the jurors they needed to use the evidence to answer three questions. First, was John the person who kicked in the door, robbed Ella Stephens and knocked her down? Second, did those actions cause her death? Finally, did John have the state of mind to make him guilty of murder—"Did he intentionally or knowingly create a high degree of risk of death or great bodily harm with knowledge of the consequences? Did he willfully disregard the likelihood that the natural tendency of his acts was and would be the cause of death or great bodily harm in kicking in this woman's door and knocking her down?" He asserted that John had the state of mind of a murderer when he "willfully disregarded" the consequences of kicking in the door and knocking Ella Stephens down, "knowing what those consequences could and would be and choosing to go ahead and burglarize this woman's home anyway."

The essence of this argument is the assertion that John Aslin contemplated burglarizing this particular person, acknowledged that she was old and had a heart condition and was aware of the possibility or likelihood that his break in would cause her to have a heart attack, then die. The assistant prosecutor's argument implicitly included all of those mental steps—that John was aware of the risk of death that his actions would pose to Ella Stephens and made a distinct decision to move forward and rob her in spite of that risk.

The assistant prosecutor essentially asserted that John—a young, intoxicated thief with an eighth grade education—had first, actual knowledge of Ella Stephens' heart condition and then the medical knowledge and analytical skills to know what action could trigger a medical episode and then went ahead and acted to create those circumstances without regard for her very life. It was a ridiculous assertion.

John's attorney emphasized to the jury what the evidence would NOT show. John did not beat Ella Stephens. John did not hold her at knifepoint or gunpoint. John was being charged with a plain robbery—not an armed robbery. There was no weapon of any kind. Ella Stephens was not tied up, handcuffed, slapped or hit. Ella Stephens did not say she was pushed or shoved or threatened. She was knocked down.

There would not be any evidence to suggest that Mrs. Stephens was physically attacked—no cuts, bruises or lacerations. He told the jury that they would see photos that would show the back door kicked in and a small table overturned near where a phone was separated from the wall. There would not be pictures of any other disturbances, no ransacking or furniture thrown about. Just an overturned end table.

The jury would need to decide if Mrs. Stephens was knocked down intentionally or accidentally, but the fact that she did not have any bruising on her body and the fact that the house was not significantly disheveled points toward it being an accident. He noted that there was a jar of money near where the table was overturned that was not taken. He said that factor should help them decide about John's state of mind.

John's attorney told the jury how John sought out Marybell Smith, asking how to seek forgiveness, that he wanted to be forgiven before he knew that Ella Stephens died. He told the jury they needed to decide whether this was a violent encounter where John knew his actions could lead to death or if it was simply a messed-up robbery where an accidental death occurred.

Robert Edwards, Mrs. Stephens' across-the-street neighbor, was the first witness called to testify. He said that Ella Stephens said she had been robbed; she appeared "petrified" and "disoriented." He noted that he asked her, "Was it a black man?" but she said the robber was white.

John's attorney had Mr. Edwards confirm that Ella's clothing was not torn; he did not see blood or any other indication that she was physically harmed.

John Henry, the next-door neighbor who allowed Ella to be brought into his home, was next. He said she had been "very feeble" and upset, "shaking just like somebody frozen with a chatter." He said she was gasping for air as she lay on the floor, waiting for the ambulance to arrive. Irene Henry gave a similar account, emphasizing that Ella was "as white as a sheet."

Stanley Hissong added a few new details to the story. He said Ella was very short—about four and a half feet tall—and she told him that a tall white man broke into her house. She pointed about a foot over her head. He confirmed that Ella said she was knocked down but that her clothes were not torn or disheveled.

Genesee County Sheriff's Deputy Daniel Atkinson was the paramedic who responded to the call. He checked Ella for vital signs, pulse and respiration, and found nothing. He began advanced life support procedures which included intubation and CPR. He worked on her for twenty to thirty minutes, but she never regained consciousness. She was dead on arrival when she reached Hurley Hospital. Deputy Atkinson actively looked for evidence of injury on Ella Stephens and found nothing.

Eric King, a Mt. Morris Police Officer, was asked to describe what he observed in her home; he said it appeared that there had been some kind of scuffle.

John's attorney objected, pointing out that he was drawing conclusions rather than merely describing what he observed. He essentially confirmed that there was some disturbed furniture near the phone and the back door was kicked in, but that was all. His input concluded the testimony for the first day.

The next morning, Mt Morris Detective Patrick South was the opening witness. He was a nemesis of sorts to John, chasing after him since he was a kid. He identified the photographs of the home that had been taken by the Michigan State Police Crime Lab. He informed the jury that a palm print had been lifted from the kitchen table near Mrs. Stephens' purse. He confirmed that the home had not been excessively disturbed and that there were delicate figurines sitting next to jars of money that had not been disturbed; the money had been left behind. He confirmed that there was no sexual abuse involved in the case.

Michael Sinke was a latent fingerprint identification specialist with the Michigan State Police. He was approved as an expert. He had FBI training and processed 65,000 fingerprint comparisons in the course of his career. Latent prints are fingerprints that are left behind accidentally. He found six identifiable latent prints in the areas were the burglar was most likely to leave them and one of them—a palm print—matched John Aslin.

He explained that he looks at various points of comparison between latent prints and known prints (the ones collected by the police department when someone is arrested) and will not declare a hit unless at least eight points match. In John's case, there were eleven matches.

Bobby Keene, who had just turned 14, admitted he was testifying under an agreement that his attorney negotiated with the prosecutor's office where, if he testified consistent with his prior testimony, he would not be charged with anything that took place on May 21, 1984. During Bobby's testimony, things happened that hinted at the coercion he underwent at the hands of the police.

Bobby said that John loaned him $2. After he went home that night, he went to his friend's house. They walked to a corner store to play video games.

"Did you tell your friend what happened that night?"

"I told him about when John was running, you know, around this bush and the money he showed me. I didn't tell him that we just robbed some old lady, like he said I did."

"Did you tell your friend that John Aslin just robbed an old lady?"

"No."

"Do you remember testifying at the Preliminary Exam that you told your friend that John robbed this old lady?"

"I believe I might have but I don't—I don't…"

"Well, did John Aslin ever tell you where he got that wad of money from?"

"No."

The assistant prosecutor was getting frustrated and read Bobby's testimony from the Preliminary Exam in its entirety to the jury. "Do you remember being asked those questions and giving those answers at the hearing"

"No."

When asked a second time, more forcefully, Bobby did not respond. The assistant prosecutor finally said, "Mr. Keene, do you wish the opportunity to discuss this with your attorney?"

The court took a short recess so that Bobby could be taken out in the hall and worked on so his testimony would fall into line. Then he was brought back in.

"Mr. Keene, are you nervous here this morning?"

"Yes."

"I'll try to slow down and take things one step at a time. Did you tell your friend that an old woman had been robbed?"

"I don't remember. Yes."

"Well, is it yes or you don't remember?"

"I don't remember."

"Did you know at that point that an old woman had been robbed?"

"No."

"Whether you told your friend or not?"

"Yes, I believe—"

"How did you know that an old woman had been robbed?"

"I believe that I heard John say it."

The judge said, "You believe what?"

Bobby replied, "That John said something like that."

"What do you remember, to the best of your memory, that John said to you?"

"When we was in the car he whispered, 'Don't say nothing about what I did.'"

"Well, did you know that there was an elderly woman involved? An old lady? Take your time."

Bobby turned to the judge and pleaded, "Can we set this for another day? Can we set this for another day, please?"

The judge responded, "What? You mean your testimony?"

"Yes."

"No."

"No?"

"No. You have to sit there and tell the truth, the whole truth and nothing but the truth."

"Can I just start over?" Bobby narrated the entire evening again and never mentioned that John made any confession to him.

He got to the point where he was with his friend and the assistant prosecutor cut in. "Now, did you tell your friend what happened that night?"

"Yes, I did mention something but—yes."

"Did you say anything about an old woman being involved?"

"Well, I said, I think an old woman was murdered."

"How did you know that there was an old woman in any way involved in this?"

"That's what I'm—that's what I can't remember. It just slipped my mind. I'm trying to think. My friend mentioned about something was happening. He said—he's bringing up stuff like—after I told him that."

"After you told him what?"

"After I told him what happened, that I seen John running around the bush and showing me all this money. He mentioned something. He said something about an old lady died over on Cass. That's what he mentioned to me. He mentioned to me that some old lady—something happened and that's where we was at the time. And I said, 'Yeah, he robbed the old lady probably.' I saw him later; he said, 'Don't say nothing about what happened that night.'" Poor Bobby tried to tell the truth, but it just wasn't good enough for the prosecutor; trying to tell the lies he'd been fed got him all twisted up.

Timothy Roberts said that John was "acting mighty hyper" on May 21, 1984 and was "rattling on about robbing an old lady." "He said that he pushed a lady down or broke into her house, pushed the lady down and kept getting up in her face and said, 'Give me the money.' And then I guess he says he pushed her back down or something and then he ran out. That's all I remember."

"Was it just you and John out in your driveway talking? Was anyone else there?"

"Me and John and my brother, John. My brother was there the whole time too." Timothy said that he and John Aslin walked together for a half mile, bought beer and went to another friend's house, but they never discussed the break in again.

It was curious that the details of this supposed confession only included details that the police collected from other witnesses.

"Did you see any money on John?"

"Just $5 though he said he had $15."

"Did John Aslin ask for your help with anything?"

"He wanted me to alibi for him. I agreed but I wasn't going to."

When John's attorney cross-examined Timothy, he zeroed in on a few key discrepancies and important details. "Mr. Roberts, do you recall talking to Detective South on June 12th, 1984?"

"Yes."

"And you told him at that time all the important information that you could, is that not right?"

"Best that I could remember."

"And did you tell him everything that happened at that point in time?"

"Everything that I remembered."

"You had said that you were not going to alibi for John Aslin, right?"

"Right."

"You told Mr. Aslin you would but you in fact had no intention…"

"I wasn't intending—no, I wasn't going to."

"And you were going to tell Detective South the truth and everything that you could?"

"Yes, but I didn't remember that at the time. I wish I did."

"Remember what?"

"That I said that, that I was going to alibi for John. Because I want everything out in the open. I don't want to get in any trouble."

Had Detective South gotten to Timothy too and scared him?

"Have you talked about this case or read about this case any place?"

"Yeah, a couple of people."

"So, you didn't tell Detective South that you told John Aslin that you were going to alibi for him on June the 12th, right?"

"Right."

"And you told him everything that was significant except that portion about the alibi?"

"Right."

"You told Detective South that Mr. Aslin had appeared nervous and worried and was acting crazy?"

"Yes."

"Would not stand still?"

"No. He couldn't."

"Appeared that he was going to cry?"

"Yes. Seemed very hurt."

"Since June 12th, you've talked about this case with other people, right?"

"Yes."

"And during those talks, it was brought up that the lady was knocked down? You heard that, right?"

"Yeah."

John's attorney was able to establish that Tim's testimony had been pieced together from other sources, but would the jury get the point?

Glenn Stephens continued to testify that John came to his home the night that his grandmother died to buy a cigarette. The assistant prosecuting attorney asked a series of questions that made it look odd that John was trying to buy a cigarette when there were stores open that sold cigarettes, yet Glenn never admitted that he was selling marijuana. Then he asked Glenn, "What did you say to him?"

"He was who I suspected so I didn't say—" Glenn planted the idea in the mind of the jury that he thought John was the one who committed the break in though he had been warned against it. It was based on the phony phone call. He said John looked nervous. "He looked shocked when he heard it on the news—that my grandmother had died on the television."

"Before that point, had you said anything to Mr. Aslin that this was your grandmother?"

"No."

"When it came on TV, did you tell him that it was your grandmother?"

"He knew it was my grandmother. I said nothing."

"How do you know that he knew?"

"He knew that my grandmother lived in Beecher and had the same name as me. We talked about it. He's known of her existence for some time." Glenn spun quite a story for the jury that completely contradicted what he said at the Preliminary Exam. He'd had time to shift his story to get around the problems he'd encountered with his testimony months earlier.

Now Glenn claimed that John knew that his grandmother kept cash in the house, though he said at the Preliminary Exam that only family members knew about that. Though he previously testified that John had never been to his grandmother's house, he now claimed that John had been a passenger several times when other people stopped by. Then he claimed that he personally told John that his grandmother had a heart attack and he was staying with her, in spite of the fact that John was incarcerated during the entire time that Glenn claimed to have been living with Ella Stephens after her heart attack.

John's attorney made Glenn admit that he'd had multiple opportunities to tell the police that John had been to his grandmother's home, knew about her money habits and knew that she had a heart condition, but he had never done so. However, the attorney really didn't go into it in much detail to clearly make the jury understand that Glenn was fabricating incriminating details to make it look like John's actions were premeditated—and that was the most important concept that needed to be clarified for the jury in the entire case.

Maybe if the attorney had gone through each statement Glenn made for the first time that day and contrasted it in more detail with the fact that those details—which were all designed to make John look like he had planned the whole thing and targeted an elderly woman— were missing in the police report and the testimony at the Preliminary Exam, it could have made a difference. Glenn Stephens' testimony was the only testimony during the entire trial that connected to the idea that this might be a case of murder rather than a horribly tragic accident.

Misty, Glenn's girlfriend, initially testified that John showed up to buy a cigarette but on cross-examination she admitted he had come to buy a joint. She confirmed that Glenn had continuously lied to the police about the issue of a cigarette versus a joint.

Marybell Smith told the jury about John asking about God's forgiveness and how she talked to him about how to pray. She stated it was the first time she had ever discussed religion with him. John was reading the prayer book when she went to bed. Sheila Hoyer, Marybell's granddaughter, said John seemed depressed the next day and asked her what homicide meant.

The next morning, the judge and the two attorneys discussed the wording of the instructions that the judge would give the jury. John's attorney urged the court to add language that would clarify that the "foreseeability of the likelihood of death" must be strong and plain for it to be murder, but the judge declined.

The attorney also objected to the court using the phrase "little old lady" instead of "small elderly lady" but the judge insisted on using his phrase, saying that Mrs. Stephens was only 4' 6".

The assistant prosecutor interjected, "Although that was the testimony, I believe the autopsy determined that she was 5'3"," but the judge responded, "Okay. Still little. Just not as little." But the difference was relevant because John was only 5' 6" so the judge again proceeded in a sloppy way that stacked the odds against an acquittal.

Two doctors were called to testify about the autopsy. Dr. David Congdon was trained at the University of Michigan Medical School; he had conducted over a thousand autopsies during his career.

"Mrs. Stephens was an elderly woman of average size—5'4" and 140 pounds—and there was nothing remarkable externally about her body except for paddle marks that resulted from attempts to resuscitate her. But internally, she had severe arteriosclerotic cardiovascular disease—hardening of the arteries. There was significant narrowing of the coronary artery—the luminar hole that her blood flowed through was only ten percent of what it should have been." The doctor essentially said that if Mrs. Stephens kept herself calm, she could manage her heart condition, but agitation could put too much stress on her physical condition.

On cross-examination, the doctor admitted that any number of things could have put stress on Ella Stephens heart—being awakened by an unexpected phone call in the middle of the night, walking to the store or taking the witness stand; it was hard to say if her need for blood to the brain would have been met in those conditions either.

"In fact, doctor, you don't know whether even absent the sudden physical or emotional stress that the prosecutor described to you she would have collapsed and died anyway, do you?"

"No, I don't know."

"And that is because the condition that she had is a progressive condition, is it not?"

"That is correct."

"It's somewhat fragile, already fragile?"

"Right."

"And whatever would cause an increased demand for blood might tip the scale and cause her death?"

"That's right."

"In fact, the increased demand for blood may be caused by less and less as time goes by?"

"Yes."

After John's attorney finished his questions, the assistant prosecutor was able to ask follow up questions. He pointed out that it would be important to consider what Mrs. Stephens had been through shortly before her collapse and the doctor agreed. The assistant prosecutor then rested his case.

John's attorney made a motion for a directed verdict on the first-degree murder charge. He was asking the judge to decide the case based on the evidence presented by the prosecutor up to that point. "I don't believe the requisite factors for state of mind have been shown by the prosecution. Simply put, judge, the state of mind shown does not rise to the level that the issue of murder should even be put to the jury. Perhaps manslaughter but certainly not murder."

The assistant prosecutor pushed back, "The People would oppose this motion most strenuously, feeling that taking the testimony most favorably to the prosecution, we have shown a wanton and willful disregard of the likelihood that the natural tendency of his behavior was to cause death. If you assume that he kicked in the door of an elderly widow whom he knew had a heart attack and terrorized her and knocked her down, got in her face, that the results that occurred certainly are within the purpose of what could be expected as a natural tendency of his acts."

The judge had listened to the testimony. If he had understood the actual law, he would have granted the motion to acquit John, but his self-made jury instructions reveal that he did not.

Beyond the judge's failure to grasp the legal concepts, there was no testimony that Ella Stephens was terrorized. There was no credible testimony that John knew she had a heart condition or even knew who she was. There was no basis to make a logical conclusion that John knew that his act of breaking into the home would lead to Mrs. Stephen's death.

The judge could have stopped the over-prosecution at that point, but he did not. "I consider it a jury question. Besides, I've already gone over the instructions with the jury."

Yes, the judge had already gone over the instructions with the jury, instructions that were misleading and inaccurate. Why did the fact that the jury had heard instructions bar the judge righting this troubling situation?

John's attorney called the detective in charge of the investigation as his first witness. He presented an eight-page transcript of the first police interview of Glenn Stephens, confirmed that there had been a second formal interview and that there had been an open line of communication between Glenn and the detective since Mrs. Stephens' death.

He asked the detective to verify that he would have added anything important that Glenn told him to the police report. The attorney asked the detective to confirm that he had talked to Glenn Stephens a half-dozen times; the detective testified that, in one instance, Glenn even contacted him to correct a previous statement.

John's attorney had the detective verify, reluctantly, that Glenn misled the court when he testified that he told John himself that his grandmother had a heart condition and that he had lied to the court about John wanting to buy a cigarette rather than a joint.

The officer confirmed that he had spoken to Tim Roberts more than once and Tim had never, until his testimony in court, mentioned that John said he pushed Ella Stephens down and was "in her face."

When the assistant prosecuting attorney cross-examined him, he said, "It isn't rare at all for witnesses to come up with new information in court than they gave the police in previous interviews."

John testified next in his own defense. He had been drinking all evening with friends in an apartment above the market where he ran into Bobby Keene. He had just drunk a pint of alcohol. He and Bobby were headed to Sue's house and a friend dropped them off nearby. He told Bobby to wait at the bar while he went to collect money from a friend, but he changed his mind on his way there. "I was in a backyard. Seen a door. Knocked on the door. Nobody answered. Knocked again. Nobody answered. I kicked the door in."

John said he couldn't remember where he was that night, but later realized that he had been to that house before. "The living room light came on and an elderly lady stepped into the doorway and said, 'What do you want?'—she said it a little bit loud. I said, 'I want some money.'" The woman stepped back where he couldn't see her and it looked like she had tripped and was getting up. She said she was going to call the police.

John was scared. "She screamed, 'I'm going to call the police,' and I kind of yelled out, 'No, please, no,' and I seen the phone and I rushed past her to the phone and as I got to the phone she fell again as I rushed right past her, she fell."

John said he didn't anticipate someone being there because no one answered the door. "She said, 'I want to call the police,' and I said, 'All I want is some money,' and she screamed, 'Okay, okay,' and walked to the kitchen where her purse was sitting on the table."

"Why didn't you just grab the purse right off the bat when you walked in?"

"I didn't notice it because the kitchen was dark."

The woman gave him some money and he ran off. John didn't know whose house he had broken into because he had entered from the backyard.

The assistant prosecuting attorney asked John how much alcohol he had consumed that night. "Two bottles of wine, three quarts of beer and a pint of whiskey."

John was feeling bad about what he had done. The next morning, he asked Tim to give him an alibi. The prosecutor had been going over John's account of what happened and John answered that he didn't remember several times. John asserted that he had been drunk and that none of it would have happened if he had been sober.

"Are you claiming that your selective memory is because of all that you had to drink that night?"

"I don't understand."

"Some things you remember very well and yet other things you don't remember at all. Is that all because of the drinking too?"

"I think so."

"Does your wish to avoid punishment and responsibility for what you did that night have anything to do with your memory problems?"

"No."

In his closing argument, the assistant prosecuting attorney reminded the jury of the three questions he had told them that they would need to answer at the beginning of the case—did John Aslin commit the burglary, did his actions cause Mrs. Stephens' death and did he have the requisite state of mind for his conduct to be murder? He asserted that the answer to the first two questions was yes.

"John Aslin admitted he was the one who committed this robbery—this is not a whodunnit. It wasn't physical exertion after John Aslin left. It was the physical and emotional stress that John Eric Aslin put on her, and no one else, that overloaded her heart and caused her death, caused it as surely as if he'd taken a gun and shot her."

"As for the third question, the People do not contend that he went into that house intending to kill Mrs. Stephens. He went in there intending to get money. That was his reason for kicking in the door. The People maintain that he operated with willful and wanton disregard of the likelihood that the natural result of his acts would be death or great bodily harm, basically that he didn't care. He knew it could happen. He knew there was a likelihood of it happening, but he was more interested in the money than in the welfare of Ella Stephens."

"I find it hard to believe that the choice of Mrs. Stephens' home was just happenstance that night, that John Aslin just happened to find himself in the backyard of Glenn Stephens' grandmother's home. There's been testimony that he knew the house, knew she lived alone, knew her money habits, and knew that she'd only been out of the hospital for six months from a heart attack. And Mr. Aslin testified he knew her."

Almost none of the testimony that was supposed to establish these facts was true; even then, the prosecutor embellished it. "I would be more impressed with his testimony of intoxication if any of the other people who were with him that night would have testified that he was intoxicated. The closest thing to any support for this claim was Marybelle Smith saying he was tipsy. I submit being tipsy is a far cry from being intoxicated to the point where you don't know what you're doing or where you are."

The prosecutor did not acknowledge that many hours had passed between the time of Mrs. Stephens' death and John's discussion with Marybelle. "Did it strike you that his ability to recall what happened that night seemed to vary depending on the nature of the question? If it was a critical question that really went to the issue of his guilt—those parts seemed hard to remember. The innocuous parts—those he remembers very well. But how he happened to be in that particular backyard, that gets a little hazy."

"You're entitled to be skeptical of Mr. Aslin's testimony. Keep in mind what he said to Marybelle Smith, that he did something bad and didn't want to get punished for it and ask yourself whether that isn't still what's on John Aslin's mind, that he knows he did something wrong but he still doesn't want to get punished for it. And ask yourself whether he's shaving the truth a little bit the same way he shaved his mustache to conceal his identity or to conceal the truth."

"Submitting Mrs. Stephens to the physical abuse and emotional terrorizing is precisely the state of mind that the law refers to when they say a willful and wanton disregard of the natural consequences that flow from your actions. He knew she was old. He knew she was frail. He knew she had a heart attack. He forces his way into her house and terrorizes her that night, not because he wanted to kill her or meant to kill her but because he didn't care. He wanted money bad enough that he was willing to totally put aside the consequences. Those weren't his concern, and I submit it isn't yet."

John's attorney countered with a plea to the jury to decide that John's actions did not constitute murder. "The reason it's particularly important to look into John Aslin's state of mind that night is shown by a situation that I think a lot of you can relate to—two brothers and one of them trips the other and the one that's tripped falls down and cuts his chin and even breaks his nose. The parents are going to be darned mad at that kid for tripping and are not going to condone his actions but you're not going to treat him the same as a kid who takes his fist and smashes somebody in the nose. There is a difference there and that difference is here too. It's the state of mind of what he has done. Nobody's asking you to excuse his actions, but we are asking you to look into the state of mind."

John's attorney presented a chart to the jury and broke down different aspects of the homicide, which he defined as "criminal responsibility for a death." He went through first and second-degree murder and manslaughter; he also asserted that accidental death was not a crime. The thing that differentiated all of these options was state of mind. He told the jury they could decide that John's actions caused Mrs. Stephens' death but that did not prove that he had the necessary state of mind to commit murder.

"He had to have knowledge, plain and strong, that his actions might cause death—strong and plain likelihood of death. This does not mean might or maybe or could have been—we're talking about a high level of knowledge here and a high degree that the natural tendency of his actions would cause death. That's what has to happen for John to have committed murder. If you find that he did not intend to create the high degree of risk but was grossly negligent and he willfully and wantonly –that means with knowledge again—disregarded the consequences that might follow –that would be manslaughter. If this death was unanticipated and unintended and unplanned and not a willful and wanton disregard of the strong and plain likelihood and not grossly negligent, we have an accidental death. Just because a robbery occurred does not mean that the death could not have been accidental."

"You need to look at what Mr. Aslin knew. If you believe Glenn Stephens, that he told John she had a prior heart attack, then you need to ask how much knowledge John had of the prior heart attack. The prosecution said she was an elderly lady and he should have known better, but the doctors told you age wasn't the big factor here. What was the big factor? Her cardiovascular system. It was a progressive situation—it did not stick out like a sore thumb."

"Even if you think John knew she had a heart condition, did he know how serious it was? Did he consciously contemplate and come up with a situation where he knew that she would die? Did he have knowledge that death could be a consequence? Even if you believe

Glenn, he moved out because she was getting better. John would have had to look inside her veins to be fully aware of the risk of death."

"The doctor said age was not the big factor, so even if you don't believe John and you think that he pushed her down and got into her face—and in hindsight you say she was old and he should have known better—you still can't get to the level where death was a strong and plain likelihood. That's what has to be shown for murder."

"Now if you believe John, the pictures of the house support his version. There were only two areas disturbed in the house and there were no bruises on her body. Even if she was pushed down, it was not enough to cause a disturbance. Don't focus on whether she was pushed down—look at the circumstances again. Look behind them. How calculated must that have been to cause her death? Even if you think she was pushed, the evidence shows it simply wasn't a violent encounter—a violent shove, up against the wall or held by the throat. What is the terror that the prosecution argued? Could John have known that his actions were going to result in anything but a robbery? Did he have knowledge—that he disregarded—that she was going to have a heart attack and her heart would be this fragile? No, he didn't, ladies and gentleman, no, he did not."

"He didn't walk in there with a gun, a knife. He was as surprised as anyone, I think. He didn't have the presence of mind. He could have run. He didn't. But did he intend to kill her or do great bodily harm? Was he aware or have the knowledge of the plain and strong likelihood of death? If he had shot her with a gun, we would have a strong instrumentality of death. When the judge mentioned arson, fire is a dangerous instrumentality, or a bomb."

"Getting from robbery to death without any significant physical activities—there were steps of age, a heart condition and death—that you don't have with a bomb or fire or a gun. We don't even have evidence of a ranting and raving maniac in this case. Tim Roberts said John pushed her down and got in her face, but he didn't 'remember' that until he got on the witness stand. It was a very graphic, specific piece of testimony, so why didn't he tell that to the detective during any of the previous times he talked to him? I don't know why he would say what he said, but I do know that there was no evidence of a major struggle."

"You might believe Glenn Stephens but I don't. He had plenty of chances to tell what he knew to the detective, yet his story changed when he testified. And he repeatedly said John was trying to buy a cigarette when it was actually marijuana. He has an obvious motive to see John Aslin punished for the death of his grandma."

"And Bobby Keene—the conversation he testified to after interrupting his testimony to talk to his attorney—was that his conversation with his friend took place at a time that was impossible because no one knew Ella Stephens had died yet. You can believe John Aslin or you can believe a kid whose testimony is at odds with the photos and a grandson who has an obvious interest in the case."

"Just because John is the defendant doesn't mean he's lying. I should have asked the other witnesses to confirm that—I take the blame for that—but Marybelle Smith said he had been drinking. Why should we believe John? Because he told us things no one else knew—things he didn't have to say. We know he asked Marybelle Smith how to seek forgiveness."

"If you don't want to believe John and instead believe the prosecution's witnesses, the situation they describe still does not show the plain and strong likelihood of death because he was not able to look into her heart. If you want criminal responsibility, the most you could say is that he was grossly negligent and that is manslaughter. If you believe John, then the death was an accident and you should find him guilty of robbery but not murder."

"The prosecution is going to talk about motive. We do know that he was remorseful and somebody that is remorseful isn't going to intend the harm that is attributed to him. He may have been careless. He may have been more than careless. But you have to have an abiding conviction that he had the state of mind for murder to convict him of that. Again, I'm not asking you to excuse him. Find him guilty of what he did. Not of what he didn't do."

The prosecutor got the last word. He said that John's attorney left off the words "or great bodily harm or serious injury" when he defined the intent for murder on 24 occasions, so the prosecutor misled the jury about the standard. He said maybe Tim Roberts wasn't asked the right questions by the detectives—that might be why he testified different from his previous statements. He said the condition of the house and the picture of the body did not prevent the possibility that John struck her—she died too soon afterward to tell.

This was a sneaky move since John's attorney would not have another chance to speak to the jury and point out that Ella had lived long enough that some indication of injury would have been present and that this assertion contradicted the testimony of the assistant prosecuting attorney's own medical experts.

"John Aslin only testified to things that were already locked in by other evidence. He was not forthright. He wasn't remorseful. Who did he ask Marybelle Smith to pray for that night? Himself or his victim? He had the state of mind to set into motion an inevitable chain of events that caused the death of Ella Stephens. He acted with willful and wanton disregard of the consequences, the strong and plain likelihood that what he was doing, confronting an elderly woman in her home, knocking her down, demanding her money, a woman who'd had a heart attack, the strong and plain likelihood that his course of conduct would result in death or great bodily harm, that makes his act murder and since it was committed in the course of a robbery, that makes it felony murder, murder in the first degree."

The judge gave the jury instructions about the elements of the crimes among their choices, but instead of using the standard instructions that had been carefully ironed out by the legislature, he created his own instructions; his version deviated from statute and were confusing.

LIFE SIX: WHERE JOHN ERIC'S NATURAL LIFESPAN IS CLAIMED BY THE STATE

THE VERDICT

The trial ended just before 1:00 pm. The jurors were taken across the street to have lunch. They returned to the courtroom at 4:40 pm to deliver their verdict. At most, they spent 2 ½ hours considering whether they should send a 21-year old to prison for the rest of his natural life—and they decided they should.

And the court rolled on as though nothing momentous had happened.

Judge Elliot gave a callous speech. "I never praise or criticize any jury verdict in any case. But I do sincerely thank you. I think both lawyers were excellent. It's an interesting case, somewhat different than the usual run of cases here, and if anybody wants to keep these instructions as a souvenir, you can."

"I think this case is close to a first on this theory of murder. It is well, I think, for young people to know that they can be convicted of murder if they break into somebody's house as was done in this case and terrorize a person to the point that they lose their life and I'm happy to see the verdict you arrived at."

After the jury left, the judge acknowledged that the sentence would be life without parole and then went home to his privileged, idyllic life.

The words that Judge Elliot's chose during the trial harmed John's case. He told the jury that John's behavior had to create a mere possibility of harm or death—but the law said it had to create a strong probability. The distance between these two phrases when it comes to a decision about a man's life in prison is a chasm where justice and injustice sit on opposite sides. The examples the judge gave—of exploding a bomb in public or setting an occupied house on fire— required an intent to create danger that was so far from any intent that

John Aslin exhibited that the judge all but assured that John would be successfully over-prosecuted. The judge's insistence on cutting his own path, rather than following the careful path laid out by the legislature, was likely a fatal blow to John's freedom. And it was discouraging that he continued to promote the idea that John had terrorized Ella Stephens. There was no basis to draw that conclusion.

LIFE SEVEN: WHERE JOHN ERIC LOSES THE BENEFITS OF A BLOODLINE

It wasn't until John was sentenced to be in prison for the rest of his natural life that he grew to understand the full scope of what he had lost—the son he had taken for granted. The children he might have had who would never be born. The opportunity to spend time with the father who came into his life for the first time to tell him who he was. The relationship between John and his father was meted out in short phone calls and sparse visits.

As for John's son, Carrie, rightly, kept him away from John. She later married a man who viewed John's child as his own. From all appearances, John's son had two good parents who provided him with a solid childhood and set him up for a happy existence. John only felt gratitude that his son might have a chance at a good life, though he also felt regret that he would never be a part of it.

Fort Benning, Georgia
1948

Boot camp was a piece of cake. Unlike the other men, Fred already knew how to take orders, keep his head down and learn survival skills. His father had exposed him to firearms at a young age and his commanders loved his stats, as well as his confidence, obedience and intelligence. Fred was rewarded quickly with leadership roles. The first two years of army life were uneventful.

But in 1951, he found himself traveling over that ocean that he had loved so much to a land that reminded him of home in some ways and would test him just as much.

Giving up a Lung for Freedom
Undisclosed location, Korea Countryside South of Incheon
1951

Fred was under heavy fire. He was pinned down and had no business making such an easy target of himself, but Billy was still moving; he couldn't just leave him laying there, getting pulverized. He had almost dragged Billy to safety when the sniper got him. Fred had been breathing hard through all the smoke and chaos, but the bullet cut his breath in half. He fell on top of his buddy and lay there, gasping, stunned and confused by the fire in his chest. Billy was lucid enough to reach out, grab the shell that was hanging around Fred's neck and jam in into the hole in Fred's chest that was hemorrhaging blood. It slowed the flow that bubbled out of the wound.

Fred had gotten the two of them close enough that Jorgenson could reach out and grab Fred's arm. As he felt himself begin to move away from Billy, he hugged him with all his might. Jorgenson was a beast of a man and pulled his brothers-in-arms to safety, then screamed for a medic to haul ass over to the wounded warriors. They would both make it home.

Charlotte, Michigan
1998
Fred Aslin

A lung for my freedom. That was what it took to give me back to myself. I survived. I was finally in a position where no one could tell me where I could go, what I could do, when I could sleep, when to wake up and when to take a shit. I thought my life was truly ending on March 7, 1951 when that bullet took my breath away, but that was when my life began. I spent my 25th birthday—marked my first quarter century on this Earth—laid up in a hospital, making plans to go home. Uncle Sam gave me a Purple Heart, but it was that seashell that I put in a glass case on my mantle. It had been blessed by the ancestors. It set me free and brought me back.

LIFE ONE: ACCORDING TO THE STATE OF MICHIGAN, JOHN ERIC SHOULDN'T EXIST

GERMANY
1952

John Albert followed Fred's footsteps by entering the Army soon after he turned 18 in 1950. His brother's intercessions with the ancestors had born fruit. Instead of being sent to the front line in Korea, where casualties were high, John was stationed in Germany. He spent his service years in relative safety.

Like his brothers, he had gone under the knife—he had not been able to avoid that fate—but unbeknownst to him, the surgeon had failed to sterilize him. The ancestors medicine proved powerful. The state had tried to take a full life away from John Albert and failed, but his lack of awareness of this failure cost him a relationship with his son and cost John Eric the benefits of a father. The state tried to prevent John Albert from having offspring, then, ironically and for all intents and purposes, took the chance of any quality of life from his only son at the age of 21.

The Prison Years 1984- ?

In the 1980s, men who were sentenced to serve a term in the Michigan prison system were sent to the Reception Center in Jackson, Michigan to await their placement in a permanent location. John was no different. Soon after his trial was complete, he found himself crammed in the back of a meat wagon with dozens of men, leg irons shackling them together, their hands cuffed.

The ride itself was terribly frightening. Their terror increased when they were awestruck by the sight of the huge prison that came into focus as they drove through multiple layers of razor wire-topped fencing.

Once inside, they were released from their restraints but crammed into an open cell with a hard, concrete ledge surrounding the perimeter—the ledge provided the only seats available. Most of the men were too afraid of the unknown to sit; they stood nervously, avoiding eye contact. An overweight guard appeared in the doorway and barked out instructions. "Listen up. Strip down to your birthday suits. Hand every stitch of clothing through the window."

Now John felt like a piece of meat, naked and vulnerable, surrounded by other embarrassed men, all unsure of what to expect next. The room was freezing; the strangers shivered, miserable and uncertain for at least an hour. Then they were called to the next step one by one. "Inmate 172869. Aslin."

John was new enough that he still got to be called by a name but eventually he would have to memorize the number and respond to it. The water that they sprayed him with, like a dog, was only slightly warmer than the room; he continued to shiver as he scrubbed with the awful-smelling delousing agent; then he was sprayed again.

At least he was given clothing after cleaning up, and a bedroll. It was an improvement over being naked, but his nerves were soon destroyed, his anxiety engulfing him, as they led him into chaos. His sense of dread began as he walked down a narrow catwalk that grew increasingly dark. John felt like he was marching into hell, and he was right.

He emerged in a five-story birdcage of madness. The more seasoned inmates screamed menacing threats and threw things at the newcomers. John had been in a lot of dangerous situations in his life, but nothing compared to the adrenaline rush of fear that overcame him.

His nasty cell—a roach-infested, corroded place layered with diarrhea-colored chipping paint—had bars on three sides. There was not an iota of privacy for using the toilet, which lacked a seat and gave off a stink that made him retch—still, his cell felt safer than being outside the bars. The walls were covered with smashed roach carcasses and boogers. The mattress was ripped and filthy.

And the place was so cold. The windows were smashed out. John could see snow blowing inside. There was a thin crust of ice on the toilet water. Birds flew back and forth along the high ceilings of the common area constantly. The place obviously felt safer to them than to the men trapped below. Evidence that thousands of men had occupied this space was all over the back wall—new names scratched over old ones. John felt like a cog in a terrible machine, numb, shocked, silent, wondering what was coming next.

John was weak in the aftermath of the adrenaline that had been coursing through him for hours; he collapsed on his cot, feeling a sliver of safety for the first time that day. Then he saw his neighbor hold out a mirror to check that no guards were on the floor. When the man was sure the coast was clear, he whipped out a device that he used to unlock his cell door in the wink of an eye. He ran down the hall to another cell, opened it and stole a television that he carried back to his space. So much for John's feeling of safety simply because he was locked in.

The first night was terrible, a waking dream. John didn't have the nerve to sit on the toilet until after dark, when he at least felt like no one could watch from across the gallery. Still, relieving himself brought no relief.

Once the lights were out, the yelling began. Men made terrifying sounds at the top of their lungs; it was hard to know if their apparent agony was real or fake. The place induced anguish, so there was probably some authentic element of stress release in all of it, but it was unlike anything he had ever heard. The sound of squeaking bed springs punctuated the other sounds throughout the night. It was a long, sleepless nightmare.

After breakfast, John was too exhausted to keep his eyes open and caught some rest.

At lunch, a guy from Flint took his cookie.

John grabbed his wrist. "You better let go of my wrist, bitch."

"You better let go of my cookie, bitch."

The cookie dropped on his tray.

"I'll see you on the gallery."

John had never been one to let a conformation fester. "Let's go. I'm right behind you."

He followed the man who headed for the hallway and disappeared around the corner. As John turned toward the stairs, his adversary was waiting. He hit before John had time to block it. John went black for a second but came to with tunnel vision and the guy was at the end of that tunnel. John ran straight at him, swinging and landing punches. They stopped and ran separate ways when the guards were called.

Later that night, the neighbor in the next cell got chatty. "Hey kid, you done good. He won't fuck with you no more, but you need to learn to block them punches with your hands, not your face. I'm amazed you don't show any bruises."

John was amazed too because, clearly, his nose was broken.

The next day, his adversary gave him a respectful nod as he walked by his table. He was shocked that John had stood toe-to-toe with him—John soon learned that Joe Jackson was nicknamed "Lights Out" due to his one-punch knock-outs. Standing up to this bully earned John enough respect to be left alone for the rest of his time at the reception center—another thirty days.

And he discovered someone had slipped his cookie in his pocket—it was crumbled up, but it was a symbol of his tenacity and it tasted better because of it.

Part of the process inmates went through at the reception center included a mental health evaluation. John had a bad feeling when he entered the office of the woman who conducted his assessment. She had her hair styled like Elvira, Mistress of the Dark, but hers was streaked with grey. Her face was pinched with sourness. She wore cat-eye glasses and peered at John over the top of them with a permanently mean expression.

"Well, Mr. Aslin," she sneered, "Where do you want to spend your life behind walls—in Jackson or Marquette? Since you're just starting out, I can give you a choice."

John didn't know anything about either option. "What's the difference?"

She glared at him, then looked down at his file and started writing. "You can go now." She didn't look up.

John asked for a court-appointed attorney to appeal his case. He might have had a chance to reduce the draconian sentence of spending the rest of his natural life locked up if that attorney had done his job, but the attorney did nothing for him. Deadlines were missed and the court never considered his case on the merits. It was another piece of bad luck that cost him too much.

The ride from Jackson to Marquette was a grueling 9 ½ hours. The vehicle that carried him was called Snow Bird because it carried inmates to the northern tundra of Michigan, across the Mackinac Bridge. Snow blew across the road, obstructing the view. John rode in a van, shackled to other men, shivering in his thin state clothing as the world froze around him.

It was dark when they pulled up to a creepy castle-like building, dark and evil. Still, it had a lighter feel than the Reception Center. But that feeling didn't last.

"Mr. Aslin, you have a non-violent history and you're young. We could send you to protective custody if you want."

John had lost almost everything, but he could still have a reputation and he would need one that would protect him for the rest of his life. If he showed weakness, it could follow him. "I'll take general population."

The gate to the cellblock was a massive steel wall that appeared to be designed to contain a dragon. Marquette was full of killers and predators.

John's cell was tiny, nine feet long and only a couple feet wide beyond the bed frame. The door had three impenetrable locks—there would be no escaping this place. There was a normal prison lock on the cell door itself, then a locking mechanism for the door that assured that, if it was left unlatched, it could not be opened; this was due to a steel rod that was attached to a huge wheel at the end of the row of cells. The wheel rolled the rod back so the door could be opened and then cranked it back so it spanned a stretch of cells and immobilized their doors. The third layer of protection was that the wheel was locked by a huge anchor chain with a monster-sized padlock. This place truly could contain a dragon.

Marquette was as quiet as a library. The men did not yell or run up and down the block. The only sounds that he heard were the click of typewriters as the men wrote letters home or to the courts or the parole board, trying to stay connected to the outside and feed their hope so it would not die. He also heard occasional humming.

The only noisy time was at 9:30 pm, when the hawkers started their rounds.

"Chili-cheese dogs!"

"Cold pop! Only a dollar! Almost out! Better get yours quick!"

"Cheeseburgers!"

The entrepreneurs were allowed to make two rounds—one to advertise their products and take orders and another to deliver and collect plastic prison money tokens. As long as they fed the guards, they could operate without harassment.

The main action at Marquette was gambling. The money was run by Ray, an old gangster and bank robber whom John had met in the Genesee County Jail. Ray's picture had been on wanted posters for years before he was caught.

Back when they were in jail together, Ray provided moral support, telling John he was being railroaded and had gotten too much time for what he did; Ray was a sympathetic ear and a good source of support. He liked John and provided him cover while he was at Marquette.

The snowdrifts in 1985 were incredible. Ray spent most of his time pacing down a 40-foot path in the yard that he had worn into the snow. All day long, back and forth, Ray appeared to be contemplating some serious shit, like a philosopher, solving the mystery of the meaning of life while guards with trigger-happy fingers watched from every direction. They were not afraid to use their guns. If a fight broke out, they would shoot a close warning shot fast, letting men know they needed to stop or face a bullet.

During his first week at Marquette, John spotted a ghost from his recent past. John walked up behind Light's Out Joe Jackson and lowered his voice to a threatening pitch. "Give me those pancakes, bitch."

Joe turned around like he was ready to go crazy and then saw it was John, who had already proven himself. He just shook his head and smiled. "You're nuts."

John walked away, feeling more at ease. That brief encounter told him that whatever had happened was in the past and he wouldn't have to watch his back and fight Joe again. It was a relief because otherwise he feared he might have to do something horrible to protect himself.

But Lights Out didn't make many friends. He constantly intimidated people, calling them bitches and using his fists to take any challengers down.

On a spring day, the basketball courts were full. The games were self-segregated between black and white inmates, but Joe Jackson was playing on the "white boy" court. He bullied other players; he was aggressive and threatening. A foot shot out and tripped him, and the mob was on him, kicking him and punching him. He got up, yelled threats at his attackers and stumbled back into the unit.

After the fight, the yard was closed. Late that night, John heard a helicopter. Rumors flew around the prison, that someone was airlifted to Ann Arbor after being stabbed. That someone was Joe Jackson.

John never heard a word about him again.

John was in Marquette when reality hit. "I'm doing life. Never getting out. This is it. Never. The rest of my life. Gone. Why do I even act sane?"

Marquette was a maximum-security place for hardened, violent criminals—not a place for young men who made unfortunate decisions that accidentally caused a death, young men who would otherwise keep to themselves if not under threat.

Living among murderers and rapists was traumatizing. His fight or flight instincts were ignited daily. John had many opportunities to work out the anger that consumed him as he adjusted to the idea that he would never again walk the earth as a free man. Sometimes he lashed out at prisoners and sometimes at guards—it made no difference so long as he hit back twice as hard when he was threatened. That was the way to keep safe; it took the edge off the stress and pressure prison life created.

John waited in line for thirty minutes to call his dad. His dad delivered some frustrating news. "I tried to visit you a few days ago. Sat there for hours but they never brought you in."

John was devastated. He had been moved to a prison in Marquette, driving distance from his father's home, but had missed the chance to finally look his father in the eye. "They never told me you were here until it was too late." This was a common ploy the guards used. It stemmed from amusement or laziness.

He had been in Marquette for four months when his counselor sent for him. She swiveled in her chair to face him. "Mr. Aslin, what are you doing here?"

"They said you wanted to see me."

"No, I mean, what are you doing in Marquette?"

"This is where they sent me."

"Your file says that you self-selected to be here. Your points are low. You could be in a different place—a less stressful place." Thanks to the kindness of that counselor, John was transferred to a Level Four facility, less brutal and dangerous.

He found himself in a place called Gladiator School, a program for younger men who posed a less-serious risk to those around them. This time, as he went over the Mighty Mac Bridge, headed south to Ionia, he was in a bus—with the same shackles as before plus belly chains. A smart-ass guard flexed his authority. "If we go over the edge, you'll all drown together. In the MDOC, the dead don't float."

The guards got a kick out of his joke, though John was sure the asshole had recycled it—he didn't appear funny or smart enough to have made it up on the spot.

The entrance to Gladiator School was a creepy rotunda with rusty chain loops on the walls. John could imagine men being fastened there in days gone by. The ceilings were cavernous. He saw men walking around in civilian clothes, dressed like they were on dates. He later found out that these were the lucky guys who were visiting with parents, girlfriends, wives, kids.

John had to prove himself anew each time he moved. After twenty minutes in holding, a twitchy guy towered over him. "You got any money?"

John looked him firmly in the eye. "Ya."

"Give me five dollars."

"I don't think so." John held his gaze.

"Alright, tough guy. I'll see you inside." The man smiled, playing it off like he was just messing around, but John knew the man registered the fact that John would fight back if the guy pushed it further, so the man moved on to an easier target.

The new arrivals walked through massive five-story blocks as men yelled from their cells. Out on the yard, men looked at the newcomers like fresh meat.

John heard his name rise above the chaos. "Aslin." It was Chris, a kid he knew back in Beecher during his baseball days. It was good to see a familiar face.

John was housed in cell 91 of an African-American wing; out of 95 men, only five, including him, did not fit in demographically.

During quiet hours, his neighbor called out, "Hey 91, what's your name?"

"Johnny."

"Hey John John, where you from?"

"I'm from Flint and I said my name is Johnny." The older man laughed.

"Yeah, yeah, John John. Pass this down to 92 for me, will ya?" John was John John from that point forward at the Reformatory.

John's profile may have been too tame for Marquette, but he was surprised to discover that he had felt safer there. The reformatory was a dangerous place. He had three options—submit to predators, fight or get himself put in lock up—the crude saying was, "Fight, fuck or lock up."

He chose to fight, always keeping a weapon handy. He ripped his desk apart, removing the steel bracket and scraping it on the floor for days until he had a wicked-looking knife.

One night, as John lay on his bunk, water flooded out of the walls. Soon the toilets gurgled and sewage shot out, overflowing. Men started shouting. They tried to stop the water, but it came from everywhere, threatening to overflow their beds. When the bottom of his mattress got wet, John climbed to his desk. That is where he spent the night, watching turds float by as water continued to gush. The next morning, after the water levels went down, guards passed a single mop from cell to cell to push the water out, but the prison didn't give the men a means to clean their living spaces.

The same thing happened the next night. John was exhausted from spending two sleepless nights sitting on his desk, but no real relief came from the Department of Corrections. He slept on a damp mattress in an unsanitized cell for the rest of the week. The experience was a typical example of the fact that every vestige of humanity was disregarded in the penal system that was his trap.

Most men inside had a hustle—they were locked up, but they still needed money for commissary or to stay in touch with the outside world. John became a one-man knife factory. He ground a large groove in his floor as he sharpened knife after knife from random pieces of metal.

The guards had an intercom system that allowed them to listen to the inmates. They heard someone bragging about some guy named "John John" who made knives. John came back from the yard and found a guard exiting his neighbor's cell. "Why does this guy's stuff have Eugene on it? Isn't his name John John?"

"No, that's me."

"Well, imagine that." The guard closed Eugene's cell door and brushed John aside to enter his cell and tossed it. He found a knife. The guard took the knife, but he left John in his cell.

"This guy tried to punk me, Bro. I need a shiv." John's friend held his hand out, urgency etched on his face. John gave him a knife that the guard hadn't found.

John had an issue with the guy that his friend wanted to take out too. The convict had been elevated to a position of authority—a porter—but he was a rampant thief. John only had one special possession that held valuable in the eyes of others—a small radio his mother had bought him. It was only $19, but it was from his mom. The porter stole it, using a broom to slide it close to the bars.

On their way to watch a Christmas movie, they ran into the porter on the stairs. John's friend hit the guy with the shiv. John worried that the man had lost an eye, but he was back on the block later that day with a large bandage on his face.

John worried they had started a war and would have to be on edge from that time forward. Rescue came from an unexpected source. Doc Strange, a powerful gang leader from Detroit, called the porter out. ""Hey, punk. I paid those white boys to get your ass. You better get off my floor."

John wasn't sure what possessed Doc Strange to intervene, but the whole place went silent. The porter froze in his tracks, then turned and left. He asked the guards to place him in protective custody and the theft problems disappeared.

Though the men were under intense pressure most of the time, there were moments of lightness. His neighbor, Washington Bey, was a radio host in the prison. His show was at night. John would plug headphones into his radio and listen as Bey spun discs. Sometimes he would hear his name.

One night, as Bey ramped into, "Love Don't Live Here Anymore," by Rose Royce, he said, "This one goes out to little John John. Stop making those shivs, boy, stop making those shivs."

When Bey got back to his cell, he pointed at John and laughed good-naturedly. "Bey, you need to stop that shit."

"Hey brother, you sowed the seeds. Reap the benefits. You no punk, homeboy."

John was lucky to land a job in the library. He began a course of self-education to make up for the time he had squandered as a younger man. It broke up the boredom and gave him some relief from survival stress.

The library supervisor was a man with a hunchback who took a lot of verbal abuse for his affliction, but he was kind and treated John with respect. They joked with each other. John was initially assigned the position of janitor, but his boss soon gave him the best job possible—working the Reference Room. John had his own office with a desk and a copier.

Working at the library provided relief from the tension of the cell block and yard, but it didn't pay enough. John was back to square one for a survival hustle. He discovered that he could draw—quite well—so he began tattooing. His work was crude, just outlines with a little shading. He did it all by hand. His tool was a pen with a needle taped to it. He dipped it in ink and made the design, one painful poke at a time, but his artistry was clear.

His "victims" showed off his work and soon he was in business. John was taken under the wing of a talented tattoo artist in his unit, Mohawk Murray, the only black man dropping ink that John encountered on the inside. Murray tattooed a dragon on John and examined the work John had done on himself. The older man laughed. "You got potential, but you need training."

One day a man on John's cellblock asked him to fix his TV—John was handy with stuff like that. John soon realized that the guy was running a scam. The man led John to his cell, pointed out the TV and stepped to the hall. Once John was examining the TV, the man reentered the cell, a furious look on his face. He accused John of dropping the TV.

"You better pay me for it now!" The man was huge. He menaced John, looming over him.

John was irrationally mad. He knew he couldn't fight his way out of the problem, so he decided to get some flammable paint from the maintenance guys. He planned to throw it on the guy and light him up. Why not? He didn't have an out date from this hell. The system couldn't take more than the single lifespan he already owed it.

Murray caught wind of his plan. "Are you frickin' crazy? That punk ain't about nothing. I'm gonna take care of this and then I'm gonna teach you how to fight."

Murray stepped next door. John heard him threaten the scammer. "You're gonna shut the fuck up about that TV or me and John John are gonna beat your ass right here. Is this over?" John heard the man cow to Murray's intimidation.

The crisis was avoided but John's ego was bruised because he didn't handle the problem on his own. Murray had parting instructions for him. "Meet me tomorrow for training."

John blew Murray off the next day, so the large man showed up in the library. "Do you know who I am, punk? My brother teaches Akido to the Saginaw Police Department and I can kick his ass. I'm gonna train you until you feel you can handle yourself without weapons or fire. Don't you dare stand me up again."

Murray became a true friend. He taught John how to block attacks, hit the throat first, then send a knee to the groin and finish it off by gouging an eye with his thumb to keep the guy down. Unfortunately, the brutality connected to the skills John was learning was a necessity for survival in prison. Soon John had skills to handle more than one aggressor—because, as Murray told him, "In prison, they never come one on one."

John's training was interrupted by a trip to the hole for the lamest reason possible. While flagging down a guard, he stubbed his toe and broke it. He yelled out "mother fucker" when the pain hit. The guard thought John was threatening him and wrote him up.

No matter how much he pled his case to the hearing officer, he ended up in the hole. He later found out that Murray mocked the guards when he was training them about feeling threatened by John. John was at risk of being placed in a different wing so the "threatened" guard wouldn't feel uncomfortable, but Murray made sure he was returned to the same place when he got out of the hole.

Then Murray got sent to the hole. Some random guy made the mistake of hitting him on the head with a lock. Mohawk used the guy's face as a battering ram against several windows as he dragged him down the block, then slid the guy like a bowling ball into several guards who were running to stop him. The guards knew better than to get in striking range. "Murray, we're not going to cuff you, but you need to walk to the hole." Murray obliged.

Later that day, a guard delivered a package to John. The small box held a tattoo gun with a bottle of ink. There was a page of instructions on how to clean it. "Murray said to take care of this for him. If you sweep and mop the floors every day, you can tattoo for the rest of the shift."

John thought he was being set up, so he passed the gun down the hall to another prisoner. But no shakedown came. The next day he was called into the guard's office. The man handed the package back to him. "Look, Murray's been saying good things about you. We feel bad about how you got sent to the hole. Don't hide this under the stairs.

That's where everyone hides their knives. We shake it down every day. We're going to look the other way about this, so just be smart. Leave it in the contraband locker. You can have it back whenever you need it."

John felt like he was in a movie—it was such a remarkable thing to have guards show a flicker of kindness. He practiced tattooing himself when he could. He did an Iron Maiden-inspired piece on his arm, then a cross and ribbon on his wrist. His forearm soon held a snake with a flying skull; a heart with a peacock was on the other side. The men on his floor admired his work and scheduled appointments.

Soon the officers knew the details of John's case and decided he was not a bad kid—he had just gotten off-track in life. They let him open a full-blown tattoo shop in the library. If an inmate wanted a tattoo, he would give his identification number to John, who gave it to the library officer who sent for the man to do "extra duty" in the library. The man would be given a pass to enter John's sanctuary in the reference section. They would listen to the radio as John honed his skills. He went from goof to legend. He had over a hundred customers and all were repeat visitors. He made enough money to never go without.

The guards on first shift looked the other way for two years. Second shift was different. Those guards ravaged his cell daily, wrote petty tickets and kept him on lockdown. John developed an acute hatred for them and had nothing to lose if he acted on it. He made up his mind that the next time he was treated unjustly, he was going to get revenge.

When he came back from the library one day and every worldly possession that he had worked so hard to accumulate was gone—every piece of clothing, the overpriced radio he had saved for and all of his drawings—he snapped and made up his mind that he was bringing his knife-making skills out of retirement. The day the knife was ready, he wrapped it in a towel. He called the biggest prick of a guard over and asked him to open the closet so he could get some soap.

Just as John was reaching for his knife, the man turned and handed him his missing belongings in a bag. "Here. Take this crap. You're riding to Lapeer tomorrow."

John turned and walked back to his cell. "God saved you," he muttered under his breath, "and he saved me too."

John
1987

Moving to the Thumb Correctional Facility felt like moving up and going home. John saw men from his neighborhood there and friends of friends, so it felt safe right away. The building was sparkling clean, having just been built. It was like buying a new car—it had a fresh-paint smell and unchipped tile.

The day after he settled in, a bus from Jackson prison arrived, full of older men from the meanest block Jackson had to offer. These men were strategically placed between the younger, wilder men as tone setters. They kept everything under control.

John's visitor list filled up. His sister was five minutes away. He saw his mother regularly—it was a mere twenty-minute drive. Life was improved until he got up the courage to tell Norma that he was in touch with his father.

Norma went ballistic. "If you talked to your dad, don't even think about speaking to us." She stormed out of the room. Family visits trickled to nothing and it was many years until he had contact with his mother again.

Robert Bowman—"Big Bow"— filled the gap. He was a beast of a man. He was serving time for shooting some police officers. He could curl 100-pound dumbbells and bench over 400 pounds. Gossip about John's case swirled around Lapeer. The mountain approached him and hurled down a command. "I want to read your transcripts." John immediately went to his cell and retrieved the transcripts for Big Bow.

The next day, John was summoned. "Kid, you're in a world of shit. You need someone to help you."

"I'm not filing an appeal. I'm getting out another way."

"Just shut your dumb ass mouth. Rodney here is taking these for a while." Big Bow nodded to a man who was sitting on his bunk holding John's transcripts. "He's going to start filing your appeal. We won't charge you but, kid, you need help. We have to keep your case alive."

Big Bow became like a father to John, chewing him out when he got in trouble, scolding him when he made dumb decisions and pulling him away when he got into arguments with fools. The older man modeled morally-just decision-making and gave invaluable advice. He helped John grow into a person who would eventually understand what integrity is and why it matters. Big Bow was a killer, but he mentored John and filled a gap that had been empty his whole life.

John had to sneak around his new environment if he wanted to tattoo. He hid his activities in the dayroom, got caught every now and then and received a minor ticket. The ticket didn't even go in his file, but it allowed the guards to confiscate his equipment while admiring his art.

But there was plenty of business. Prison was so boring that getting tattoos gave people something to do and helped inmates cultivate an image that might intimidate an enemy. People also got tattoos to bond with their gangs.

John's talent got him in trouble, but it also saved him. So many men were indebted to him that no one bothered him anymore. He was winning when it came to peace of mind, but he was losing financially. He would build up his stash of possessions—electronics, coats and clothing—only to have them confiscated over and over because they were purchased with what was considered ill-gotten gains.

Soon he added drawing and painting to his repertoire. When he sold a piece of art, no one could take the things purchased from the proceeds away from him.

One day, while John was out on the yard, he heard screaming coming from the other side of the fence that surrounded the prison. A distraught woman ran directly toward him. She wore a nightgown; she had filthy bare feet and wild eyes. He hair was knotted and tangled. She threw herself against the chain-link and held on as her legs collapsed.

She hung there, crying. Two orderlies weren't far behind. Each grabbed an arm and dragged her away. John locked eyes with her as she receded toward a series of dark buildings that he could see off in the distance.

"What is that place?"

"Lapeer State Home. Its full of imbeciles and crazy people." John wouldn't know for several years that the neighboring institution had played such a tragic role in his life, but the place repulsed him nonetheless.

Once he was aware of it, he couldn't help noticing the spooky turrets that were visible from his window. After he got a job in the prison laundry, he was further repulsed by the place. The laundry had a contract with the institution next door. The sheets that were sent over from the Lapeer Home smelled of feces and dog food. He imagined that the residents to the north were not cared for much better than he was.

In spite of the benefits of being at Thumb Correctional, John had a well-connected enemy who worked there—a guard who knew Ella Stephens. This guard's influence and malice toward John revealed itself regularly.

John's entire unit—except for him and two men labeled as predators—were transferred to Level Two, a more pleasant and less-restrictive environment. John was sure that he had been left behind due to the intervention of the guard who was connected to Ella Stephens. The man's name came up over and over again as guards tossed John's cell and picked and prodded at him, hoping to keep him miserable. John was confident that the guard prompted his brothers-in-arms to harass John.

John worked out with Big Bow. He wanted to get big and strong—transform his scrawny young self into someone that people—prisoners and guards—would think twice about bothering. He was able to order synthetic steroids, adrenal and pituitary gland pills and mega weight gain to supplement his efforts.

He thought he would get big and healthy—little did he know he was about to go crazy. He gained weight, started benching increasing amounts and started losing control. His muscles were cut, veins popping out, but his emotions were popping out too. He yelled at people and picked fights. The anger at being locked away for life was harder to contain as he consumed the supplements.

One day, when an officer argued with him, John flung a chair across the room. "Come on. Get your crew in here and let's fight. I'm tired of all of you picking on me, taking my property."

John threw every chair in the unit at them and even a few tables. By the time he was out of ammunition, seventeen officers were waiting to take him down. They beat the crap out of him, all the way to the hole. His face was scraped against brick walls, he was bent around light poles and his shoulder was dislocated. The cuffs cut into his wrists. He was stripped naked, shivering in an empty cell, bleeding all over and still he wanted to fight. The pills had done a job on him, turning him into a walking hormone with pent up anger at the world blazing out of him.

In addition to his out-of-control hormones, he was depressed—

isolated from his mother and sisters, generally cut off from the world. He was lonely. The only reminder that he wasn't forgotten was that the guard connected to Ella Stephens was intent on making his life in prison even harder.

One day, the guard brought the husband and wife who owned the house that Ella had lived in to John's cell. The woman squealed with surprise. "Oh my god, it's John Aslin."

"I told you I had a surprise for you, Mom." the deputy said with satisfaction. "I'm making sure he's really well taken care of."

John realized that this man had been behind much of the hostility he had been shown by deputies in the recent past, even before he had taken steroids. Fortunately, he didn't have to deal with the problem for long. He was on the move again.

John
1989

John crossed the Mackinac Bridge again and arrived at Chippewa Correctional, otherwise known as Upper Regional Facility or URF which was commonly known by insiders as U-R-Fucked because the guards there were masters at playing mind games with prisoners and URF prisoners were violent and dangerous.

John was no sooner checked in and eating his first meal when a guard called out, "Who is Aslin? Is there an Aslin here?"

"Yes, sir. That's me."

"We've been waiting for you." There was arrogance and menace in his voice.

John leaned over and pointed at the man's butt. "There's a big hole here. I can see that."

"I'll be seeing you around, Aslin."

URF Level 4 inmates were potheads, pillheads and predators. They were crammed into tiny cells. The whole facility was small—only one basketball court, one small weight pit and one picnic table.

But his dad lived nearby. Regular visits from his father and stepmother, Fannie, calmed John down. He tried to stay out of trouble.

A familiar face walked up to him one day. It was his unit counselor from Lapeer. The guy had transferred north. "Your case was the topic of a lot of discussions down state. A lot of people disagreed with how your case went down. I want to do something for you. Give me six months with no misconducts and I'll get you into Level Two."

John kept his nose down and stayed ticket-free, then sent the counselor a kite, which is the name from the paperwork prisoners have to fill out to make a request, and the man followed through. John would be in the safer unit for three years.

He was still settling in when one of his new neighbors approached him. "I heard you're the best tattooist in the state. I got a buddy who got one and its real messed up. I need you to fix it."

John was firm. "No way. I just came off Level 4. I'm not going back. I don't need any trouble."

Ten minutes later, a guy showed up; he revealed an awful tattoo and unloaded $40 in groceries and a nice radio with headphones on John's desk. "Come on, man. Help me out. All this will be yours. I got a good lookout. You won't get caught."

It took a couple of hours, but John fixed his problem. The guy was so happy that he kicked his bunky out and moved John in. "Johnny, you ain't even got to work on anyone but me. I'll pay you every week, Bro." The guy owned a party store on the outside and always had money in his account.

Things went well and then one day his bunky was gone, carted away by deputies. He was close to his out date, but his wife had ratted him out—she told the prison he was incarcerated under an alias in Michigan and was a fugitive from Florida. She didn't want him coming after her when he was released because, though she had kept money in his account, it wasn't as much as it should have been based on how well their business was doing. She knew he would be mad when he figured that out.

John was busy for the next three years, accumulating fifty new customers. He was talented, so they lined up. He tallied many tickets too. If he turned someone down because he was too busy, they would tattle to the guards; the guards would shake his cell down and take all of his stuff.

He got good at spotting the ones who were likely to cause trouble by the tantrums they threw. As soon as they left, he would immediately clean out his cell. It was a cat and mouse game and he was a cat at heart, so he learned how to win.

Things were better when he started working on some of the officers but holding off a crackdown on his tattooing business couldn't eliminate the fact that URF was becoming increasingly violent.

A theft ring had been stabbing many men so that it could steal their food and personal belongings. Everyone knew who was doing it, but no one was brave enough to say it out loud. One crew member was a customer, so John had an escort when he carried his purchases back to his cell. He was safe for the time being, but he knew how quickly the power dynamics could shift.

He decided to make a change. John asked to transfer back to Lapeer. He would be closer to home and in a safer place. His counselor filled out paperwork to send him to LRF, thinking that was the code for Lapeer. John was surprised when he, instead, ended up at the Lower Regional Facility in Muskegon, Michigan, located in the north west corner of the lower peninsula, far from Flint to the south and his father to the north.

John made an appointment with his new counselor. "Why did I end up here?"

"It says that you wanted to come here—the paperwork says LRF."

John groaned. "I was supposed to go to Lapeer."

"Well, you're stuck here now."

John settled in and opened shop. He was back in the tattoo business, but a pattern emerged. Instead of paying him for his work, several in a row told the guards that John had threatened to kill them. It was a bizarre turn of events since he had threatened no one. He was put in the hole, where he couldn't collect on his debts.

After this scenario repeated three times, the prison gave up and shipped him to Lapeer. He was elated. He was going to a place full of friends and this time he would be in Level 2 with them.

John
1993

His nemesis, the deputy who had haunted him for years, was waiting at check in when John arrived. He took John's file, waved it cockily in front of his face, and moved it to the Level 4 pile. This meant that John would be placed in more restrictive housing with more dangerous people.

There was no basis for it—John was ticket-free. The deputy claimed, with a straight face, that Level 2 was full. His cruelty knew no bounds. What he really meant was that there was no comfortable place for John in Lapeer so long as he worked there.

When John was settled in, a guard showed up at his cell. "Aslin, I was told to shake you down good."

John held his tongue as he stepped out into the hall and relinquished his space. The guard took John's every worldly possession except for an empty bag, a single sock and some state towels. John's legal work was crumpled into a ball.

Two hours later, the same guard returned. "I was told to shake you down again in case I missed anything."

John stepped to the door. "I'll give you what I got left if you want to step in here."

The guard heard the threat in the words. "Kid, I know you know what's going on. Don't take it out on me. It would be plain stupid to hit me. The sergeant and the president of your fan club will be on vacation next week. I'll give you everything back then. Just don't blame me. Let's you and me get along and I'll help you out." John chose to trust the guard even though his heart was telling him not to.

On Monday, John was called to the officer's station and every bit of his property was returned to him. The guard, his secret ally, whispered words of encouragement. "Here you go, kid. Now just chill out. Don't throw any chairs at us. We're on your side."

John focused on appealing his case, working many hours to complete the paperwork. He sent it to the prison library to be copied. When he went to pick it up, it was missing. In fact, it had never arrived. He was frantic and furious.

Red Taylor, known as a mean guard who was not to be messed with, tried to calm John down. "Let's go talk in your cell." When they arrived, he motioned for John to go in first. "We need to talk, but don't you swing on me."

John went to the far side of his cell, waiting to hear what the man had to say. "I found your paperwork in your enemy's office."

John exploded. "That piece of shit! He's trying to stop me from filing my appeal, reading my legal papers, telling his family what I'm doing before the courts even know."

Red Taylor put a hand on John's shoulder. "I'm getting your stuff back and things are about to change for you. No other officers are going to be his pawns anymore." The harassment was tamped down after that.

Soon after, John was elected Unit Representative. This gave him an opportunity to attend the Warden's Forum. When he was given permission to speak, he had his question ready. "Why was my legal paperwork missing for days?"

His nemesis jumped up. "I took care of that, Aslin!"

"I beg your pardon. I wasn't speaking to you."

"If you think you're going to come in here and become a political activist, you're going to have a rude fucking awakening."

John placed a shocked look on his face. "I didn't use profanity when I was speaking and my question has not been answered."

His adversary stormed out of the room. The guard who was running the meeting turned to John. "John, why are you still in Level 4?"

"I was told that there hasn't been an open bed in Level 2 for two years."

His questioner shook his head. "I'll look into that."

Later that night, a guard delivered a message to John. "You have fifteen minutes to make it to Level 2 before count or you won't be coming over there."

John grabbed his legal work and pictures and left the rest of his things without looking back. He felt happy for the first time in a long time—he was returning to his friends and would be free of his enemy's grip.

The man who had haunted him since he began serving his sentence died of cancer not long after that.

For the most part, John was treated with respect by the other officers once he moved. He spent many comfortable years, relatively speaking, on Level 2 in Lapeer.

Lapeer Correctional had a vibrant Native community. John attended services and began to reclaim the heritage he had lost in the midst of his parents' chaotic relationship. The older Native men mentored him, helping him build skills to help him deal with his troubles in better ways, ways that wouldn't lead to self-destruction. John absorbed the history of his people. Learning about the struggles of others pulled him outside of his own misery. He developed compassion for the suffering his people had endured as their rights were disregarded.

As he self-identified more and more as Native American, a new source of harassment opened up. On a daily basis, he would hear some form of, "What makes you think you're an Indian?" but instead of punching back, he was able to take the challenges in stride and press on.

He remained in contact with his father. He was still stuck in a living hell, in prison for the rest of his life for a non-violent crime, but he was starting to feel complete. Parts of his psyche were starting to heal.

1994

Dear Mr. Aslin,

May I call you John? I heard about your situation from a friend at church. She knows your mother. Your life must be hard. I thought it might be nice for you to have a Christian woman praying for you every day. I would like to become your pen pal. Would that be okay with you? Please write me back if you get a chance.

Yours truly,
Sharon (but call me Sherry)

Dear Sherry,

It's been a while since I got such good news as to think that someone on the outside had put me in their prayers. It means so much to me. I try to focus on the good in the world whenever I can. Knowing that you are sending prayers up to the Heavenly Father on my behalf will bring me a moment of peace every time I think of it. I would be honored if you would call me John because that might mean you see me as a friend. I would love to be pen pals. I have enclosed a picture I drew of a bird I saw out in the yard. I hope you like it.

Your friend,
John

Dear John,

What's it like to spend all that time locked up? I got stuck in an elevator for twenty minutes and thought I was going to have a panic attack. I started imagining that there was no fresh air and that soon I wouldn't be able to breath. I imagine that your cell is not much bigger than the space I was in. Am I wrong? I'm going to have to ask you to write to me at another address. My husband found one of your letters and got sort of jealous. I told him that I was just trying to brighten your life by showing you the light of Christ but he doesn't go in much for church like I do. I don't want to abandon our friendship so please just send the letters to my friend Carrie. She'll make sure I get them.

Yours truly,
Sherry

(P.S. The drawing of the bird was lovely. You're very talented.)

Dear Sherry,
Prison would almost be boring if it wasn't so dangerous. I have a routine to fill my days and keep my mind away from dark places as much as I can, but I can never completely relax around here. Situations can turn violent, even deadly, without any warning. I spend my time reading, drawing and giving tattoos to other guys. If you see a tattoo out in the world and find out that the person got it in a Michigan prison, there's a good chance it's my work. I'm able to make a little spending money by doing the tattoos and drawing greeting cards for guys to send to their sweethearts. Did you like the bear I sent you? I thought that bear and I could talk to each other when I was a kid. He was kept in a cage outside a store up near Rose City. Every time I saw him, I felt like he was asking me to open his door. One time I stole a car when I was a teenager and I drove up there to set him free. I got in a lot of trouble, but I thought I was on the righteous side of that adventure. I never found out if they caught him or if he escaped for good. I like to think that he is out there living the life, but he's probably long dead. I read in a book that bears live about twenty years in the wild and forty in captivity. The first time I saw him was about twenty years ago. If he's still around, I wish he could come return the favor for me. I look forward to your next letter.

Your friend,
John

Dear John,
I have a new address that I wrote on the envelope. I didn't want to tell you this before, but things have not been safe at home. I finally had to leave. A recent "incident" was the worst of all. I finally couldn't take it anymore. I'm embarrassed to say that I have a big bruise on my waist

and quite a shiner on my left eye. I couldn't hide in the house long enough for it to heal, so I had to admit the truth to Pastor Luke. I was so worried God would be upset with me for abandoning my marriage, but my pastor said I need to pray and ask for guidance. He said it's okay to leave for now so I can make a safe and peaceful home for my child, especially since Richard smacked her when she tried to stop him from coming after me.

Pastor Luke wants me to bring Richard to the Lord but he's seen this kind of thing before. He says God will understand if I file for divorce. If Richard won't become a Godly man, then he and I are "unequally yoked" and I can't live that way. I liked the bear a lot.

Yours truly,
    Sherry

Dear John,
    Richard has been stalking me. He stood outside my new apartment and yelled vile things. Several of the neighbors stopped being friendly. I have an appointment to see a lawyer this week.

Yours truly,
    Sherry

Dear John,
    I did it. I filed for divorce. I feel scared and relieved at the same time.

Yours truly,
    Sherry

Dear Sherry,
    It hurt my heart to think that anyone could hit someone as nice as you. Richard does not deserve to be your husband and I think God will understand your decision to divorce him. Please know that I will be praying for your safety and that you will have peace of mind about your choice.

Your friend,
    John

Dear John,

After all of these months of writing, I have decided it's time for a visit. I'm hoping to come next week. It will be nice to finally meet my pen pal who has been so supportive during my difficulties.

See you soon.

Yours truly,
Sherry

John kept his hair long, a remnant of his youth and a tribute to his Native American heritage. He carefully combed and braided it into a single strand so it would look neat when he met Sherry. He looked at himself in the mirror carefully for the first time in a long time, practicing a smile that he didn't often use.

He was self-conscious of his teeth, which looked crooked to his eyes, so he always tried to smile with his lips covering them. His full smile was more sincere; he tried to balance his competing goals— hidden crooked teeth and authenticity—as he waited for the guard to retrieve him for the visiting room.

Interest in him as a human being had dwindled in the outside world. He got few visits, mainly his mother and sister, Linda, who lived near Lapeer, Michigan, where he was housed. His father (who wrote him faithfully) and step-mom made the long drive from the Upper Peninsula a couple times a year. Sherry's would be the first "social visit" in over a decade.

John saw Sherry sitting in the second row of chairs as soon as he entered the room. She gave off a nervous energy, a shy person battling her instincts in an attempt to appear bright and cheery. Her light brown hair was cut short. She had bright blue eyes—similar in color to John's own but where his were piercing, hers sparkled.

She stood when she realized he was there. Her lips turned up in a warm smile. With her high heels, they stood eye-to-eye. She was too pretty for words. John found himself turning shy himself.

He stuttered out a hello and sat down across from her. "You made it." His smile grew so wide that his lips couldn't contain it. His hand reflexively brushed up to hide his teeth. "I was worried that the weather might've made you change your mind."

"I've been driving in Michigan long enough not to let the weather hold me back."

"How were the roads?"

"They were fine." She whispered, "Why are you covering up your face?"

John reluctantly put his hands in his lap. "I didn't want you to have to look at my crooked teeth."

"I think they look fine. They give you character. Your life has been a bit crooked, but you can still smile at me."

John relaxed. Sherry had no idea how much her kindness meant to him. He went months without having a gentle act directed at him. The closest he came would be when a hardened convict might grunt approval when John finished laying down some ink. There were a few warm and friendly guys inside, but not many. The only employee who was ever nice was the nurse in the medical unit, but he hardly ever saw her. He was starved for experiences that made him feel human.

"I can't believe you got dressed up to come and see me. Were you slipping and sliding in those shoes when you walked in?"

Sherry laughed. "Yes, I was having a time, but that gentleman over there offered me his arm and walked me in." Sherry nodded toward an elderly man who was visiting his son.

John noted that the civility of the father had not been passed down to his angry son, who was known for starting fights. "That's good. It'd be nice if he could walk you out too."

They had gotten through chatting about the weather. John was eager to keep the conversation going, eager to hold her there as long as possible. Having visitors was the closest thing to a vacation that he might ever get.

"How are you handling life as a single mom? Is Richard leaving you alone?"

"Yes, I think he has a new girlfriend. I'm old news now. My daughter wants nothing to do with him, so I really don't have to worry about seeing him. It's been really nice." She laughed, but John could see that there was a bit of pain lingering in her eyes.

They chatted for hours. At the end of the visit, she asked him if she could pray with him. Normally he might have felt self-conscious to pray in front of other inmates. Prison was a tough place and any show of weakness in any moment could have dire consequences, but he noticed that the other men in the room seemed softened by their contact with normalcy. He nodded and bowed his head.

"Dear God, please keep my friend safe. Let him know he's your child, that you love him and are looking out for him. In the name of your son, Jesus, amen."

Sherry continued to visit, initially a couple times a month and then every week or more. She brought John clothes that she picked up at the Salvation Army store and books she thought he might like to read. One day, she brought him another visitor. "This is my daughter, Amber."

Amber was the opposite of her mother at first glance. She wore all black, her clothes carefully layered and torn to give an effect of not caring about her appearance, but her carefully applied dark eye-liner, collection of piercings and the multiple tattoos that lined her arms spoke otherwise. She tried hard to appear tough and aloof. She struck a pose of boredom, sitting back with her arms crossed. This brought her most prominent tattoo into full view.

John pointed to the design that covered her arm. The part above her elbow was the torso of a beautiful mermaid with long hair and a tail that narrowed to the crook of her elbow, then morphed into a snake that was curled around a syringe. Bright spots of blood dripped from the end. "You get that tattoo from Charlie at Moondogs?"

"Oh my God, how did you know that?" The standoffish seventeen-year-old was suddenly bubbling with friendliness.

"That's my design. I sent Charlie a drawing of it." John had designed the piece for a friend who was struggling with a secret addiction. The mermaid represented the view that the addict showed to the world and the bottom served as a reminder of the struggle that brewed below the surface. "Can I see his work?"

Amber held her arm out. John saw small pinpricks dotting her inner elbow, hidden by the ink. Amber saw him notice her secret and drew her arm back, shrinking back into an uncomfortable posture. Sherry excused herself to use the bathroom a few minutes later.

"Does your mom know?"

Amber shook her head, worry washing over her face. "It's not a big deal. I've got it under control. Besides, she would just try to pray it away. That's what she does." There was an edge of frustration in Amber's voice.

"Your mother loves you very much. You're the reason she filed for divorce. I think she would have let your dad keep hurting her but when he hurt you, she had enough."

Amber was a regular guest. She and John developed a ritual where he would examine Amber's arms when her mom stepped away and encourage her whether they were blemish free or not, but unmarked skin was becoming more frequent.

Several months later, Sherry showed up alone. "I need to talk to you about something." She had such a serious look on her face that John was immediately nervous. His stomach flip-flopped. *She's not going to visit anymore. I wonder what happened.*

"My friends don't approve of this little arrangement we have."

I knew this was too good to be true.

"I talked to Pastor Luke and he said we have to make some changes."

John was deflated. Sherry represented the only goodness in his life; he'd fallen for her. Her visits and letters provided him with more happiness than he'd had in years. "I understand."

Sherry was sweet and "Christ-like," but she could be spunky too. "I don't think you do. I'm about to ask you to marry me. If we get married, no one will be bothered by the fact that I've decided to devote myself to you."

John was speechless. He gave her a full-toothed grin. "I wasn't expecting that."

"You must know that I've fallen for you, John."

"I'd hoped but why would you want to latch yourself to me? I may be stuck in this place for the rest of my life. You're a young woman with a lot of living to do."

"It's important to me that my church friends respect me. I think they will if we marry. I hope you decide to say yes."

"I would be a lucky man to have you as my wife, but I need to think about it. I need to make sure this is a good idea for you. I love having you visit and having you to talk to and write to, but this place is hard on relationships. I don't want to rush into this selfishly and have you be miserable in the future."

Shelly visited several times a week. She opened each visit with a question—"Did you make up your mind yet?"—and closed each one with a prayer.

Three weeks later, when she asked the question, John said, "Yes and yes."

Prison weddings are somber affairs trying to masquerade as joyous occasions. Sherry had to jump through a lot of administrative hoops to make their marriage official. First, she had to get a marriage license and write a letter to the prison chaplain to schedule a date. Then John had to write a kite to the Chaplain to confirm his desire to get married. Then Sherry had to have her guests fill out applications and get approved to enter the prison. It was a challenge, but Sherry could be very determined. It took about a month, then everything was set.

Sherry and Amber were through security, but Sherry's cousin, Barb, unfamiliar with the process, lagged behind. A guard walked by as she was being frisked.

"Barb, is that you?"

"Hey, Ronnie, long time no see."

The man froze and stared her down. "What're you doin' here?"

Barb was the oldest daughter of a hard-nosed cop and no one familiar with her family would have expected to see her visiting a prisoner. "I'm here as a witness for my cousin's wedding?"

Distaste flashed over the guard's face. "Is she a bit slow? She's marrying a con?"

Barb was not one to buy into sweeping generalizations. The guard's comment got on her nerves. "Mind your business, Ronnie. The heart wants what the heart wants."

Barb watched a guard do a hack job on the small cake Sherry had brought in for the celebration. He systematically inserted a knife in it from every angle.

"What the hell?" exclaimed Barb. "Are you all that paranoid?"

The guard gave her an icy glare, issuing a warning in a steely voice. "You best keep your opinions to yourself unless you want to go back out the way you came in."

Ronnie was hovering. "Don't mind her, Branner. Her pop's a cop. She thinks she's hot shit but she's all right."

Branner finished rearranging the cake. It didn't look as pretty as it did when it was carried through the front door, but it would still taste good.

The women entered the visiting room, which had been cleared for the small ceremony. Sherry had borrowed a suit for John; he was waiting for her, beaming. The black jacket and blue tie matched his dark hair and bright eyes.

He whistled softly. "Damn, Sherry, I didn't think you could ever look more beautiful than you always do, but I was wrong."

She smiled. "You watch that language, Mr. Aslin, before I change my mind."

Fred
1996

Fred made it to 72 years old, in spite of all the things that happened to him that should have wiped him out. The state had tried to make him irrelevant and though it had succeeded in taking his bloodline away, he survived. He married a widow and raised her sons like his own. But he was feeling his age. It was time to plan for a journey to the happy place—it could come at any time. He made an appointment with his attorney.

"Hi Fred. What can I do for you?"

"I'm feeling my age. I want to make a will, get my affairs settled."

They discussed his wishes. The conversation wound its way around to what had happened over a half century before at the Lapeer Home. His attorney was shocked. It was a story that came out of nightmares, not something that could have happened to the man sitting in her office.

"We should get your records. See if we can learn more about what happened."

The records showed how the state had tried to justify the sterilization. Fred always thought that he and his siblings ended up at the Home because they were poor. He didn't know that even more than that, it was because they were Indian.

The Aslin family had fallen victim to the burgeoning Eugenics movement that gained momentum in Michigan in the early 20th Century. The details of that movement incensed Fred, once he learned the truth behind his tragic childhood.

Battle Creek, Michigan
1914

The series of unfortunate events that lead to the Aslin children being abducted by the State of Michigan started in the bizarre little mind of John Harvey Kellogg. John Harvey liked to tinker. He tinkered with cereal recipes and medical patents, but he especially liked to tinker with human beings.

When he was still a boy, he fell under the influence of James and Ellen White, becoming their protégé. The Whites were enticed to relocate their publishing business to Battle Creek after being offered financial support by the Kellogg patriarch, John Harvey's father. The Whites employed John Harvey when he was quite young; he became closer to them than their own children.

The Whites were two of four founders of the Seventh-Day Adventist Church; the Kellogg family were among their staunchest supporters. Because they believed that the return of Jesus to Earth to redeem the faithful was imminent, the Kellogg children only attended school for a short period of time—education would not be necessary in the afterlife.

John Harvey, however, read extensively and was self-taught. He began working for the Whites when he was twelve years old and, by 1864, he was editing and proofreading their publications regarding health. By 1875, John Harvey completed his medical training at the University of Michigan and New York University Medical Schools. The following year he was put in charge of the Battle Creek Medical Surgical Sanitarium.

It goes without saying that John Harvey accomplished some impressive things in his life, but he laid the groundwork to create tragedy in the lives of many people. Seventh Day Adventists advocate for a vegetarian lifestyle and John Harvey zealously pursued the discovery of creative new foods to supplement the group's diet. He is credited with creating granola (thank you, John Harvey) and the modern concept of breakfast cereal—namely, Corn Flakes. He was the first person to patent meat substitutes made from nuts and grains; he patented acidophilus soy milk in 1934. The best thing that has ever been attributed to him is the credit for developing peanut butter, although this high honor has been attributed to several others as well.

John Harvey held numerous medical patents, improving devices that administered light therapy and massage and provided therapeutic exercise, as well as radiant heat baths. Hydrotherapy and heated operating tables were among his inventions. But he also developed an instrument for the removal of the ovaries, and it is this device that opens a window into the dark recesses of his weird little mind.

John Harvey averred all things sexual. When he married Ella Eaton in 1879, they immediately installed themselves in separate bedrooms. During the next 41 years of a marriage that ended due to Ella's death, their union was never consummated; they had no biological children, though they adopted seven and fostered over forty youngsters.

John Harvey's anti-sexuality obsessions pervaded his life. He believed in eating only bland foods because they were less likely to excite sexual desire. He promoted circumcision of boys—not babies—without the use of anesthesia so that they would remember the pain and be discouraged from masturbation. He believed that the clitoris should be treated with acid so that any stimulation of it would be painful. And he believed that only certain people should be allowed to procreate.

John Harvey tracked advances in plant and animal breeding occurring around him and thought that the same techniques could be applied to the human population to create a superior race. Sound familiar?

In 1914, he organized and hosted "The First National Conference on Race Betterment" at the Battle Creek Sanitarium. It was well-attended by powerful people, including U.S. Senators from two states, a state senator from as far away as Oklahoma, the Vice-President of the New York State Board of Charities, the Director of New York Life Insurance, the President of the American Medical Association, the Director of Good Housekeeping Magazine, the directors of the Michigan, Kentucky and Indiana State Boards of Health and the former Minister of Agriculture from Ireland. Prestigious academics were also in attendance. The President of Harvard and Northwestern University Medical School, the Superintendent of the Chicago Schools, the President of Fargo College and twenty other college administrators sat in the audience. The leader of the YMCA was there as well as, oddly enough, Booker T. Washington. There were numerous social workers, clergy members and juvenile judges occupying seats.

Kellogg walked confidently to the podium and began the swirl of ugliness that would impact the Aslin family line for generations to come. "Thank you for attending the First National Conference on Race Betterment. Man has improved the production of eggs in hens, milk in cows, turned sour little apples into hundreds of delicious varieties. Humans have created wonderful new races of horses, cows and pigs. Man has improved every useful creature and useful plant with which he has come into contact by breeding out defects. The efficiency of the trotting horse was improved 50% in a century. Why then should we not also have a new and improved race of men?"

There was a smattering of applause.

"The average attitude toward human eugenics is well illustrated by the story of a New York merchant who had four full-blooded dogs and two young sons. A friend asked, 'Why do you give your personal attention to your dogs and turn your sons over to a tutor?' The man replied, 'Well, my dogs have a pedigree.'" The auditorium erupted in a chorus of chuckles.

"The idea of a new human race may seem absurd, but the suspicion has been creeping into the minds of thinking men that humans may not be making real and permanent progress. Many of today's savages descended from ancestors who possessed relatively elaborate civilizations. The possibility of degeneration of the white races of Europe seems to be worth some consideration. We are subject to the general laws of evolution and are as likely to degenerate as improve. Our bodily structures and mental capacities have not progressed beyond those of our immediate forefathers, the ancient Greeks. Does the reason of the average man of civilized Europe clearly evidence progress when compared with that of the man of the bygone age?" He paused to let that question sink into the minds of his receptive audience.

"A noted evolutionist has predicted that future man will be a bespectacled bald-headed and toothless individual of infantile proportions and diminishing intelligence. Advances in disease control have simply served to keep alive a large number of feeble infants who would otherwise have perished. The result has actually served to diminish the average strength and vigor of the race. The effect of natural selection in weeding out the weak is diminished. The world can be rescued from the control of the physically, morally and mentally decadent only by rigid application of the principles of eugenics."

"Life on this planet is so constituted that it can only progress by the survival and propagation of the biologically fit and the elimination of the unfit. Insanity and idiocy are increasing. Diseases of vice, alcoholism, drug habits, suicide and violence are spreading rapidly. The number of vagrants and paupers is increasing. Mental unsoundness, lunacy, idiocy, imbecility and feeble-mindedness may be traced to hereditary influence in 90% of the cases. The birthrate of the thrifty and healthy is in decline while families of the incompetent and parasitic working-class average 7.4 children per family."

"So far we have lacked the moral courage to openly recognize and fight this scourge. We possess enough knowledge to create a new race within a century if principles of scientific breeding are put into actual practice. If we could remove the drag of the mediocre on ancestry for only a few generations, we could eliminate regression and create a stock of exceptional men."

"Degeneracy is rampant on earth. Every day the tree is planting its roots deeper and spreading wider its death dropping branches, but eugenics can rise like a light tower in the darkness." His audience ate the whole thing up like a bowl of Corn Flakes.

Lansing, Michigan
1923

It took almost a decade, but Kellogg's plan took root when the Michigan Legislature passed a bill that allowed for the "compulsory sterilization of anyone adjudged feeble-minded by a probate court." This meant that a judge, without even seeing an individual, and upon the word of someone who may or may not care about or even personally observe the person being discussed, could order that person to be sterilized. The bill allowed virtually anyone to make application for sterilization of a third-party, whether acting in the interest of the "defective person" or the public.

This bill was drafted by Professor Burke Shartel of the University of Michigan Law School. It was supported by Victor Vaughn, Dean of the University of Michigan Medical School and by the very president of the university, Clarence Mitchell. The purpose of the bill was to limit the ability of certain undesirable populations to muddy the genetic pool with their undesirable DNA. Poor Indians fell into the very category of peoples who needed to be eliminated. Certainly the U.S. Supreme Court would step in and reverse this miscarriage of justice, wouldn't it?

US Supreme Court, Washington DC
1927

The Marshall of the Court solemnly entered the gallery and made the same announcement he made every time the Court was in session.

"The Honorable, the Chief Justice and the Associate Justices of the Supreme Court of the United States. Oyez! Oyez! Oyez! All persons having business before the Honorable, the Supreme Court of the United States, are admonished to draw near and give their attention, for the Court is now sitting. God save the United States and this Honorable Court."

The marshall announced the case that would solidify that the Aslin children were screwed. "Please give your attention to the first case, Buck v Bell."

Attorney I.M. Whitehead (aptly and actually named) spoke half-heartedly on behalf of his client, a poor woman who was purportedly institutionalized based on claims that she was feeble-minded; she had actually been detained due to her promiscuity. "May it please the court, I am here on behalf of my client, Carrie Buck, whom the State of Virginia has petitioned the court to sterilize. The inherent right of mankind to go through life without mutilation of organs of generation needs no Constitutional declaration. We would ask this Honorable Court to deem the statute that provides the authority for this request a violation of Ms. Buck's Due Process Rights under the Constitution of the United States and to deny Virginia's request."

Mr. Whitehead's adversary, Harry Hamilton Laughlin, had the last laugh. "May it please the Court. Ms. Carrie Buck belongs to the shiftless, ignorant, and worthless class of anti-social whites of the South and this propensity has been traced back to three generations of her line. She provides a typical picture of the low-grade moron. She is promiscuous and has already birthed two bastards. Virginia prays that this Honorable Court will see the wisdom in allowing it to proceed with ridding the race of degeneracy by preventing the feeble-minded from procreating and allowing the state to involuntarily sterilize Carrie Buck so that society will not have to suffer or support any more of her degenerate progeny."

Justice Oliver Wendall Holmes delivered the verdict in the case. It did not fall on the side of protection of the vulnerable. "We have seen more than once that the public welfare may call upon the best citizens for their lives. It would be strange if it could not call upon those who already sap the strength of the State for these lesser sacrifices, often not felt to be such by those concerned, to prevent our being swamped with incompetence."

"It is better for all the world, if instead of waiting to execute degenerate offspring for crime, or to let them starve for their imbecility, society can prevent those who are manifestly unfit from continuing their kind. The principle that sustains compulsory vaccination is broad enough to cover cutting the Fallopian tubes. Three generations of imbeciles are enough. Virginia shall be allowed to sterilize Carrie Buck."

Fred was furious when he met with his lawyer after reading his file. His court-appointed "guardian" didn't even attend the hearing where a judge rubber-stamped a request to sterilize Fred. The records showed that Fred wasn't allowed to be present either. According to state paperwork, he was still, officially, a "mental defective."

"They termed us feeble-minded idiots and wrote that our children would be like us or even worse. Do I seem like a feeble-minded idiot to you, someone who can't live a normal life and raise a family?"

"No Fred, you don't."

"My brother, Ted, fostered over 100 kids. I raised my wife's boys from being babies. They were wrong about me, about Ted, about all of us. What can I do about this?"

Fred and his attorney made a plan. He wanted an apology. None came.

He was so infuriated at the insult that he filed suit against the state of Michigan, seeking compensation.

John
1996

John and Sherry settled into a routine. She showed up three times a week, ending each visit with a prayer for his safety. Most of the time, she chattered about events from her week. Not much good happened in his life, so he did not have much to offer beyond telling stories from his past, but he knew how to keep the conversation going, enjoying the minutiae of her life. He was a good listener, picking up on details and asking questions.

One day his curiosity caused the conversation to take a fateful turn. "Do you believe that God hears your prayers and guides you?"

"Yes, of course I do."

"That's something my beliefs and yours have in common."

Sherry paused. "What do you mean?"

"My tribe believes that when we offer up prayers in our ceremonies, the Creator hears them and provides us guidance in our dreams or at ceremonies."

Sherry was startled. "What in the world are you talking about?"

John was taken aback by her reaction. "We believe that God exists in everything. The wind, the animals, the trees."

"God can never talk to you through a tree. If you think a tree is talking to you, that's the devil." Anger infused her voice as her body stiffened.

"I don't think God talks to me through trees. I just respect trees, birds, the earth, the wind, the rain. Everything that is alive has a life force coursing through it and deserves respect because that means God is in it."

"John, this sounds crazy to me. Like witchcraft."

"But Sherry, your own God gave the Ten Commandments to you through a burning bush."

"That's different. And what do you mean—my own God? Isn't he your God too?"

"Yes and no. I just think of God in a different way."

Sherry was visibly upset, her voice shaking as she ended the visit abruptly. John didn't see her for a full week. When she finally came back, the brightness was gone; she delivered an ultimatum in a flat voice. "I talked to Pastor Luke. He says you have to become a Christian, give up that nonsense about praying to trees and animals or the wind or I have to end the marriage."

John was saddened by her pronouncement. "I never asked you to change a thing about yourself to earn my love. Never even told you that something you think or believe is wrong. Learning about my tribe and its ways has made me a better person, more connected to my father and my past. I can't just give it up."

"If that's how you feel, I guess there isn't anything else to say."

The "Dear John" letter came in the mail soon after.

Dear John,

I checked with the court. If you file the divorce, they'll waive the filing fee because you're a prisoner. I can't afford it so please take care of this as soon as you can. I've met someone. I need to be freed of this situation so I can move on and live my life.

Sherry

Animals were drawn to John. At Michigan Training Unit, a murder of crows would wait, just over the fence, until John opened his cell window and threw them chocolate cookies. There was something magical about the fact that they remembered him and waited specifically for him each day at a certain time.

When he got back to Lapeer, he had a pet groundhog that lived in a ditch drain. As soon as John sat down at the picnic table in the yard each morning, Stubby, named such for his lack of a tail, would waddle over and put his front paws on John's knee, eating carrots and celery out of his hand.

A family of raccoons would show up in the afternoon. They weren't as trusting as Stubby. They came within a foot, but if John tried to pet them, they hissed and let him know he was pushing his luck.

At any given time, John had at least one snapping turtle in his cell. The seagulls would pick them up from the creek and drop them on the basketball court, trying to crack their shells open. John would rescue them and keep them inside to heal and grow, feeding them bugs and grubs that he would dig up in the yard until they were too big and heavy for the gulls to target. Then he would release them into Stubby's drain so they could make their way back to the creek.

One day, as he stood, enjoying the feel of the sun on his face, he saw something small moving toward him. He held very still. A tiny deer mouse hopped on top of his shoe. It looked up at him. He leaned down and picked it up, put it in his pocket and took it back to his cell.

Vern lived with him for five months. He was a good companion and John trained him to do tricks. One day a guard showed up. "John John, someone said you have a rat living in your cell."

John just laughed and tapped on the desk. Out walked little Vern, with his adorable ears that were bigger than his head. Vern hopped on John's hand. "Really? Does this look like a rat?"

"I'm sorry, but we have to take him outside." John walked his little friend to the edge of the yard and placed him in the grass. Vern stood there, looking at John as if to say, "Really, Bro? Why are you doing this? It's wild out here." Then Vern gave a mouse shrug and disappeared through the fence. John never saw him again.

John was furious. He knew that his neighbor, whose eyes had gotten as big as eggs when he saw Vern, had turned him in. He stopped in front of the man's cell. "Someone else has a rat living in their cell too!"

Fred
1998

The court dismissed Fred Aslin's lawsuit, stating that the statute of limitations had expired. Five years prior, the Michigan Supreme Court had ruled that a man whose eye surgery had been bungled, but who didn't discover the truth about what had happened to him until 26 years later, could sue for compensation. In that case, the court ruled that statutes of limitation "do not ... extinguish a cause of action before the plaintiff is aware of the possible cause of action," but that sentiment was not extended to the Aslin family.

The Michigan legislature could have taken action to assist Fred, but it did not. The passage of time could have been overlooked, as it was for Holocaust survivors in 1999.

Good Morning America and 20/20 ran a story about Fred's cases but no apology came.

John
1998

"Aslin, report to the unit desk."

When John got to there, he received a message that set him back because he knew what it meant— "Call Fannie Aslin." It meant that his father no longer walked the earth.

He called Fannie.

"Johnny, he's gone. I'm so sorry. Getting to know you brought him a lot of happiness. You be sure to keep in touch with me. You're my son too."

It was pouring rain. John went to the yard, sitting off in a corner. He felt safe to release his grief because the rain obscured the tears streaming down his face; not many people were outside anyway. He was able to see the highway, cars speeding by while he was going nowhere.

He had been given such a small amount of time with his father. They never got to do anything meaningful together. His father had only been able to visit him a handful times—not a lifetime's worth.

John released his sorrow for the years he had and did not have with his father and the future possibilities that were now gone. Still, in the small amount of contact they had with each other, his father tried to help him. He set John on the Native path, gave him cultural purpose and gave his life a song, a reason to continue to improve himself. Connecting with Native elders helped him become a more reasonable and responsible person.

He was startled when he finally looked up and saw his Ogema—leader of the Native American circle in the prison—headed straight for him. "John, I heard about your father. Are you okay?"

"Thank you but yes."

The older man squeezed John's shoulder, then left him to his memories. John was surprised—he had told no one that his father had passed away but the Ogema had known why John needed comfort.

Soon after his father died, John's sense of the world was altered by the TV. "Hey, Aslin. Take a look. This guy's from Michigan; he's got your name."

The guest on "Good Morning America" was named Fred Aslin. He was suing the State of Michigan for forcibly sterilizing him. He resembled John's dad.

He appeared on 20/20 and told Diane Sawyer a terrible story. "My brothers and sisters and me—we were all held by the State against our will. We were not feeble-minded. They forced sterilization on us before they would set us free. None of us were able to have children. All because we were Indians."

What about me? John was distraught, his heart breaking for the childhood his father endured and kept to himself. He called Fannie. "Johnny, he just didn't like to talk about it. It caused him so much pain that he tried to push it deep inside. But he knew you were his. You look like him and talk like him and act like him—even though you'd never been around until we met."

Fannie collected articles for him. He pieced together what had happened. As he gained a deeper understanding, he regretted his father's death even more. Learning about John Harvey Kellogg and the impact that the neighboring property—the Lapeer Home— had had on his life was the hardest thing he endured in prison. He should have had a huge family. He should have been surrounded by cousins when he was growing up. But his family had been stunted. His generation had been erased by the state's exploitation of his vulnerable relatives when they were on the cusp of beginning their adult lives.

Charlotte, Michigan
Fred Aslin

I've done some research about the Home, as you can imagine. It started when I had a health scare and decided to do some estate planning. That journey caused me to go looking for my records and I found them. Reading them laid me low. Coming to the realization that you don't have any natural heirs is a chilling thing.

They sterilized each of us when we hit 18. A whole generation wiped out with a flick of a scalpel. They said we weren't captives—that the fences were merely decoration—but they fenced in our minds.

When Peter tried to leave to avoid the operation, they hunted him down like an animal, gave him a sound beating and forced him under the knife. The only way we were getting out of that place was by giving up our future and our freedom. They fixed us like we were dogs and then forced us boys into the military. First me, then Peter, Ted and John. We served our country well, but our country did not serve us.

I had it in me to be a father. A good one. I had a loving pa and was ready to pay that forward. I met a good woman and raised her boys like they were mine. I made myself a future in spite of the government's best efforts to destroy it. Ted was a Sergeant in the Marine Corps and became a foster parent to over 100 kids. We survived and made a difference; we proved them wrong.

John

The only good thing that the coverage of Fred Aslin's case brought John was the return of his mother. She talked to him about his father for the first time, the bitterness stripped away. "You're his alright. All his sisters had your blue eyes."

In spite of the hurt he was subjected to his whole life at his mother's hands and heart, he forgave her. When she was difficult, he chose not to argue with her. She was his mother—the only one he would ever have; for better or worse, he was drawn to her. He recalled how he had kissed her goodnight every night, well into his teen years. He had always craved her love, even at the worst of times.

John relished having Norma's undivided attention during her visits. He saw her in a new light and took responsibility for the impact his choices had on her; he recognized how the stress was aging her. He treated her with the patience and kindness she had never shown him.

John wrote Fred Aslin and received a response. "They say you're my nephew but I'll never know because you never got a DNA test. Sorry to hear that you are serving the ole Life without Parole. You'll probably never get out, so I will say I wish you the best." The letter left a bit to be desired in the heart-warming realm.

The next day he got a letter from a woman he had never met.

Dear Mr. Aslin,

I had the "pleasure" of reading the letter Fred Aslin sent to you before it went out. I want to apologize on his behalf. He's just not that great at being nice at his age, after everything he's been through. I knew your father. He told me a lot about you. I would be happy to write to you and send you some information about your dad and the lawsuit that Fred has against the state. Let me know if you are interested.

Take care.
    Deborah Green

Dear Deborah,

Thank you for your letter. It hurts me that my family is so fractured. Learning about all the damage that was done is hard enough but being locked up and unable to seek out my aunts and uncles is even worse. It was hard for my dad to talk about his past, so it would mean a lot to me if you could help me fill in some of the blanks.

Your friend,
    Johnny Aslin

Deborah sent him a pile of newspaper and magazine articles about the Home in Lapeer where his father spent his captive childhood. She sent a copy of Fred's lawsuit. Everything he read ignored his existence. The story was repeated over and over that none of the Aslin siblings had produced children.

It hurt John deeply to be rejected by his uncle. But he knew in his heart that his father had accepted him and loved him. Before he died, his father made sure that John was enrolled as a member of his tribe. John had the birth certificate with his father's name to prove that he

The Nine Lives of John Aslin

was his son. He focused on his father's actions toward him and took what comfort he could from the results. He knew that his father's generation must have been emotionally damaged by institutionalized childrearing.

Deborah continued to write, telling John to pay Fred no mind—he was embittered from the difficulties that life had thrown his way and his unwillingness to accept John was not personal. She was so nice to John. Her letters were kind. John assumed she was Fred's girlfriend. They wrote letters back and forth for several years until Deborah wrote that the house that she shared with Fred had burned down and they were moving to Indiana. Then the letters stopped.

Fred
2000

In January of 2000, Fred made an appointment with James Haveman, the director of Community Mental Health in Michigan. He received a personal welcome. "Mr. Aslin, come in. Can we get you something to drink? How about a cup of coffee?"
"That would be nice. Thank you."
"What can I do for you?"
"Well, sir, I'd like it if you would sit and listen to my story."
James Havemen smiled warmly. "I can do that."
A few weeks later, a letter arrived that made Fred weep.

Dear Mr. Aslin,

I was very dismayed to hear your first-hand account of what you and your family members suffered while in the custody of the State of Michigan. Though many years have passed, your pain is clearly still very fresh. I would like to offer my personal apologies. It is clear that the treatment you and others received was offensive, inappropriate, and wrong. Thankfully, we have learned from the horrors of the past.

Yours,
James Haveman, Director
Michigan Department of Community Health

Fred appealed the dismissal of his court case and it took several years for the appeal process to conclude. Attorney General Jennifer Granholm's office delivered a cold response when the case ended unsuccessfully for Fred.

"We do not condone what happened to the Aslins. We do not believe that what was done at that time was proper by today's light, and it probably shouldn't have been proper in 1944. But the statute of limitations has run out long ago."

The Attorney General's action against Fred's case represented a truly unequivocal failure to bring justice to a family that had suffered so much. Jennifer Granholm was the officer of the state who was in a position to bring justice to Fred as part of her responsibility to protect the citizens of Michigan—she probably shouldn't have used the word probably. Jennifer Granholm would play a part in John Eric's life as well.

John
2005

"How you doing today, Johnny?" Mandy was a young guard who showed kindness to the men. She was aware of John's case and thought he had been over-sentenced. She encouraged him when she could. "Don't you give up now. My mom plays the lottery every day. Once she wins, I'm gonna hire Johnny Cochran for you and get you out of here. I read your file. We all know you deserve a chance at life."

Attention from an attractive female guard draws jealousy. There was nothing but compassion and encouragement in her words, but the warden received several complaints that accused her of crossing the line. The solution was to get rid of John.

After twelve years, plans were made for John to become another facility's problem. Officer Frank, a warm man who had always counseled John to choose wisdom, woke him up. "Hey, Johnny. Pack up. You're shipping out today." He held his hand out as though he was going to shake with John, but he pulled John in for a hug. He was one of several guards who had shown John sympathy and helped him grow from a young foolish idiot into an adult with a conscience. "It's been good getting to know you. I hope to see you again someday."

Since their reconciliation after his father's death, Norma had visited her son every three months. It wasn't a lot of contact, but it was better than being shut out. It was clear to him that his mother was declining. Each time he saw her, her eyes were emptier than they had been on the visit before.

In January of 2006, he was transferred from his comfort-zone in Lapeer to the Michigan Training Units in Ionia. Norma could not make the trip there, so the last time he saw her was Christmas of 2005.

John hated Ionia. His art supplies—paints, brushes and leather—were confiscated as dangerous contraband. He had no legal way to make money, so he took a job cleaning units for $17 a month—a demeaning job that lowered his spirits because Ionia was disgusting.

Much of the filth resulted from the fact that the guards would not let the men out of their cells at night to go to the bathroom. The prisoners were forced to resort to urinating in bags and pouring the contents out their windows or tossing the bags of piss into the common area. The guards forced younger, more vulnerable inmates to clean the mess up, waking them at 5:30 am so they could have everything up to snuff before the administrators rolled in. The building wreaked of urine and body odor. Blood sat on the ground after a fight and no one cleaned it up. John was perpetually nauseated by the stench.

And the place was chaotic. He had not been in such a vicious place for a long time, where the guards constantly screamed at men and degraded them at every turn.

John wrote letters to the governor and the E.P.A., claiming that the condition of the prison created an environmental hazard, where bacteria and bloodborne pathogens festered, putting the health of everyone at risk.

Prison staff responded that his claims were frivolous. They punished him for writing complaints by restricting him. He felt powerless and less than human. He wondered why he even tried to change things.

A few weeks after his letter-writing campaign, something that felt close to a miracle happened. A maintenance crew came through and power-washed the entire building. The place was transformed into something that was potentially appropriate for human habitation.

John felt a smidge of satisfaction at the change he had put into motion. A guard passed by his cell and tossed a directive over his shoulder. "Aslin, get your shit packed. You're riding out." He had stuck his head up too high and was being put in his place. He was being sent to Kinross, otherwise known as the "Killing Fields."

They thought that they were punishing him, but he felt like they were sending him home. Kinross was located in the Upper Peninsula of Michigan, next to the county where his father was born. It was tribal country. He was closer to his people. There was a strong Native Community in the northern prisons. He hoped that he would find mentors in Kinross and learn even more about his tribe.

Kinross boasts the largest outdoor area of any Michigan prison. The buildings were large too. When John got off the bus, he breathed in the fresh, crisp air and enjoyed the sound of the wind. A guard pointed him toward the temporary housing gym.

A clerk greeted the new arrivals at the door. He waited in line until it was time to give his name. "You're John John?"

"Yes."

"There are some Indians out there waiting for you." John saw a group of men relaxing on the grass in the yard. They were all Anishanabe—he knew one of them from his travels through the maze of prisons during the past twenty plus years. Most had long, dark hair, similar to his own. They stood to greet him, shaking their left hands— the side that they believed was the side of the heart. A left-handed shake indicated trust.

"We've been waiting for you." John felt like he could breath— especially after the inhospitable stay in Ionia. To have a community that welcomed his arrival was an unexpected blessing.

The wooded yard had trees that spread out as far as he could see. The anxiety that Kinross rumors had caused him receded. His welcome committee took him to a large set of bleachers filled with Native men. They were waiting just for him. He shook dozens of hands and took a seat among them as they invited him "into the circle." John discovered that the Ogema was a distant cousin. John felt like he could truly belong to this group. He had never experienced anything like it— being a member of a pack of brothers, a family that looked out for each other and did things as a group, ensuring that no one went without.

Norma had been through a lot of health issues. She underwent surgery to open up the veins on both sides of her neck. One of her lungs was removed. Her energy faded. John focused on being sweet to her, joking around and refusing to engage in any bickering. He tried to behave like a grown up and heal their relationship.

His conscious decision to treat her well brought him some peace when she passed away in August of 2006. John received a letter from Norma the week she died, just as he was preparing to leave Ionia. The handwriting was so shaky that it was hard to read.

He called her after he arrived at Kinross, knowing it might be the last time they would speak. "Hi Ma. How you doing?"

"Not so good, Johnny. I only have a few days left. I might as well spend it being nice to others."

"So you've known all along that you've been so mean to everyone?"

Norma laughed at his joke. "Yeah, I know."

They chatted for a while. He shared news of the community he had found in his new home. She was so weak. She asked him to call every day—she only had a handful left. Soon his phone time was up. "Bye, ma. You take care. I love you." He was glad that those had been the last words she heard from him.

He tried to phone the next day, but someone blocked his calls. It broke his heart. When she died, even though he hadn't been parented well, he felt alone in the world. No father. No mother. Entering prison at the age of 21 can stunt a person's development in many ways but being parentless made John realize it was time for him to grow up and stand alone.

A few days later, his counselor told him to call his family. The phones at the facility weren't working. John, frantic to speak with someone from home, went back to the counselor's office and asked to use the man's phone.

"I don't care about the phone trouble. I'm not letting you use my phone. Now get out of here."

These are the types of experiences that strip away the humanity of incarcerated men—when the capacity for compassion does not even extend to the death of a parent. John was devastated. He returned to his cell and collapsed on his bunk, lost in grief. Five hours later, a second-shift guard heard that his mother had died and came to check on him. "You okay, Johnny? Didn't your mother die?"

John poured out his disbelief about being denied a call home. The guard looked upset and motioned for John to follow him. He argued with another officer until he had a set of keys in his hand. He took John to the counselor's office and picked up the phone. "I need an outside line. John, what is the number?"

When he confirmed that Linda was on the phone, he handed John the receiver, walked out and closed the door behind him, giving John the privacy to grieve.

John never ceased to be amazed by the rare flares of kindness he encountered in the inhumane places where he was trapped, though, in truth, they just involved people treating others that way that humans were supposed to be treated. Humane acts seemed remarkable. Because it rarely happened, any attempt at humanity stood out.

Later that week, he got his mother's final letter. She had written on one side of the page and Linda had written on the other. Norma said she was happy for him, that he should be content up north among people who shared his heritage. There was a hundred dollars tucked inside. John held on to that money for a long time, not wanting to spend Norma's final gift.

By the time John Eric Aslin arrived at Kinross Correctional Facility in 2006, smack dab in the middle of the woods of Michigan's Upper Peninsula, he had lived in nine other prisons over a span of twenty-two years. His mother died a week after he arrived, making him a 43-year-old orphan who had almost no contact with the outside world. Very few family members survived. Anyone he might have called a friend hadn't written in years.

With his parents gone, John was faced with the reality that he was truly on his own. Whether he made his way forward in this strange world and created a semblance of a life or gave into despair was his responsibility alone.

He had survived as a talented tattoo artist for years, but the Michigan Department of Corrections decided that tattooing involved dangerous contraband. Men who were caught doing it were sent to the hole, something that could mess up an inmate's life and John was getting too old to deal with the uncertainty. John never knew where he'd end up after a stint in solitary. He simply couldn't risk it.

Once an artist, always an artist. He had marketable skills. Before he learned to tattoo, he'd survived by drawing greeting cards for men to send to their moms and sweethearts. So when an old biker named Custer taught him leatherwork—how to tool and dye the pieces to create art—it proved his best skill yet.

The profit margins were low because his materials had to be

purchased with a hefty "prison tax" added. The prison made money off the backs of prisoners and their families. Women trying to support children on the outside would still send their men money so that they would have a little something extra—little being the key word as $100 a month in a prison wouldn't buy much. Men would spend too much money calling home at ridiculous rates.

The Michigan prison system was not only inhumane and brutal—it was economically exploitive. Anything an inmate purchased was marked up excessively from what it would cost in the real world; many of these over-priced items were of low quality and volume. Still, John made $700 in profits in six months selling belts, purses and Bible covers. He gave up laying down ink for good.

The move to Kinross brought an unexpected blessing. John's stepmom, Fannie, was able to visit him regularly. John craved nurturing contact. Fannie treated him like he was her own. She gave pure love and support, very different than what he had received from the mother who raised him.

One day Fannie showed up with an extra guest—Deborah Greene. Deborah sat at the end of the table. She was quiet, taking everything in, but that would change. Meeting Deborah changed his life—at least for a while.

Deborah wrote John a letter that week, asking if he would like her to continue coming to see him. He responded yes. Even though they hadn't spoken much when she came with Fannie, they had a good rapport as pen pals.

Deborah, who was retired, lived within driving distance of the prison. She was seven years older than John and lived with his Uncle Fred. "What does Fred think of you visiting me?"

Deborah laughed. "Did you think he's my boyfriend?"

"Well, you live with him. You have for a long time."

"I'm his caregiver. I used to be married to his step-son."

John and Deborah made each other laugh. They grew close. Deborah flirted with him; he flirted back. It was nice to have someone on the outside who cared about him, was attracted to him and enjoyed his company. Things accelerated from friendship to more.

"John, you know I love you. Why don't we get married?"

"I would marry you in a heartbeat, but you know I might never get out. That's no life for you. It would be hard."

Being married to a lifer was guaranteed to disappoint and John did not consider foisting his problems into someone else's life a casual decision.

"I have everything I need and you're an important part of my life."

John was touched. "I want you to think about it, but if you decide you still want to, I'll marry you. I love you too."

"I'm going to start giving you $300 a month so you won't have to go without."

"I don't need you to do that."

Deb chuckled. "If you knew how much I got every month, you'd be mad that I only offered to give you $300. And as far as you never getting out, we need to do something about that."

Deb was an unexpected blessing, a bright spot after years of darkness. John was grateful for her presence in his life. It felt good to have someone in his corner.

John wrote letters to attorneys, hoping to get help with his case. He typed the letters individually and sent them into the world. There were one hundred of them; he didn't receive a single response. He remembered that his mother's attorney was now a judge. He wrote to him, asking the Hon. Geoffrey Neithercut to recommend an attorney. The judge gave him two names. He wrote them both. One responded.

Dear Mr. Aslin,

I received your letter. Even though your appeal options have been exhausted, you have the ability to file an application for the governor to commute your sentence. I would be willing to help you with this. Please let me know if you would like to move forward so that we can schedule a visit to discuss your case.

Respectfully,

Attorney Jill Creech Bauer

"Deb, I got a response from a lawyer! She said she can file an application to have my sentence commuted. The governor has the power to let me out."

Deb was speechless. They had commiserated weekly about the difficulty of finding an attorney to take his case and suddenly one had appeared.

"I'll get you the money. I have a piano that I don't play anymore. I'll sell it!"

Having an option that might result in John's release made it possible to plan a life. They picked out a house. Deb bought it with her proceeds from selling the house that she and Uncle Fred lived in.

Deb sold the piano and some of John's artwork and scraped up enough for the legal fees.

The desire to get out was more complicated by the increasing peril of life in a Michigan prison. Though Kinross had been a good place for him when he arrived, the environment was changing. The smoking ban—indoor and out—that was imposed on February 1, 2009 caused the men to go a bit crazy. A solid half of the prison population smoked. It was one of the few luxuries prisoners had when it was suddenly taken away. Stress levels among prisoners and staff rose precipitously.

At the same time, numerous gang members transferred to the facility. The environment became more menacing. Though Deborah brought lightness to his life, he was in a dark hole when he was away from her. He spent most of his time in hobby craft, working with leather and painting pictures. He appointed himself caretaker for the native area, keeping the grass cut down and tending the garden. He grew onions, peppers and carrots to enhance the cooking the men did in their cells with makeshift set-ups. He grew sweet grass, sage and wintergreen for ceremonies and kept watch over the cedar trees.

John and Deb sent documents to the attorney and an application began to come together. When it was ready, they held their breath and sent it in. John was scheduled for an initial video interview as a part of the parole board process. He did his best to answer the woman's questions, though he could barely speak at times as he tried unsuccessfully to choke back his tears of remorse and humiliation over the stupidity he had shown as a young man that had resulted in such tragedy. But he felt tremendous hope and pride, that someone recognized value in the man that he had worked hard to become in spite of so many setbacks. If the screeners had not seen a change, they would have rejected his paperwork.

Soon John learned that he would be interviewed by a psychologist. An investigation into his prison record was initiated. The reports came back strongly in his favor. Hope was filling him up, making his steps light.

But then he didn't hear anything for almost a year. During that time, he was an artistic machine, determined to make pieces that Deb could sell in order to replenish the money she had spent to hire his lawyer. He painted countless canvases and tooled leather items that would fetch a high price.

And then something amazing happened--success. He was scheduled for a full-blown parole hearing —if the parole board had decided there was no merit in his case, they would have denied his application and filed it away, but they wanted to see him in the flesh, take his measure and see if he deserved to be set free. It was an opportunity that not many lifers received, and he appreciated the chance to plead his case.

John couldn't wait to tell Deb the news. She was the only reason he would be heading down state to argue for his freedom. He ran to the table where she sat waiting for him. "Deb, honey, I have great news. I got a public hearing. They're sending me down state. That is the final step before a recommendation is sent to the governor."

John
2010

In August, his Native brothers gathered to wish him well before he climbed aboard the bus that would carry him back to the Michigan Training Unit to await his public hearing.

Nothing had changed. Ionia was a madhouse. The young men rioted; soon after he arrived, the entire place was placed on lockdown for five days. John sat in a steaming cell, directly in the path of the sun. There were no fans. The air hung, stagnant and heavy with body odor from sweaty men. No one was allowed to shower. The smell made him nauseous.

The guards didn't allow an iota of respect to invade their treatment of the prisoners. Orders were yelled and every interaction was viciously emasculating. Most of the inmates were so drugged up as a result of the generous distribution of meds by the mental health program that they didn't even know where they were.

John hunkered down, kept out of the way; he meditated and prayed that he would make it through the public hearing without ruining his opportunity at a second chance.

Deb followed him downstate, but her behavior was odd, cold. Their visits were silent and awkward. They had waited so long and worked so hard to get to this point, but it seemed to bring her no joy. He didn't know what was wrong, but he knew that he had to brush it off and focus on the parole board testimony. It was a life or death situation—

a life of freedom versus a death behind bars.

By the time the hearing date arrived, John had been locked in his cell for ten days without showering, with the sun beating down on him and a diet of only cheese sandwiches. The original five-day lockdown had stretched into ten when the men rioted in the yard immediately after being released.

John's stress levels were unbearable. His blood pressure medication hadn't been sent with him; his anxiety climbed as the medication left his system. He had to force himself to keep calm, preserve this chance, keep his mouth shut. He was in a position that many men would have appreciated, so he stayed curled in his bunk, facing the wall and focusing on the hearing.

He was finally allowed to shower the day before his appearance. The next day, he walked to the public hearing room in shackles. He entered with leg irons that were so tight that they made his ankles bleed. When he mentioned it to the guard, the man laughed. "They're supposed to hurt." His wrists were bolted to a band around his waist. He hobbled into the room, tears of shame rolling down his face.

John was led into the room, between rows of chairs full of citizens who were there to observe his hearing. The parole board was seated behind a long desk at the front. He saw a few family members out of the corner of his eye. He could hear whispering and crying behind him, but he had been warned not to look around or make eye contact with anyone; he kept his eyes pointed straight ahead, waves of humiliation overwhelming him.

"Please state your name for the record." John paused, about to carefully enunciate his name. "I need to remind you that this is being recorded."

"John Eric Aslin."

Remember. No excuses. You must take responsibility for what you did. Every word you say will be turned around and examined from every possible angle. Speak carefully. Any inconsistencies will be viewed, not as mistakes, but lies. His attorney's words hammered through his head once again as they had over and over since he knew he would have a hearing. Deb sat in the back; though he was tempted to look at her, he knew that any impulsive action, even one as small as looking for what might be the only loving face in the room, could be held against him. They might think he was trying to intimidate the family of the victim. He held himself erect and stared forward at his inquisitors.

The next few questions were routine, intended to confirm several basic facts about his case. Then, bam! He was hit with his first doozy like a slap on the face. "Why did you target Ella Stephens?"

I didn't target Ella Stephens. I didn't "target" anyone. I was an abused kid— a mere 21 years old. I was entering my seventh year as an alcoholic. I was drunk. I was stupid. I was drunk. I was young. I was drunk. I had no one in the world who looked at me with love in their eyes my whole young life. That's not an excuse, but I was drunk. I regret. I regret. I regret. I would do anything to undo this. I would like to be free, but I would rather that she be alive if I was given a choice.

He recalled the panic when he heard her frightened voice coming down the hall, how he froze, then sprinted past her to escape, making unintended contact and knocking her down. He had paused to help her up, but his looming presence over her, reaching out to her, had caused her to gasp in fear, thinking he intended her harm, not help. How it had momentarily broken his gentle heart, but then he fled from fear of the terrible mistakes he was making. He still was brought back to that moment every time someone in the visiting room wore hairspray. One sniff and it sent him reeling back through time.

"I was 21. I needed money. My mom had kicked me out. I had no home, no food, no cash. I didn't think anyone was home. I broke in. When Mrs. Stephens came out to the front room, I didn't mean to knock her down. I had no intent to harm her. When I found out she died, it broke my heart."

Would they accept that answer? Would they think he had failed to take responsibility? He was responsible. He was responsible every day. The weight of Mrs. Stephens' life sat on his chest every morning. When he opened his eyes, he saw her face. In the beginning, she looked at him with disappointment, anger, a lust for revenge, but over the years she had softened. Now she looked at him with wonder, that he had been frozen in place for more than 9000 days and she was frozen with him, waiting to untie her fate from his.

"What have you done to improve yourself in the past 25 years?"

I'm sober. You might think that a prisoner can be nothing but sober, but you would be wrong. It is easy to get drunk in prison, but I've been sober for over twenty years. I'm an artist. I'm a mentor. I'm peaceful. I'm compassionate. I was sent into this hell to become an animal, but I've maintained my humanity. I'm ready to be free. I'm ready to be free. I'm ready to be free.

"During the past 25 years, I've matured. Though I got some tickets at the beginning, I haven't had a ticket for years. I'm heavily involved in the Native American community at Kinross. I mentor younger men, try to straighten them out. I spend a lot of time making art—leatherwork and painting, drawing."

The hearing was grueling. The board members fired questions at him, homing in on any inconsistencies between the written record–his transcripts and file—and the things he said. After it was over, one of the members walked up to John, using a tissue to wipe tears that John could not reach himself from John's face. As the man placed some extra tissues in John's hand, he leaned in and whispered, "Never give up hope, young man. Never stop trying to do right. Hold on to hope. It's the only thing that will get you by."

John was taken to the visiting room when the hearing was over. He was recovering from his emotions when Deb burst into the room and beelined for him. She was livid. "Why did you tell them you knew whose house you broke into?!"

She had no idea how taxing the experience had been and how difficult it had been for him to focus and answer rather than be rendered catatonic by the fear that he would fail. "I did what I had to do. I needed to take responsibility for everything."

Deb was obsessed with that detail and kept coming back to it. Then she left, without expressing any emotion or support, and flirted with the guard on her way out in a way that John knew was designed to hurt him.

Something had changed. He didn't know what, but he knew things were not the same between them. When John got back to Kinross, he uncovered a piece of the Deb puzzle that brought him understanding. She had taken up with another inmate who was taking college classes. She helped him with his homework. When she might have been concentrating on her husband and supporting him through the most important moment in his life, she was in a hurry to get back to the hotel to talk to her boyfriend. She continued to pick fights with John. His source of positivity and support slipped away.

Kinross was turning into a warzone. Stabbings were a common occurrence, but they were covered up by the prison. Critical incident reports were buried; men were not taken to the hospital to receive the treatment they needed. Instead, they were patched up in-house, amateur stitching of faces and necks. Once the men were stable, they were transferred to another locale. Nothing was done to hold assailants accountable because it justified the need to hire more guards and further restrict the movement of men inside their caged existence.

And it didn't hurt that bribes flowed freely to guards so that they would look the other way. Leaders of gangs encouraged young members to engage in violence as part of their initiation, so there was often no rhyme or reason to who became a victim. It was all for a show of toughness.

John had to look around every corner and be ready for an attack, even though he kept his head down and didn't cause anyone trouble. Because John returned from a public hearing, he was placed in a new unit. It was the most violent place in the facility, the center of gang activity, with the highest amount of drug use, stabbings and violence. He felt like he was being tested, targeted for failure. He struggled to keep his cool while he waited for the parole board's decision.

The guards in his section were assholes. One guard walked up and down the floor hollering out "Mr. Stone Wall Road," which was Deb's address. John was furious, but he calmly walked to the desk, leaned over and quietly informed the officer, "If you ever yell my family's address out around all of these freaks, we are going to have a real problem."

The guard was bewildered, surprised to be confronted by an inmate. It ended up working in John's favor as word got around from the offended officer repeating the story. Soon after, on his way to the visiting room, another officer stopped John, one with Ojibwe ancestry. "You know someone on Stone Wall Rd.?"

"My wife."

"I've got lots of family out that way." It was an area where a lot of tribal people lived. John realized they might be connected somehow.

"I have lots of ancestors from these parts."

"Aslin. Huh."

A few days later John showed the officer a document. "This here's my family tree. I've got relatives buried on Mackinaw Island. Here's one from 1870, another from 1890. Fact is, there are about 40 of them. My people are all over up here."

A few weeks later, John was moved to a safer unit.

One night, a large bang woke everyone up—a gunshot! The lights came on. Suddenly the unit was freezing. John opened his window. The men had all, in a show of solidarity, flooded the space with fresh air to clear away the smoke so that the guards wouldn't be able to find out where the gun was. John also opened the bathroom windows on his way outside—the guards had ordered the unit cleared so officers could search for the gun.

A few days later, a man approached him, referring to his opening of the bathroom windows that night. "Thank you, Brother. That was good looking on your part."

"That's just what we do."

After that, John was treated well on his new unit until that man was dragged off by the guards a few months later. Some rival must have ratted him out.

As usual, the players always changed and the violence increased.

But there was some incredible news to balance it out. The parole board recommended that John be released. It was a miracle, so rare and unexpected. If he had been able to convince a panel of experienced decision-makers that he deserved to be released, wasn't the Democratic governor who was finishing up her final term likely to be merciful and set him free? His life was in Governor Jennifer Granholm, formerly Attorney General Granholm's, hands.

While John waited for his parole decision, he was offered a chance to move to the unit that housed his Indian brothers; he jumped on it. As he was packing his cell, a guard under the influence of a roid-rage fit, paused in front of his cell. "You moving, Aslin?"

"Yep." John kept placing his things in a box.

"No one asked me if you could move, bitch." The man slammed the cell door and stormed off. He blocked John from moving. John tried to stay out of the man's way, avoiding trouble as he awaited his commutation papers, but the man wouldn't leave him be.

Later that week, the officer entered his cell and stepped up to John like he wanted to fight. John had no choice but to meet him. He leaned into his face. "Hey mother fucker, I don't need your permission to do my bit so what's up?"

The guard backed off. He was used to bullying men and having them cower. The officer turned and fled, yelling, "Get the fuck out of my unit!" He slammed the door on his way out. John's bunkies were freaked out, staring at him like he was insane.

The place was about to make him crazy just like all of the men around him. But standing up to the bully worked—he got transferred to the Native floor. A few months later, he ran into the guard. "Hey Aslin, how you doing? Thanks man. I was just having a bad day."

John could have filed a complaint about the guard, but he didn't. His willingness to take the guard's behavior in stride gained the guard's respect.

LIFE EIGHT: WHERE JOHN ERIC LOSES HIS CHANCE AT A SECOND CHANCE

2010

When the letter from Jennifer Granholm arrived, John was afraid to open it. He took it back to his cell until he gathered the courage to break the seal.

Jennifer Granholm denied John's commutation, against the recommendation of the parole board, the prison psychologist and other people who had weighed in on his request. How would John go on? How would he tell Deb?

He almost chose to stand his wife up in the visiting room—he was numb from the news and didn't know how to go on. When he saw Deb waiting for him, the life drained out of his eyes and his stomach twisted. Should he not tell her?

"What's wrong? What's going on?"

So began the longest and saddest visit of his life, but she didn't seem that surprised. Looking back, he wondered if she already knew.

His life had changed again. All the hope that had buoyed him up was gone. He laid in bed for days, turned toward the wall where no one could see the tears that would not stop leaking from his eyes. What could have caused Granholm to turn him down?

Eventually he acknowledged that it was over. Granholm was on her way out. The new governor wouldn't be likely to release someone like him. It was time to pick himself up, act like a man.

Prayer circle was his refuge. He shifted his perspective and doubled down on continuing a meaningful life despite his setbacks. His rock-hard faith in doing the right thing carried through his days but his nights were filled with self-doubt.

His environment was spiraling faster than his inner self. The stabbings increased to two or three a day and this count didn't include the face slashings. It was maddening, yet nothing was done to calm things down.

But John was back with his wolf pack. He focused on making a difference as a leader in that world. They hung together, ate their meals as a group and played baseball. Their team had been winning for years; even though they had old players, they just worked together to cover them—it was a metaphor for the Indian community itself. His wolfpack brought balance to his life that he could not find in other ways.

Ravens were prevalent in John's life and dreams. When he returned to Kinross after the public hearing and later, after his commutation was denied, he often sat on a bench in the yard in the freezing cold. He was alone with his thoughts, giant flakes of snow enveloping him in a fluffy silence.

A huge raven sat on a pole and watched him. John would speak to him. "Anii, brother." The bird stared, as if truly curious, turning his head from side to side. He was a pretty specimen, large and blue-black, even purple, in the sun. He came every time John was in the yard. No sooner would John sit down than his friend would land on a nearby tree or pole.

Sometimes John laid prayers in the snow at the edge of the yard and walked back to the bench. His friend would encourage him. "Gork, gork, gork."

John left food for him about twenty feet out from where he sat, but the bird would fly off. "You're not tricking me," the raven seemed to say.

John stood and left, calling, "It's yours if you want it." After John was a safe distance away, the raven would eat the food.

John felt completely alone. As winter pressed on, he shoveled a path to the sweat lodge, hoping to meditate his pain. He named the raven Pete. Pete watched him from the roof of a nearby shed as John built the fire and heated the stones. John talked to Pete about his troubles; Pete looked like he understood John's sad heart and bruised soul, turning his head from side to side like he was thinking of solutions and only wished that he could speak them.

Pete's presence healed John. He looked forward to spending time with his winged friend. Soon Pete followed him to the housing unit and sat in front of his cell window. It was so strange. How did that bird know where John's cell was? A few weeks after John was moved to a unit on the first floor, John was awakened by "Gork gork, gork." Pete paced the ground outside his window.

What John heard was, "Get out here, Bro. Let's hang out." John took some food outside—tuna and rice—and placed some on the ground for Pete. Pete flew down and walked in circles around it, pecking at it and jumping back into the air as if the gift frightened him. He flew to the tree, came back, circled, and approached the food again; it was like he was engaged in a ceremony. Finally, he took a bite but flew up to the tree to actually taste it.

Pete must have realized that John was his friend because, when John put the rest of his meal on the ground, Pete flew back and ate it all. Pete was special. John felt that the wounds from the denial by Governor Granholm, that were deep and raw, were healing as Pete touched his heart and guided him toward peace.

John moved back to the unit that he was in before he went downstate for his public hearing. Sure as shit, he was awakened by "Gork, gork, gork," just outside his window, but now Pete had a sweetheart with him—a skinny, ruffled yet poised partner who watched everything from a nearby pole.

John placed cookies on his sill and Pete carried a piece back to his girl, whom John named Patricia. Within a week, Patricia came to the sill to get her own food. Having two birds follow him around made John feel good about his daily life. He felt special. Soon they entered his dreams, where he could pet their shiny, feathered heads.

Each day, John woke up and went to his window. Pete would be on one pole and Patricia on another. As soon as John opened his window and talked to them, they flew over. Pete strutted back and forth, proud of his large frame and the single white feather under his neck. Patricia puffed up her chest as though asking John to admire her now shiny feathers. The chicken bones and scraps that he collected for them in the kitchen made them healthy and strong.

John regularly told Deb about the ravens, until the day she snapped. "Don't you dare waste my time on the phone talking about those stupid birds."

John was silent for a whole minute, deeply hurt. His entire life was composed of praying, creating art and feeding his friends, the ravens. Deb's attitude about them was a sign that she was already gone. He was grateful that he was less lonely than he otherwise would have been because of Pete and Patricia. They were changing his life and buffering him from the break-up of his marriage. They made up for what he was missing in his human relationships—he felt kinship and kindness radiating from them. A man in pain can say things to a pair of ravens that he would not be able to say to another person when he needs to remain invulnerable in prison.

Just the sight of the ravens would make him smile, as they tracked him from hobby craft to his cell—they would be waiting on the window ledge when he arrived. They even attended prayer ceremony. Soon the whole prison, including the guards, knew Big Pete and Patricia by name.

His marriage was coming to an end. The other inmate who Deb had been communicating with told her John was swindling her, that he was dangerous and did not present his true self to her.

"Why does the MDOC website say that you committed premeditated murder? You're hiding something from me. You're not telling me everything. If you're hiding something from me, I'll leave you."

"Deb, honey, you have my transcripts. Every damned page is there for you to read yourself. I'm not hiding anything. Just read them."

"Randy," the man whose homework she was doing, "said he found out some things about you that should make me fear for my life."

"How can I convince you that I love you? I have been faithful to you for eight years. I haven't even written to another woman without letting you know ahead of time. If I was so dangerous, I would be in trouble all the time. I don't know what I can say that will make a difference."

His trial transcripts were returned to him soon after.

"Did you read them?"

"No. And I don't have a place to store them anymore."

John took the transcripts to hobby craft and tore them up, three pages at a time. What was the point of hanging on to them? His appeals were exhausted. The papers he held in his hands carried pain and heartache. Deb was leaving him, he was sure. No one outside the prison walls would even remember he existed. There would be no help from the outside to keep his case alive. It took him most of the day to destroy them and then they were gone forever.

When the divorce papers came, he just threw them away. She could have what she wanted. John had given up.

John's attorney made a final effort to change the outcome of the commutation case. She wrote to the governor's husband, whom she had met several times.

Dear Mr. Mulhern,

My family has been a great supporter of your wife. We campaigned for her, marched in parades, handed out literature, and provided financial support during both terms. We believed in her and backed it up with our time and resources. I have had the pleasure of speaking to you on several occasions, once when you spoke at the Consortium on Child Abuse annual dinner in Flint. My eight-year-old daughter sang that night and her voice drew you back into the room even though you had to leave. Your decision to linger showed me that you are authentic and care about people.

My personal experiences with you have given me confidence in my belief that you live your life with integrity. Because of that, I am writing to ask you to do me a favor which literally involves saving someone's life. I am involved in assisting an inmate named John Aslin. John was incarcerated for life due to the fact that his crime was used as a test case for the expansion of the felony murder law in the 1980s. He was a young man who grew up in horrible circumstances and developed a drinking problem.

At 21, while intoxicated, he broke into a home to steal a purse. The elderly occupant was frightened by the break in, had a heart attack and died. John never laid a finger on her but was convicted of felony murder. He has been in prison since 1984, but he has not had a major ticket since the late 80s and has had a stellar record for at least the last 10 years.

Since becoming incarcerated, John established a relationship with his father for the first time in his life and learned that he is Native American. He has been able to connect with his tribe and become very spiritual and centered. He focuses on living a good life in an effort to somehow balance the tragedy that he caused in the past. He is authentically remorseful for the death of this elderly person and tries to compensate for this bad choice daily. He has an established record of mentoring young inmates and providing them with advice and guidance to live a better life.

John is also an incredibly talented artist and has kept himself intact mentally and emotionally through working with paint and leather. At one point, the majority of prison tattoos in the system were his handiwork. John had everything in place to become a productive member of society. He was recently married to a woman who retired from the state after a career of working in the mental health field who has the background to support him in his adjustment to society, he had a place to live and he had work lined up both selling his artwork and working at his tribe's casino.

He had been cleared by a psychologist and got a green light from the parole board, yet an aid in the governor's office denied his request. I know that things can fall through the cracks and I am hoping that is what happened in this case and that it is not too late to give it a second look.

There is no purpose to continuing to incarcerate John Aslin. He will continue and expand his mentoring activities if he is released. He wants to have the opportunity to be productive and give back something to his community. This will never happen if he remains locked up. If you actually met John, you would see how he has grown into a gentle, sensitive man and how he is wasting away, yet has so much to offer.

In the past, I have taken time out of my busy life to help your family reach its goals. My family is fully behind the goal of working toward the release of John Aslin and I am asking you to give our goal a little time and cause someone to take a second look at this case.

I know I may sound dramatic, but John has one life to live and, though he is nearing 50 years old, he has not lived yet. He made a single terrible choice that had tragic consequences and he deserved to be punished, but not for his entire life. Twenty-six years is enough. Please help me secure his release.

Respectfully,
Jill Creech Bauer
Attorney at Law

An e-mail reply came on December 22, 2010.

Jill,

I went to my PO Box for the first time in a couple weeks today and found your compelling letter. I am not sure whether anything else has transpired with respect to Mr. Aslin. I will try to pass the request along tomorrow. I must say that it is so late in the term/year that if nothing has happened yet, I cannot hold out much hope. Most folks on the governor's staff have left for vacation and for new jobs. The vast majority of the time has been spent on transition activities for the governor-elect.

The governor and her legal counsel have worked hard and closely with the parole board, and you have probably read that she has been more lenient than any governor in memory. But each of those pardons took huge amounts of time and were in process for a long time. So, again, I will pass it along, but I am not even sure whether anyone will have time to read it at this point. I commend you on your advocacy, and I hope that if nothing works out now for Mr. Aslin that something will in the next administration.

Thanks again for reaching out.

Dan Mulhern

John
2014

John's best friend, Ronnie, was having trouble in his unit. He discovered a gang plot to rob his 70-year-old bunkmate and intervened to stop it. The upper level of the gang had not sanctioned the hit, so the younger men who had hatched the plan cancelled it. Now there were some unhappy men in the lower ranks of the gang who wanted revenge on Ronnie for getting them in trouble with their bosses.

John, as the leader of the Native community, said he would look into it. He didn't have time to take care of it before he and Ronnie were attacked in the yard.

They were swarmed by a mass of men. One swung over John and slashed Ronnie's neck. Another man grabbed Ronnie's jacket and pulled it up, throwing Ronnie off balance. Both John and Ronnie went down on the ground. A supply truck pulled up and lightly beeped the horn, sending some of the men running but not all of them. John turned to face the remaining men, but they suddenly ran off when the guy wrestling with Ronnie took off too.

Blood squirted out of Ronnie's neck as John pulled him up and applied pressure with a corner of Ronnie's coat. Ronnie was in shock, but he could walk. "Go, dammit, go to healthcare."

John placed Ronnie's hand up where it would keep pressure on his wound and turned him toward the building.

John was covered in blood and in a dangerous spot. He would be the next target—likely in the next 24 hours, especially if the guards got involved. He needed to get inside and get the blood that covered his clothes, shoes and skin cleaned up. He kept his eyes low as he passed through two officers, one of whom was carrying a camera and pointing to where the attack had happened. It was strange. No one in charge paid him any mind, yet every eye in the yard was on him.

John stripped off his clothing. "Get these washed fast, Bro." The guy who worked the laundry counter gave him a nod. John went directly to the gang leader of the men who had attacked. "What the fuck was that?"

The man was shocked that John had the balls to come into his cell. "It wasn't me, Johnny."

John went to his own cell and locked the doors. Within a few minutes, his Indian brothers were there. "Are you okay? What do we need to do?"

"I'll take care of it." He just had to make it through the next 24 hours and take care of it before a hit was put on him.

He talked to various leaders—African American, Latino and others and found out who was responsible. The hit on Ronnie was not sanctioned. The men were told to leave Ronnie alone, but if they did decide to go after him, they were not to do it in front of John and were not allowed to put John in danger because he was the Ogema. It would be disrespectful to the Native community to do such a thing.

For the next few weeks, other leaders escorted him as he moved through the prison, letting him stand with them in the yard or walk with them in the halls.

Ronnie was sent away.

Not long after, a mass of guards ran toward the weight pit. The gang had taken action to teach the man who had disrespected their authority a lesson. Soon someone was placed in the small ambulance that was kept in the yard.

An Incan man snickered. "There goes our problem."

Still, John was traumatized by seeing the violence so close up. For months, he had a rush of adrenaline every time he turned a corner and saw huddling groups of men.

John
2015

Getting the community set up, and to the point where the ceremony would take place, had been like a chess match. John made a move forward and the prison complex blocked him. Constitutional protections, however, are powerful things; pipe ceremonies and the like are religious traditions that are protected by law. Prison policies are designed to completely dehumanize the men who live within their walls, but the authorities could not strip the Native community of their religious activities.

The sweat lodge had been established. The pipe ceremony had happened, with cultural leaders being allowed on the grounds—just as priests and clerics were—and tobacco had been brought in despite the "smoke-free" ban that was in place.

John was the Ogema, the leader of the Indigenous community, and he had received ceremonial pipes and an eagle feather to commemorate his position. These items were kept on his body at all times so that nothing would happen to them—to ensure they didn't disappear like so many things did. These items were more likely to be "misplaced" by a guard than another inmate as John had earned the respect of a vast number of interest groups in the prison population and was generally left alone.

Left alone, that is, by other inmates; he was fair game to the guards. Triumphs over the status quo do not go over well in prison and a reckoning was coming—he had accomplished some goals, so he was taught a lesson by being transferred to the prison across the street.

The day before he was transferred, Pete flew down and paced in front of John's window. He seemed to know his friend was leaving. John threw him some food and he pecked at it like a sad little kid. It broke John's heart. He would never see this brother again, a bird that had brought such a marked improvement to his life.

John still carries one of Pete's feathers in his medicine bundle, where he keeps his herbs and prayer items, so that a part of Pete will always be with him. Which ancestor had sent the ravens to him when he needed to heal? Whomever it was, Pete's existence reminded John that there were spirits monitoring his welfare.

Chippewa Correctional was supposed to be a dangerous place. John had been at Kinross for years, building up his network. Moving a few miles changed quite a bit of his daily life. All of his art and leatherwork supplies had been taken from him before he left Kinross. As he made the short trip to Chippewa, a distance he could have easily walked, he realized that he was starting from scratch in every respect—no friends, no community, no way to pass the time, nothing.

Everything that he owned was placed on a table. They were taking no chance with people coming from Kinross. Every piece of paper was examined, every food wrapper opened, every piece of clothing squeezed and pulled. All of it was run through a metal detector and all electronics were taken apart. It took hours.

But then he was on the floor and his hopes rose. There were Indians waiting for him. "Welcome, Bro." The unit was clean and solemn.

A guard barked at him. "Take your hat off. That's not allowed here."

Another yelled at him for walking down the hall with his toothbrush sticking out of his mouth. "You can't have anything in your mouth when you walk the halls. You're lucky I don't write you a ticket."

John had to laugh. Men were getting maimed and killed a few miles away and these fool guards were worried about enforcing petty rules. Maybe this place wouldn't be so bad. Maybe they had done him a favor by sending him to a less dangerous place.

John attended prayer circle the next day with six other men. The indigenous community was not being run well. An owl feather was used for prayers. John's ancestors wouldn't enter any space that had an owl feather—owls have ominous energy. John secured an eagle feather to replace it and brought his family pipes to lead a pipe ceremony. Many of the men shed tears.

Soon after, the Ogema was caught stealing the tobacco they prayed with to fund his drug habit. He was voted out. John was elected to replace him. The men wanted revenge on the former Ogema for violating the sacred rites, but John enforced his authority. "None of you are allowed to harm him. We're even going to let him attend the circle. His voting rights will be stripped because his judgment is clouded by drugs, but he'll be safe."

The group grew to 25 as other men were transferred from Kinross. John got to work, organizing the Native American community and planning the annual Ghost Feast Smudge. The Ghost Feast was hard to coordinate because food had to be prepared off-site and brought in, something that was no longer allowed. However, at the insistence of the Department of Cultural Reparations liaison, it would happen. The men would eat an authentic Ojibwe meal, some of them for the first time, and there would be a drum ceremony and speakers from the tribe would attend to give encouragement to the men.

The path to the smudging ceremony had been like a war dance, where John stepped forward, pivoted to avoid a thrust meant to push him back then twirled and moved forward. He used visualization to keep himself from getting discouraged as the prison administration made every micro-step as difficult as possible.

The unit officer stood in the doorway to John's cell, a cocky grin on his face. "Aslin, I notice you've done some good things for the Indians in here, what with the pow wow and all." He pulsed his hand in front of his face and made a war call like someone in an old movie.

John didn't react.

"Too bad you won't be here for any of it."

"How's that?"

"We're transferring you. The day before. You'll just miss it." The petty cruelty of the prison system struck again.

John was going back to Lapeer, which might at least allow Linda to visit him. Maybe some of his old friends would still be there. He hoped it would be a positive move since he was losing a lot by transferring downstate.

It was relaxing to watch the scenery fly by—the variety of his scenery had been so limited over the past 30 years. The bus rumbled along through the gorgeous fall colors. John took in every detail—deer peeking through the woods along the barren highway, new models of cars and new buildings sprinkled amongst the familiar sights.

The trip to St. Louis, Michigan took about five hours. That was the location of the holding center where men were sorted out and sent to their new locations. Inmates were placed in 16' by 20' cages with a single, long wooden bench and no bathrooms or running water. They had to sit and wait.

The close proximity to strangers, coupled with little supervision, meant that tensions ran high and anger cut through most interactions. The officer escorting John walked him by the Lapeer cage.

"I'm supposed to go in there. I'm going to Lapeer."

The man flipped through the clipboard he was holding. "Nope.

Coldwater. Its right here—LCF."

"L doesn't stand for Lapeer?"

"No. Lakeland. In Coldwater." *Dammit, why were these counselors so fucking sloppy and ignorant when it came to these important details that impacted men's lives?*

Coldwater housed new arrivals in pole barn dorms with open rows of bunkbeds. Young gang bangers circulated, disrespectful, loud little fools trying to establish themselves, fueled by fear and anger. Theft was rampant since everyone's stuff was out in the open; it was easy to swipe belongings when they had to be left behind for meals and appointments.

The place was noisy and chaotic. Gangs swarmed their target's living space, twenty strong, right under the cameras; the guards didn't intervene. John was in a disciplinary unit, something designed for immature men who hadn't learned how to navigate life in prison. Why was a 55-year-old man with twenty ticket-free years under his belt in this place?

John talked to his counselor about being moved and got no response. After six months, he finally wrote the warden. She forwarded the letter to the deputy who told John he wasn't going anywhere.

In another thirty days, he wrote the warden again. "I thought you informed your deputy that I should be placed in housing more appropriate to my age and misconduct record."

Three days later he was moved to a converted closet—no windows and barely any space but much better that the zoo he had lived in for seven months.

Eliminating the endless chaos allowed John to take the measure of his new home. He sought out the Native community and found it in disarray. The Ogema was a white man with no proof of his heritage. He controlled five other men claiming to be Indigenous, but they didn't know anything about the rites and traditions. John soon determined that the group existed because claiming to be Indian allowed them to grow tobacco; they were selling it for profit.

When he tried to join the group and make it more authentic, they barred him from joining the circle. Strange, harassing things began to happen. John would be awakened in the middle of the night by deputies who were responding to health care kites that he had allegedly written saying that he was bleeding. Another time, officers arrived in response to a non-existent stab wound.

The officers did not know John and thought he was creating drama. He tried to explain that the handwriting on the kites, though consistent, did not match his.

He could confirm that the claims of physical injury weren't real, but the claims of mental health troubles were harder to prove false. One night, he was dragged from his cell in cuffs—an anonymous tip claimed he was hearing voices and threatening to hurt medical staff and others.

Fortunately, the staff realized that the same handwriting had been on kites that maligned a variety of other men, so John was not held responsible. This was good news. He needed to keep his record clean.

He had recently connected with an organization that wanted to help him file for commutation. The Citizens for Prison Spending had compiled a list of Michigan prisoners who deserved release and John was in the top 25. They were assisting him in filing the paperwork and he could not afford to have anything odd in his file.

Because he suspected that the former Ogema was behind the trouble, he stepped away from the Native community and focused on his release.

John
2016

John's application was ready to file. The parole board clerk gave him a hard time and made him change some details; it made aspects of his application inaccurate, but John was intent on having the documents accepted so he followed directions. This resulted in his case being presented to the parole board as a premeditated crime.

The advocate organization worked hard to have the error corrected, but the clerk didn't update the computer in a timely manner. The parole board was presented with inaccurate information and denied his application as being without merit. The governor didn't receive the list of meritorious commutations that the organization compiled until John had already been denied.

John called to talk to the clerk. The clerk's response to the effort to correct the record was arrogant—"The letter will be placed in your file for your next application." The man knew that John couldn't file again for two years.

It was time for John to rebuild a life in prison. He determined to challenge the false Ogema. Being disconnected from his heritage weighed on him, so he decided to take control of the wayward circle. The other men were scared to stand up to their leader because they had seen the chaos he had visited on John, but they backed John anyway. "John John is right. We should change this. We should change that."

John taught the men how to sing, play the drums and lay proper prayers. There was an uptick in the false kites but then the Ogema got paroled. The nonsense stopped—well, almost. When they went to collect their eagle feather, they discovered the Ogema took it with him—something he had been entrusted with that belonged to the community. It was a terrible thing to do within the constraints of the culture.

John was elected Ogema. He established a seven-man counsel so that the group would never be ruled by a tyrant. The community grew to seventeen men—brothers, family, a source of strength to survive.

In 2018, an inmate transferred from Kinross. "Johnny, I've been asked to deliver a message for you."

"From who?"

"Gork, gork, gork." The man laughed. "Your damned big ass raven follows the Indians you knew around. They feed him. They said, 'Don't worry. He misses you.'"

John sees ravens everywhere. He greets them with, "Hello, Brother." When they appear in his dreams, he pays attention because there is something special being communicated. Ravens have the power to heal him.

John's attorney had an idea of how to get John released from prison. She emailed the Genesee County Prosecutor.

"I've come up with a way to get Mr. Aslin back into court for a resentencing but my idea will only work if your office doesn't object. I would like to file a motion to resentence based on the brain research cited in the legislation that has caused other juvenile life sentence cases to be reviewed. The research tells us that the human brain is not fully developed until age 25 and normal development rates can be impacted by trauma. Mr. Aslin had trauma in his childhood, including being hit by cars multiple times before age 10 and getting into a car accident as a teenager where he hit his head and was knocked unconscious. If the brain is still developing until age 25, limiting the application of the brain research to defendants under the age of 18 is simply arbitrary. In fact, the State of California has chosen to review cases for defendants 23 and under for this very reason. Will you work with me to assist Mr. Aslin in seeking release?"

Weeks went by and there was no response. She reached out to a high-ranking member of the office. After a few back-and-forth e-mails, she received her answer. "I'm sorry but the prosecutor really has no interest in reviewing this and would continue to oppose any resentencing."

John
2019

John came to the attention of an older couple. They visited him faithfully for two years, advocating for his release and helping him sell is artwork. He eventually referred to them as "Mom and Dad." It raised his spirits, gave him hope.

He looked for ways to spread the positivity he was feeling. He took on projects—designing a large card for a young shooting victim. After having fifty men sign it, he sent it to the girl who had been injured in a drive-by.

Mom and Dad assembled a small group of supporters. One of them sent John a bag of sweets and instructed him to share them with the men in his unit—she wanted them to know they weren't forgotten. He insisted that the men whom he shared the sweets with each create a handwritten thank-you note to teach them gratitude.

Then he conceived of a truly great project—a day of peace, 24 whole hours without violence. He called a meeting with other religious leaders in the prison. The Nation of Islam attended as well as Moorish, Melanic and Suni members, Christians, and Catholics specifically, Buddhists and Pagans. Everyone agreed to support the event. John approached the gang leaders and asked for a commitment of support. Then he wrote to the warden and got permission to move forward.

The event made him proud. Fifteen speakers from the outside would attend, encouraging the men and imparting wisdom, vocal music and Indian drums. He also advocated for Native men in other facilities when their troubles reached his ears.

A man who was dying of cancer received cultural care thanks to John's intervention. John focused on doing good things despite his predicament—looking outward instead of gazing inward and losing hope. If anger threatened to overtake him in his frustration to get things done, he would release it. If he had learned anything, it is that lightness and darkness cannot exist together. John chose to live in light.

LIFE NINE: THE LIFE OF THE CAT—
THE ONLY ONE LEFT

EL GATO

When John's spirit animal, the Lynx, was revealed to him, he felt the cat buried deep inside him come alive. The Lynx is a keeper of secrets, an important skill inside the walls of a prison. In Ojibwe lore, if someone wants to know a secret, they have to ask the lynx because he sees everything in the woods and doesn't talk easily. John's observational skills and his discretion had helped him gain respect and had kept him safe.

John had long been called "El Gato" on the handball court. A good handball game required fifteen minutes of constant running and jumping. At 57, he could defeat much younger men. He was fast and agile, even though his joints complained after the games. Though he had slowed a little in his fifties, the cat still had moves. He wasn't really as fast as everyone thought he was, but he was good at judging where the ball was going so he could maneuver to get to it.

Handball had been a part of John's life since he entered the prison system. His success in the sport mirrored his growth and maturity. As a young man, all an older player would have to do is get John's temper up and John would lose. Sometimes he would purposely hit the ball on the roof in anger, ending play for everyone.

As an older man, he could recognize these tactics and remain calm. Handball takes intense concentration and cooperation with a partner. It's all about reading angles, finessing and keeping a cool head. He had to be able to read where the ball would land, get his body to that spot and hit the ball so it would go to the place that would be hardest for the other side to reach.

If he hit the ball too hard out of frustration, he made it easier for his opponents to return it. He excelled at a "kill shot"—which would make a guy run from the back of the court to try and catch a ball that was already dropping before he got there. The ball would hit the floor flat and just roll away.

Handball was not a game of power; it required brains, focus and speed. He could never take his eyes off the ball—but this was a natural skill for a cat.

The handball courts tended to be populated by Natives and Latinos. They were crowded in the summer. On nice days, men gathered for tournaments—radios blaring upbeat music—salsa, classic rap or classis rock—unless an errant ball took the radio out.

John and his partner, "Machette" Martinez, usually won tournaments organized by inmates from the recreation department. If an inmate was in charge, the men would play their hearts out for a bag of chips. If it was an official prison-sanctioned competition, many packs of ramen noodles would be on the line. Either way, the handball court was where his true cat nature was on display.

The lynx can be clairvoyant, seeing things before they come to pass. Many years before, John had dreamed that his sister was lying on a table and screaming. It was very vivid. He couldn't see what was happening, but there were a lot of people standing around and Amy was calling out.

John was disturbed by the vision. It was during the time that his mother had banned him from calling because he was in contact with his father, but he was so worried that he called Norma anyway. He hadn't talked to her in over a year, but she told him something had happened the night of his dream. This is how he found out that Amy had a baby. He knew what his mother was going to say just as she was saying it. He didn't say a word about his dream, not wanting to sound like a fool.

There were other times during his life that John has dreamed about something before it happened. Sometimes it made him uneasy and sometimes it was life-affirming. It let him know there is at least a little magic in this world.

John has a troop of animal friends at Coldwater too. He tamed some squirrels and chipmunks to the point that they run up to anyone now. There is a trio of crows that come to the prayer circle daily to munch on raw ramen noodles and stale cookies.

But the best thing about Coldwater is the dogs. Its a training unit for service animals. The inmates also take in rescues that need to be acclimated before they can be adopted out. The first day that John woke up in the greyhound unit, he felt something wet on his ear. He freaked out and jerked awake. It was 5:00 am.

Chixi, who was being trained by a neighbor, had escaped her cell and beelined to John, whom she had met the night before. He was so touched.

"Chixi, what are you doing here?"

She wagged her tail and tried to lick him, then jumped in his bunk and tried to snuggle in. She kept coming back. He was touched that, out of thirty cells, she chose to return to him, even if she kept waking him up too early. She greeted him daily with a "Hey buddy, I know you'll play with me" vibe.

Chixi was not the first, and she won't be the last. The dogs at Coldwater know that John Aslin, though he is a cat, runs a dog-friendly cell.

The Ojibwe follow the guidance of the Seven Grandfathers: Humility, bravery, honesty, wisdom, truth, respect and love. What if John had grown up with this legacy instead of the broken, alcohol-infused anger and chaos that peppered his formative years? What if he had not been a fatherless son?

Imagine with me what John Aslin's life might have been if his people had not been targeted for extinction. If his natural connection to the earth and her creatures had flourished. If his mother and father had not turned from each other, preventing him from knowing who he was for so long. Or what his life could still become if he is set free.

John Eric Aslin was born among the First Nation People. Like them, he has faced difficulty and overcome many circumstances and attempts to destroy his spirit. He lost his way as a young man. Yet he is Lynx Man, a cat with nine lives.

The time he has spent thus far on this earth has used up eight of them, but he has one left. Like his people, he survives. He contains the spirit of his ancestors, many of whom were warriors, who lived with honor. His father was put under the knife, yet John exists. His mother nearly died yet lived to bring him into this world. His childhood was one of abuse and trauma, but he has lived long enough to make peace with his past.

He created sorrow in this world. He caused a life to end, deprived his own son of a father, lost his parents while he rotted away in prison, lost many Indian and animal brothers as he traveled through the penal system and has nearly lost hope as it is chipped away each day of his life sentence.

Thirty-six years in a cage. He has survived things that would have broken many. Eight lives of his feline nine gone. One left. Will it end in a cell? John releases tiny sparks of hope into the universe each day, hoping that someday he will move freely through the woods, climb a mountain, fish in a stream. Become the Lynx.

AFTERWORD

The manuscript for this book was completed at the end of January 2020. My original plan was to publish it on April 30, 2020 to commemorate John Aslin's 57th birthday. As the text was undergoing editing and feedback from readers, the Covid-19 crisis hit. As the virus swept through the Michigan prison system, John Aslin's facility was one of two locations where the toll of the virus was particularly harsh. Lakeland Correctional Facility in Coldwater, Michigan experienced a high level of infection and death; overcrowded conditions at the facility made it impossible for men to shield themselves from infection.

John tested positive for the virus in late April 2020. It was a harrowing time for him and for the people who care about him, but I am happy to report that he has recovered. His knowledge of herbs and traditional medicine helped him weather the illness. As of June 2020, he has been dominating on the handball court, tending to his garden and leading the indigenous prison community at the Lakeland Facility.

The risk of death that John faced when he became ill only serves to highlight the necessity for John's release. Had he succumbed to Covid-19, he would have been denied a deserved second chance at life. His sentence really would have become a life sentence and his life would have ended at the age of 57.

As I finalize this manuscript and ready myself to release it into the world, I am daily tracking the Black Lives Matter protests that have erupted after the tragic murder of George Floyd at the hands of the police. The deep flaws in law enforcement that have worked their way into the American consciousness in the last few weeks expose a system that is merely the entry point into the nightmare of incarceration in America that disproportionately impacts minority men, including indigenous men like John.

The current protest movement may be focused on the policing systems now, but it will eventually need to turn its attention to the courts and the prisons. These are the places where past victims of racist criminal justice policies are stuck until those policies are recognized for what they are and replaced with just and unbiased rules.

John Aslin does not have the time to wait for change. He entered prison on the cusp of adulthood and, in eight years, he will be old enough to call himself a senior citizen. If you believe that John Aslin should be released, please spread word of his predicament to everyone you know.

John applied to the Michigan Parole Board for commutation of his sentence in June, 2020. In order to increase his chance of success, please voice your support for his release to the following:

Michigan Governor Gretchen Whitmer
P.O. Box 30013
Lansing, Michigan 48909

Michigan Attorney General Dana Nessel
P.O. Box 30212
Lansing, MI 48909

Genesee County Prosecutor David Leyton
900 S Saginaw St
Flint, MI 48502

Sign up for my email list on my website (jillcreechbauer.com) to receive a **free short story**, notifications about my upcoming books, updates about John's case and information about an upcoming podcast (tentative launch date September 2020), "The Nine Lives of John Aslin." The podcast will dive deeper into topics touched on in the book, such as eugenics, the destruction of native cultures in the 20th Century in the U.S., juvenile justice and prison reform. You will also hear more about John's life from the man himself.

If you want to provide financial support for John's release and receive bonus content and updates about John, find us on Patreon (mid-July, 2020) at Jill Creech Bauer.

You can add your signature to a petition for John's release on Change.org by searching "Free John Aslin." John has an application for release pending with the parole board and a well-supported petition could make a difference in his case.

Please leave an honest review of this book on Amazon and Goodreads. Reviews help readers discover independent authors.

ACKNOWLEDGEMENTS

I am grateful to my husband, James Bauer, the Honorable Brent Bartholomew and Susan Strayer for their conscientious feedback on early drafts of this book. The time that a reader gives to an author is a generous gift and my appreciation is sincere.

ABOUT THE AUTHOR

Jill Creech Bauer grew up in Flint, Michigan and now lives in Salt Lake City with her husband. She has three adult children. She practiced law in Flint for a dozen years before becoming a full-time creative. In addition to writing, she is an abstract painter, aspiring screenwriter and amateur filmmaker. "The Nine Lives of John Aslin" is her first book.

Get a free short story by joining the email list at jillcreechbauer.com. You will also receive updates on John's case, future publications and other projects.

CPSIA information can be obtained
at www.ICGtesting.com
Printed in the USA
FSHW020758121020
74182FS